Burning the Breeze

THREE GENERATIONS

❊ *of* WOMEN *in the* ❊

AMERICAN WEST

Lisa Hendrickson

Afterword by James E. Pepper

University of Nebraska Press   Lincoln

Publication of this volume was assisted by a grant from
the Friends of the University of Nebraska Press.

Library of Congress Cataloging-in-Publication Data
Names: Hendrickson, Lisa, author.
Title: Burning the breeze: three generations of women in the
American West / Lisa Hendrickson; afterword by James E. Pepper.
Description: Lincoln: University of Nebraska Press, 2021. |
Includes bibliographical references and index.
Identifiers: LCCN 2020057473
ISBN 9781496227928 (paperback)
ISBN 9781496228758 (epub)
ISBN 9781496228765 (pdf)
Subjects: LCSH: Businesswomen—West (U.S.) | Women-
owned business enterprises—West (U.S.) | Dude ranches—
West (U.S.) | Tourist camps, hostels, etc.—West (U.S.)
Classification: LCC HD6054.4.W48 H35 2021
DDC 338.7/6179656092520978—dc23
LC record available at https://lccn.loc.gov/2020057473

Set in Fanwood Text by Mikala R. Kolander.
Designed by L. Auten.

To Sherry Merica Pepper, who opened her arms,
her heart, and her family archives,

and to my parents, who encouraged me to explore the world

Burning the breeze:

Western slang for "riding at full speed"

Contents

Illustrations

Introduction

This is the true story of a strong and determined woman—a woman who shunned the traditional American women's roles of her day and blazed her own trail. Chances are good that you've never heard of this Montana native, but her tale deserves telling.

In the middle of the Great Depression, fifty-one-year-old Julia Bennett arrived in New York City in 1931 with no money and an audacious plan: to hunt down easterners who could afford to spend their summer at her brand-new dude ranch. Julia, a big-game hunter known as "a clever shot with both rifle and shotgun," flouted convention as she struggled to build a guest ranch. Through sheer determination and force of personality, she became the first independent woman in Montana to own and operate a dude ranch. She eventually built not just one but two successful dude ranches—one in Montana and one in Arizona—attracting world-renowned celebrities and artists who affectionately called her the Boss.

Julia's grandmother and mother—pioneers both in action and spirit—set Julia on this road to independence. During the Civil War, Lizzie Nave Martin and her seven-year-old daughter, Lulu, set out from their home in war-torn Missouri with little more than a yoke of oxen, a covered wagon, and the clothes on their backs. Lizzie's husband had died, leaving her destitute and with a mountain of debt to repay. Desperate to make a living, she and her daughter headed out on what would become a ten-month journey to the Montana Territory, hoping to find opportunities in the newly minted mining town of Virginia City. They faced countless heartbreaks and obstacles as they started a new life in this 145,000-square-mile territory that at the time was home to fewer than twenty-one thousand people.

Lulu would go on to marry at fourteen, raise Julia and four more children, and manage a remote 1,200-acre ranch—often while her husband, Benjamin Franklin Bembrick, was hundreds of miles away tending to his immense cattle herd.

The Montana Territory was not a place for the weak. Many who left nineteenth-century America to try their hands out West didn't stay. Blizzards, droughts, rugged terrain, wild animals, and clashes between the new settlers and Native tribes were among the many challenges that defeated them. But Julia Bennett's family came from hearty stock.

Montana novelist Dorothy Johnson once noted, "I think the people who headed West were a different kind of people. Somebody said in a long poem that the cowards never started and the weaklings fell by the way. That doesn't mean that everyone who went West was noble, brave, courageous, and admirable because some of them were utter skunks, but they were strong."[1]

In the past, western stories generally have focused on the adventures and exploits of men, but today the accomplishments of pioneering women are coming to the fore. Take, for example, Caroline Lockhart, a novelist and former East Coast investigative reporter who owned a working ranch in one of the most desolate areas of Montana. She declared to a newspaper reporter that "petticoats are no bar to progress in either writing or ranching."[2]

Jeannette Rankin, the first woman elected to the U.S. Congress in 1916, was another Montana woman who defied convention. A prominent woman's suffragist and antiwar activist, she revealed her ambition in an early journal, writing, "Go! Go! Go! It makes no difference where, just so you go! Go! Go! Remember, at the first opportunity, go."[3] Interestingly, Julia Bennett herself earned the soubriquet "Go! Go!" from *Chicago Tribune* cartoonist Carey Orr, who was a frequent guest at her ranches.

Bonnie Reilly, also raised on a Montana ranch, observed, "We didn't worry about whether something was 'ladylike.' We just did what had to be done."

Julia Bennett, Lulu Bembrick, and Lizzie Nave Martin surely would have agreed.

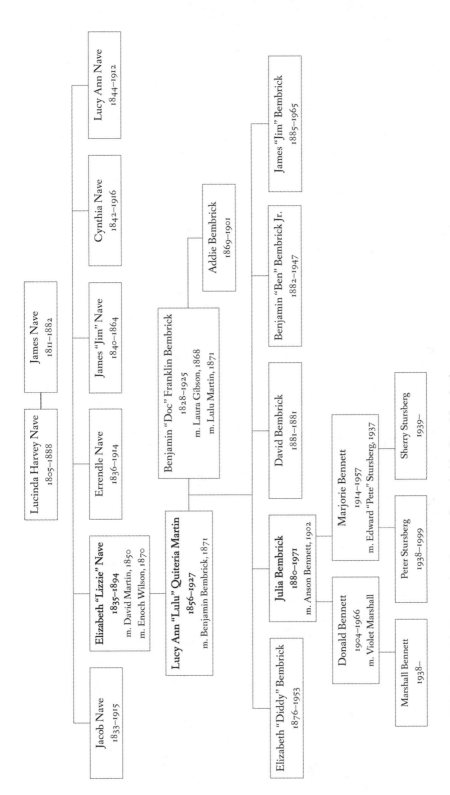

1. Nave, Bembrick, Bennett family tree. Compiled by Lisa Hendrickson.

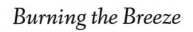

Burning the Breeze

Part I

The PERILOUS JOURNEY

Chapter 1

In Western dramas [authenticity] must consist of cowboys, with
their chaps (pronounced shaps), their wide-brim (or ten gallon,
as we say here) hats, a kerchief about the neck and high-heeled,
fancy boots. Though the outfit be utilitarian, it is also held to be
romantic by those who have the West close to their romantic hearts.

—*New York Times*, March 1, 1931

On a chilly February morning in 1931, Mrs. Julia Bennett, who just
a few days earlier had arrived on a train from her native Montana,
stood by the front door of New York City's Northern Pacific Railway
Office. She didn't know a soul, and she had only enough money to
last a week—if she didn't eat much.

Despite these daunting circumstances, Julia, a striking fifty-one-
year-old woman with an aquiline profile and dark-blonde hair, exuded
an air of confidence. She sported a spotted cowhide vest, a silk neckerchief, and a black felt bolero—and since she was now in Manhattan,
she had exchanged her cowboy boots for a pair of black pumps that
added a few inches to her five-foot-four frame.

"I had never been in a big city alone," Julia wrote many years later,
"and when I arrived in N.Y. I was so frightened I didn't know what
to do." Those who knew her said she was fearless. But on this wintry
day in 1931, she was desperate.

Julia Bennett was in Manhattan to find guests for her new dude
ranch, the Diamond J—the first in Montana to be exclusively owned
and operated by a woman. Her timing could not have been worse.
The stock market had crashed sixteen months earlier, and the economy was continuing its rapid downward spiral into what soon would
become known as the Great Depression.

Unemployment stood at nearly 16 percent, and food riots were beginning to break out in some parts of the country. "There was hardly a man or woman in the country whose attitude toward life had not been affected . . . in some degree . . . by the sudden and brutal shattering of hope," wrote historian Frederick Lewis Allen that same year.[1] In nearby Central Park, homeless men had set up an informal camp in its recently emptied reservoir. They derisively named it Hooverville, after the president of the United States.

The richest Americans, however, still owned 40 percent of the nation's wealth, and it was this elite group that Julia Bennett, an accomplished big-game hunter, was targeting. A veneer of prosperity still was evident at the intersection of Fifth Avenue and Forty-Sixth Street, where she stood outside the Northern Pacific office. In these parts of the city, women dressed in fur coats and had the means to shop at Saks Fifth Avenue and join their friends for lunch at Schrafft's.

Julia herself had no steady income and hadn't laid eyes on her ne'er-do-well husband, Anson, in more than a decade. Although their son was now grown, she was raising their sixteen-year-old daughter alone. Julia urgently needed money to pay off the $13,000 she had been loaned by a group of Montana businessmen to finance the construction and outfitting of her new ranch, which she had designed and built with the help of a few out-of-work wranglers. She was planning to open it to guests for the summer season in just four months. Thirteen thousand dollars was no small change—it was the same amount it had cost Charles Lindbergh to finance his solo flight across the Atlantic four years earlier and about $200,000 in today's dollars.

"I was broke, and way in debt, so I realized I must get the ranch booked, but how?!" Julia wrote. Times were hard throughout the country, but they were especially bad in Montana, the only state that had lost population in the previous year's U.S. census.[2] Although penniless, what Julia Bennett did have—in spades—was energy, charm, and resourcefulness. And she hoped that some of the wealthy East Coasters she planned to meet still had enough money to spend their summer out on the range, living their idealized version of the cowboy life.

Back in Montana, Julia wore jeans and a plaid flannel shirt while hunting and working on her ranch, but here in New York she dressed as if she were starring in a motion picture Western. She knew what she was selling.

Chapter 2

Only in New York is it possible to be in the midst of millions of
persons and be completely alone. . . . Romance and phlegmatism
are next door neighbors. Nowhere else can you find a three-
story house in the shadow of a 102-story skyscraper. You
can find gilt or gold wherever you go. . . . It is infinitely the
place where you "pay your money and take your choice."

—James Atwell, *Mason City Globe Gazette*, June 18, 1931

Julia Bennett was all alone in this city of nearly seven million people.
But she managed to find a tiny, inexpensive short-term apartment
and then immediately set to work. "I had one contact," she wrote,
"and that was a lady that had written me asking me to mail her a
brochure." The lady's name was Mrs. Taylor, and she lived, Julia
wrote, in a town called "Prinston." Julia may not have been aware
that Princeton, New Jersey, was the home of Princeton University
and that it would require yet another train ride to get there.

Julia certainly did not know that Mrs. Taylor was Bellevernon
Taylor, the wife of a wealthy real estate developer who—in addition
to their residence in Princeton—also owned a $400,000 mansion in
Grosse Pointe Farms, Michigan. Julia decided to telephone her, and
Mrs. Taylor invited her to dinner, telling her she would meet her at
the Princeton train station.

Boarding the train at the two-block-long beaux arts–style Pennsylvania Station in Manhattan, Julia arrived about an hour later at the
Princeton station, near the entrance of the university. Mrs. Taylor
had come to fetch her in a large automobile driven by the family's
chauffeur. "I looked so green she walked right up to me and asked if
I was Mrs. Bennett," Julia wrote.

The chauffeur drove them a few blocks to the family's stately pre–

Civil War brick home, where Julia spent the evening showing Mrs. Taylor photos of the Diamond J and describing the beauty of her ranch. Mrs. Taylor expressed interest but said she would have to speak to her husband. She asked if Julia would require a deposit if they decided to book.

"Oh, no," Julia replied.

✣

For the next three days, Julia stayed in her apartment, hoping to get a call from Mrs. Taylor. At the end of those three days, the phone rang. "She called me and said they had decided to come. There would be two adults and one child for the summer."

The amount of the family's stay would total $5,000, which in 1931 was enough to buy five Model A Ford Town Cars. Mrs. Taylor told Julia she would send her a "small deposit."

The next day, an envelope was delivered to Julia's apartment. Inside she found a check for $1,000.

"I could hardly believe it," she wrote, in what might have been one of the world's biggest understatements.

The thrill didn't last long. Even if Mrs. Taylor and her family spent the summer at the Diamond J, one booking clearly would not be enough to make ends meet. Julia would have a multitude of expenses. She'd have to hire wranglers to saddle up the horses and lead the guests on horseback rides, as well as local girls to clean the cabins. She'd have to buy saddle horses and supplies, provide transportation and entertainment. She calculated that she'd need at least a dozen bookings to break even, and she had just exhausted her one and only contact.

"I didn't know where to go from there," wrote Julia. But she was undaunted. A Christian Scientist, her faith supported her pragmatic and optimistic nature. She fervently believed in founder Mary Baker Eddy's philosophy and read passages from her book *Science and Health with Key to the Scriptures* every day. "If you wish to be happy," Eddy had once preached, "argue with yourself on the side of happiness; take the side you wish to carry, and be careful not to talk on both sides, or to argue stronger for sorrow than for joy. You are the attorney for the case, and will win or lose according to your plea."[1]

As she walked through central Manhattan, Julia could see the shimmering spire of the one-year-old art deco–style Chrysler Building—the tallest skyscraper in the world—rising to the south. Soon it would be surpassed in height by the Empire State Building, whose steel girders already were climbing skyward. Even in the middle of the Depression, these buildings telegraphed prosperity. And Julia was confident that there must be people in New York who could afford to spend the summer of 1931 at the Diamond J.

She recalled that someone back home (perhaps it was the wealthy Chicago businessman Julius Butler, who had hired her to cook for several summers at his own Montana ranch, the Nine Quarter Circle) had told her to call a friend in New York. That friend's name was Mr. Wright, and Julia thought he might be able to offer some advice.

She telephoned and introduced herself, telling him that she was in New York to book her dude ranch. Wright responded with a laugh, saying, "I've never heard of a dude ranch," but added that he would stop by to meet her. When he arrived, she told him about the Diamond J. "He didn't see how I could book anyone staying in the place I was," she said, and he suggested she move to the Roosevelt Hotel at Forty-Fifth Street and Madison Avenue. The hotel, built seven years earlier, was just down the street from Grand Central Terminal and was advertised as "a rendezvous of smart New Yorkers."[2] The immense sixteen-story building encompassed an entire city block and was linked to the train station by an underground tunnel. Its three limestone-and-brick towers held more than one thousand rooms.

Wright told Julia he knew the hostess at the Roosevelt, who might be able to help identify some potential "dudes" to fill her ranch. That very afternoon, Julia strode into the Roosevelt's elegant balconied, marble-columned lobby and booked a room for herself, although she knew that unless she booked more guests, she wouldn't be able to pay the bill when it came time to leave.

After checking in, Julia headed straight to the Northern Pacific Railroad ticket office, just two blocks away, where she hoped to attract the attention of people planning summer trips out west. Fifth Avenue was bustling. Double-decker buses with spiral staircases competed for lanes with cars and taxicabs, all directed by traffic cops sporting double-breasted suits and white gloves. Julia strode into the office and left copies of her newly printed Diamond J brochures, which she had sat up most of the night finishing before leaving for New York.

The front cover featured a pen-and-ink drawing of a cowboy holding a saddle, while the back cover highlighted the ranch brand—a horizontal diamond shape with a J in the middle. A sketch of a young woman who closely resembled Julia's lovely teenaged daughter, Marge, sat smiling in the hook of the J, wearing a cowboy hat and chaps.

"A Country of Romance," the brochure read. "Pack trains with competent cooks and guides lead you over the dim trails of Indians and cowboys, that have not been widened, to hidden retreats and remote fishing streams."

After leaving her brochures at the Northern Pacific office, Julia devised a plan, perhaps with the advice of Mr. Wright's hostess friend. The Roosevelt was full of meeting rooms; she reserved one. She planned to entice guests with what she called a "show" that highlighted the Diamond J, along with Montana's mountain landscapes and pioneer history. Wright loaned her a movie projector so she could show a film of the ranch she had brought with her. But brochures and films alone might not do the job. She decided to liven up the presentation with cowboy music.

Enter a young man named Woodward Ritter. A twenty-six-year-old who had studied prelaw at the University of Texas, Ritter had in the past few years turned his sights to the world of entertainment. In 1928 he'd sung cowboy songs on Houston radio station KPRC and then headed to New York to pursue a career, urged on by his brother-in-law, who told him that a few years in the East "would be good for a Texas boy because it moved a little faster and gave you a different outlook."[3] Now he was playing the role of cowboy Cord Elam in the production of *Green Grow the Lilacs* at the Guild Theatre on Fifty-Second Street (which later would be the basis for the musical *Oklahoma!*). The cast included, according to the *New York Times*, an authentic "contingent of hell-for-leather cowboys, who would just as soon shoot you as look at you. (This is said only in good, clean fun.)" Many of them had been discovered the year before at the World's Championship Rodeo, held at Madison Square Garden.[4]

How Julia discovered young Woodward Ritter and snagged him to moonlight in her "show" at the Roosevelt is a mystery. However, she told a newspaper reporter during a trip to New York the following year, "All the best cowboys can be found right here in Manhattan, twangling their guitars and singing lonesome songs about the prairie in Harlem night clubs."[5] All she wrote in her unpublished memoir was, "He came in his cowboy outfit and sang songs at the shows for me." Ritter might have worn the same checked shirt, red bandanna, and felt cowboy hat that he donned for the play. Maybe he crooned "Git Along, Little Dogies," which he sang as a chorus member on Broadway. Julia recognized talent when she saw it, but little did she—or anyone else at the time—know that he was on his way to becoming the Hollywood film star and best-selling country singer Tex Ritter.

Julia's efforts began to yield results. Although she didn't have a publicist, she was a savvy marketer. Just two months after arriving in New York, she was featured in the women's section of the *New York Evening Post*, which billed itself as "a department devoted to the interests of the alert modern women of the modern world."[6] Perhaps her standout western duds had attracted the attention of a reporter.

The article, headlined "Dude Ranching Is Becoming a Profitable Profession, Says Julia A. Bennett, Who Runs One Out in Montana," included a large photo of the Diamond J, along with a smaller one of Marge sitting on a cabin railing, a cowboy hat crowning her stylish bobbed hair.

"In her room at the Hotel Roosevelt she undertook to tell us the other afternoon why she believes that a Western background is essential for successfully running a dude ranch," noted the reporter, Marion Clyde McCarroll, who also was the first woman ever to receive a press card from the New York Stock Exchange.[7]

"I've been on a horse since I was four years old," Julia told McCarroll. "My father used to take me out with him when he went hunting. I'd ride behind him until he shot what he was after; then he'd swing me around in front and the animal would be slung over the horse in back and we'd go home in triumph with some good fresh meat."

Like the article, Julia's promotional brochure also conjured up vivid images of the Wild West: "We are also near the mystic Vigilante Trail ... and Alder Gulch, the richest gold strike in history. ... Here Virginia City, the second capital of Montana, grew over night and in its mad gold days when Plummer and his road agents held their reign of terror, the streets thronged with miners, trappers, Indians, fur traders, stage drivers, road agents and settlers in covered wagons."

Julia Bennett knew her subject well. Among the settlers arriving in Virginia City in 1864 had been her young, recently widowed grandmother Elizabeth Nave Martin and her eight-year-old daughter, Luly. They were fleeing their home in northern Missouri, where a civil war within the Civil War had turned neighbor against neighbor and left them with no apparent option—other than escape.

Chapter 3

I David R Martin being of sound and disposing mind and memory
but considering the frailty and uncertainty of human life do make
publish and declare this to be my last Will and Testament.

—David R. Martin, December 5, 1862

One Thursday in early November 1862, Elizabeth Nave Martin
walked through the front door of Bell and Leeper's Mercantile in
Chillicothe, Missouri. David, her husband of eleven years, was at
home on their farm, dying of consumption.[1]

David and Lizzie (as her friends and family called her) lived about a
mile northwest of Chillicothe, the largest town in Livingston County,
with a population of three thousand. During her visit to Bell and
Leeper's, where the Martin family had a credit account, Lizzie spent
$6.02 on two and a half pounds of rice, a pound of coffee, and a pair of
socks. She also selected fabric and trimmings for her sewing projects:
three and a half yards of bleached muslin, four yards of cotton velvet,
one and a half yards of dotted swiss, and some ribbon. She may have
been planning to use the muslin to sew her husband's burial shroud.

Lizzie was twenty-seven, with a round face and long dark hair that
she wore parted in the middle and pulled back to the nape of her neck.
David was eleven years older. Lizzie had married him when she was
only fifteen, and it is easy to see why she found him attractive. He was
handsome, with large eyes, an angular chin, and wavy brown hair that
reached the top of his collar. A teacher, he owned more than eighty
acres of land not far from her parents' large farm. Three years after
their marriage, he was appointed by the county court to serve as the
county's commissioner for the state's new public school system. And
three years later, Lizzie had given birth to their only child, Lucy Ann
Quiteria Martin—known to everyone as Luly.[2]

2. (*left*) Lizzie Nave Martin in 1864, the year her family headed west. Lulu Martin Bembrick photograph album, Sherry Merica Pepper private collection.

3. (*right*) Lizzie's husband, David Martin, undated. Lulu Martin Bembrick photograph album, Sherry Merica Pepper private collection.

The Martins' physician, Dr. C. A. Williams, had visited their home nearly every day since late July, trying to cure David's tubercular cough. In October Dr. Williams had taken the additional step of calling in his brother and partner, Dr. J. S. Williams, for a consultation, but the prognosis was not favorable. Lizzie was no stranger to the devastating effects of consumption—the disease had killed her older brother Jacob's first wife, Sarah, a few years earlier.

After making her purchases, Lizzie returned home to care for her husband, who, by this time, must have known that his time on earth was nearing its end. On the fifth of December, he wrote his will, leaving all his possessions to "my beloved wife . . . and my daughter." Dr. Williams continued to make near-daily house calls. His final visit was on December 16—just two days before Lizzie and David's twelfth wedding anniversary.

Barely one week later, David took his last breath. His passing was recorded in detail in the family Bible: "D. R. Martin departed this life on the 22nd day of December at 3 o'clock P.M. 1862, near Chillicothe, aged 38 years, 11 months and 18 days."[3]

Meanwhile, back at Bell and Leeper's Mercantile in Chillicothe, James Leeper added another charge to the Martins' bill: $2.00 for "dig[g]ing grave."

It would be a very bleak Christmas for Lizzie and Luly. Although David had gone to the effort of writing a will (with the same Mr. Leeper serving as its witness), he had stipulated that all his "just debts be first paid," with the balance going to Lizzie and Luly.[4] But there was no money left. The family debts totaled more than $300. David still owed the principal on their farmland and had large, unpaid bills for lumber and merchandise. Lizzie also now owed Dr. Williams $82—$1.50 for each of the fifty-one house calls he had made during David's illness, as well as for the times earlier that year when he had come to extract a tooth and to prescribe Smith's Tonic when Luly was feverish.

Missouri law entitled the new widow to keep a few things: "all her implements of industry, beds, wearing apparel, provisions, &.c., requisite for the family; also, kitchen furniture to the value of twenty dollars, and any other personal property to the value of two hundred dollars," as well as any property she owned before she was married.[5] But Lizzie also now legally assumed David's substantial debt, and creditors soon would be knocking on her door.

"For many women, a husband's death brought his creditors down on the estate like vultures," wrote one Civil War historian.[6]

Lizzie Nave Martin was no exception. And there was yet another complication. Her youngest brother was a Confederate guerrilla.

Chapter 4

Missouri was almost equally divided in political sentiment.
One neighbor was arrayed against another.

—Mrs. Maggie Stonestreet English, *Reminiscences
of the Women of Missouri during the Sixties*

On August 13, 1862—just about four months before the death of Lizzie's husband—federal authorities had arrested her twenty-one-year-old brother, Jim, as a guerrilla. They accused him of driving a wagon that carried a wounded member of Poindexter's Army, an unofficial Confederate militia. Three friends and neighbors swore under oath (in statements recorded by the omnipresent merchant and clerk James Leeper) that Jim had been forced to drive the wagon against his will.

A young neighbor named Sarah Dowell testified that Jim was working in her father's field, "stacking timothy hay," along with her father and another man. She said Poindexter's Army pressed into service her father's wagon and teams and three other horses to take them two miles away to the Grand River, where they said they would let them return home. Two other witnesses told similar stories, though they weren't entirely consistent. The observation by all three that Jim was "in his shirt sleeves" may be telling. While they—as well as Jim—swore that he was pressed into service involuntarily, Union soldiers may have seen things differently. "Civilian clothes were the mark of the guerrilla," notes historian Michael Fellman.[1]

The provost marshal of Livingston County wrote to his superior, "I understand that [Nave] claims to have been pressed in as guide by Poindexter when he was in this county. I do not believe it."[2] Another witness told officials that a day earlier, he had seen Jim "in Poindexters [*sic*] camp at Springhill" and heard him offer Poindexter a barrel of pickled pork. He added, "Nave appeared perfectly willing for Poindexter to take the pork."[3]

The day after his capture, Jim, tagged as a "straggler from Poindexter," was taken to the Union garrison in the neighboring county of Linn, where he was loaded onto a railcar with thirty-eight others and transported to Gratiot Street Prison in St. Louis. The prison—a former medical college, school, and private house—housed not only Confederate army prisoners but also male and female "spies, guerrillas, [and] civilians suspected of disloyalty."[4]

Just three days later, Jim was transferred again—this time to Alton Military Prison in Illinois, the same prison from which his brother Errendle had escaped a month earlier. While there, Jim wrote a series of letters to Union army officers, requesting "to appear before you to have our cases investigated."

Jim claimed that he and a neighbor were hauling hay when Poindexter ordered them to transport a wounded man, telling them that if they refused, he would keep their horses and wagon. "He made us go about 30 miles before we could get released," Jim wrote, claiming that as he and his neighbor made their way home, a regiment of "Federals . . . pressed us to haul their ammunition and after serving them about half a day they took our team from us and turned us in to prison."

Fourteen Livingston County men signed a letter swearing that Jim and his neighbor were "quiet and orderly citizens" and that "since this rebellion has broken out they have been living at their respective houses engaged in their ordinary and legitimate pursuits and have never engaged in any act of hostility to the government of the United States but on the contrary have been loyal and true."[5]

While awaiting a response to his appeal, Jim was stricken with an acute bacterial infection called facial erysipelas. It was fatal to many prisoners at Alton, with symptoms that included a severe red rash, high fever, chills, and vomiting. In early November Jim was transferred back to Gratiot Street Prison for treatment.[6] On November 6, 1862, as Lizzie's husband lay dying, the acting assistant surgeon at Gratiot Street recommended to the provost marshal that Jim be released on parole "to go to some good institution to recruit his health," adding that Jim was "convalescing now but very low" and that he required "good attendance and careful nursing."

Two days later, Jim was paroled to Sisters Hospital in St. Louis. As a condition of his parole, he was required to report to the provost marshal. "Sir I am laying sick yet and unable to report in person as soon as able I shall report in person," he scribbled on a piece of paper. On November 24 he was ordered to report weekly. He asked to be exchanged for a Union prisoner and sent home. Jim's wish was granted, but as a condition of the exchange, he was barred from military service.

The Nave family's Confederate sympathies, which were no secret in Livingston County, may well have made them the target of Union loyalists. But there was no shortage of rebel sympathizers willing to ignore—or even actively aid—Confederate guerrillas, also known as bushwhackers. In a note to his superior, one Union army captain wrote of his frustrations:

> This trip has again proven to me the perfect folly of chasing bush-whackers while the country is full of law-abiding citizens to harbor and feed them. . . . While none of us would molest and injure the innocent, and in all cases look upon the ignorant with a great deal of charity, yet we can but look upon those who still insist that they are rebel sympathizers with scorn and contempt. We know that it is this class who are now drawing the life blood out of our glorious Union.[7]

In 1862 life for everyone in northern Missouri, not just the Naves, was bleak—and becoming more violent by the day. Nearly twenty Civil War battles already had taken place in the state, and neighbors were pitted against neighbors in the bloody struggle. Lizzie and David lived just east of Jackson Township in the northern Missouri county of Livingston, a hotbed of Confederate sympathizers. "In 1862 all Jackson Township was in a state of war. . . . Hardly a day passed without a skirmish," noted the author of the *History of Caldwell and*

Livingston Counties two decades later. "There was a great deal of bushwhacking. Men were shot at in the fields, on the highways and even at home."[8]

Amid this chaos, Lizzie and Luly were now on their own. As executrix of her family's estate, Lizzie was required by the court to file an inventory of possessions. The assets included not only their thirty-acre farm but also forty acres David had purchased in Franklin County, Missouri, before their marriage, along with a lot in Golden City, Colorado. Now their house and properties would have to be sold to pay creditors.

They were at least fortunate that Lizzie's parents, James and Lucy Nave, lived nearby on their 360-acre farm. Soon after David's death, Lizzie and Luly moved in with them. Lizzie was an excellent seamstress, and she may have been able to earn some money from sewing. She periodically made trips to the Chillicothe courthouse to pay what she could on the debts. But times were hard.

They hadn't always been that way.

✤

Before the war, the Nave family had prospered. Sometime in the early 1830s, Lizzie Nave's grandparents and their eleven children had traveled more than seven hundred miles from their home in Cocke County, Tennessee, to join family members who had settled in the gently rolling hills of northern Missouri. A decade earlier, Congress had incorporated Missouri into the Union as a slave state, in what was known as the Missouri Compromise.

Lizzie's father, James, had married her mother, Lucy Ann, in 1832. Lucy Ann was six years older than her husband and, starting at the age of twenty-eight, had given birth to eight children over eleven years. Two of them died in infancy. Lizzie was the second eldest, born on April 22, 1835. When she was still a toddler, the family moved to a small town founded in 1833 by her father's brother, Jesse. Located in what soon would be named Livingston County, it was fertile land, "a piece of earth surface shaped by nature for beautiful farms."[9] There,

Jesse Nave had built a cabin with two rooms, opening a trading post in one, and became postmaster of the town soon known as Navestown. A few years later, Jesse renamed the town Springhill, apparently annoyed that many butchered his name by addressing their letters to "Knave's Town."

The area, which boasted several springs that never froze, was heralded as "a hunter's paradise." An 1886 edition of Livingston County's history noted, "Game was so plenty that it was often shot for mere pastime." Bears, panthers, wildcats, and even "huge timber wolves were for a time unpleasantly numerous. Every settler depended to a greater or less extent on his rifle as a means of supplying meat for his table."[10]

By 1850 James and Lucy Nave were well established in the county. Their oldest son, Jacob, helped on the farm. Lizzie and her younger brothers, Errendle and Jim, attended school, while the youngest Nave girls, Cynthia and Lucy Ann, stayed at home with their mother.

Along with the farm, James Nave operated a ropework. Hemp, one of the most important crops in Missouri at the time, formed the rigging for boats that plied the nearby Missouri River and bound the massive quantities of cotton harvested in the South.[11] Perhaps because of his Tennessee roots or his business interests, Nave was one of many Missouri Democrats stridently opposed to the calls for an end to slavery. While there's no documented evidence that he owned slaves, his thinking was in line with other Livingston County men who attended a rally in Chillicothe in the summer of 1849.[12] A Democratic newspaper claimed that the men's objection to the abolition of slavery was not "a contest between Union and Disunion" but rather "a contest between the fanaticism of the North, contending for a usurpation of power, against the slaveholding States of the South, standing up for their constitutional rights and equal justice."[13]

By 1850 about three-quarters of Missourians had southern ancestors.[14] The Naves were longtime members of the Methodist Episcopal Church South, which split from its northern counterpart over the issue of slavery back in 1844—a division prompted by the church's censure of a bishop who had become a slave owner through marriage.

In November 1851 James Nave was among the key players in a public meeting held at the Chillicothe courthouse "to adopt measures to counteract the malign influence upon the slave population of this county which certain secret Northern abolition emissaries are supposed to be producing upon their minds."[15] They were referring to emissaries of the Methodist Church North. Nave was one of six on a committee that wrote a preamble and resolutions resulting from the meeting. The resolutions, which endorsed using force if required to keep the emissaries from their midst, were signed by the mayor of Chillicothe, the clerk of the circuit court, a member of the Missouri House of Representatives, and local merchants, including James Leeper.[16]

During the run-up to the Civil War, Missouri declared itself neutral. Delegates to the state's 1860 Constitutional Convention voted to remain in the Union. But in that year's presidential election, only 10 percent of Missouri voters cast their ballots for Abraham Lincoln. Outgoing governor Robert Marcellus Stewart, who supported the cause of the North, proclaimed, "Missouri is a peninsula of slavery running out into a sea of freedom."[17] But his successor, Governor Claiborne Jackson, refused to allow the secretary of war to conscript Union soldiers from Missouri and worked behind the scenes to support Missouri's secession.

By 1861 the Missouri Legislature opposed federal efforts to coerce the seceding southern states "into obedience." It resolved that "if there is any invasion of the slave States for the purpose of carrying such doctrine into effect, it is the opinion of this general assembly that the people of Missouri will instantly rally on the side of their Southern brethren, to resist the invaders at all hazards and to the last extremity."[18] In August 1861 Federal commander John C. Frémont declared martial law throughout the state.

When the Nave family first arrived in Livingston County, "every man regarded his neighbor as his brother, and feeling his dependence exercised a proper amount of forbearance," wrote one historian.[19] By 1861 this was no longer the case.

Chapter 5

There will be trouble in Missouri until the Secesh are
subjugated and made to know that they are not only
powerless, but that any attempts to make trouble here will
bring upon them certain destruction and this . . . must
not be confined to soldiers and fighting men, but must
be extended to non-combatant men and women.

—Missourian Barton Bates to his father, U.S. attorney
general Edward Bates, October 10, 1861

James Nave and his sons were on the side of the South—the "Secesh,"
or secessionists. They were among the majority in Livingston County
and especially in Jackson Township, where they lived. Since June
1861, Federal troops had occupied Chillicothe, and they were finding
the Confederate guerrillas "greatly annoying. . . . All knew the county
thoroughly, all were desperate fighters, and for some time they held
Jackson township as completely as the Federals held the rest of the
county."[1]

In August 1862 the state had ordered military-age men to "present themselves before the authorities and enroll as either 'loyal' or
'disloyal' to the United States and State Governments." Men who
identified themselves as disloyal were required to surrender their
weapons and to refrain from participating in the conflict. They were
allowed to remain in their homes and businesses as long as they continued "quietly attending to their ordinary and legitimate business
and in no way give aid or comfort to the enemy."[2]

Two of James Nave's nephews added their names to the list of those
declaring themselves disloyal.[3] And Lizzie's two younger brothers,
Errendle and Jim, were among about two hundred Livingston County
men who joined the Confederate army.[4] Three days before Christmas

in 1861, at the age of twenty-five, Errendle enlisted as a private in the Third Regiment of the Confederate Missouri Infantry, Company F. By February 12, 1862, an official report noted that he was "left sick in hospital Springfield, MO. Never heard from."[5] But within three weeks, Errendle had rejoined his unit and was fighting in the Battle of Pea Ridge in Arkansas, where, according to his daughter, "he was wounded in the shoulder and laid on the battlefield for four days while Union soldiers kicked him as they passed by."[6] He was captured on March 8, the final day of the battle, and sent to the military prison in Alton, Illinois, where his brother Jim also would later be held. On a Friday night in July, Errendle and thirty-five other prisoners disappeared in a daring escape. A Louisville newspaper reported that they had accomplished the feat "by digging a hole commencing from the head of the bakery, . . . used as a bathroom for the prisoners, and passing under a shed and out under the prison walls."[7] He was never recaptured.[8]

※

During the summer of 1863 in Missouri, some Union loyalists sought out Confederate sympathizers—robbing their homes, stealing their food, even murdering them. The situation had been tense for several years. A young girl named Mary Sheehan Ronan, who in 1861 was staying with relatives on their plantation in St. Joseph, Missouri (about sixty miles west of the Naves), remembered, "I heard members of Cousin John's family say, for they were in sympathy with the cause of the South, that Union soldiers had come in the night, stolen the horses, and driven the darkies away. One terrifying night we children were aroused from bed and dressed in readiness to flee; I heard whispering that the soldiers would surely come and turn us out and burn the house."[9]

Along with the real stories of hardship, rumors were abundant. One Union private from Wisconsin wrote of his unit's arrival in Gainesville, Missouri: "The inhabitants of Gain[e]sville had almost all fled in terror from the approach of the 'Northern Hessians.' Here we first heard of those stories which have preceded us during all our hitherward march—that we were burning and robbing houses, destroying property, imprisoning or killing all males from twelve years upwards—and much more of the same trash."[10]

But it wasn't only Confederate supporters who were fleeing. In a letter to his brother, one Unionist wrote, "If I could get away from here I would go in a minute but there is no chance. . . . God only knows what these times are coming to. . . . Property is not worth anything."[11]

Although there are no records that explain exactly what happened to the Naves, family lore holds that their land was confiscated. Whatever occurred, during that summer of 1863 all of them—except young Jim—decided to leave Missouri and make their way together in a long and treacherous journey to the western frontier. They may have thought they were leaving heartache behind, but they had no inkling of the danger, hardship, and pain they would confront along the way.

Chapter 6

This is the great emigrant route from Missouri to
California and Oregon, over which so many thousands
have traveled within the past few years. The track
is broad, well worn, and can not be mistaken.

—Capt. Randolph B. Marcy, *The Prairie Traveler*

In late August 1863 Lizzie Martin and Luly, who had just turned
seven, climbed aboard their wagon and headed to Atchison, Kansas,
about one hundred miles west of their Missouri home. They had
decided—along with nearly five hundred others—to join a massive
wagon train heading westward to the Idaho Territory, where gold
had been discovered in a desolate spot called Alder Gulch about
three months earlier.

The Nave family had decided to join the many thousands of
Missourians fleeing from the horrors of war. In some of the most
ravaged towns, most of the population—both pro-Union and pro-
Confederate—left. Some moved to less vulnerable areas of Missouri,
others to Illinois or Iowa or their native homes in the East or South.
Still others decided to escape "America" altogether and head west
to the new territories. "Nearly all of the southern families have left,"
wrote one young Missouri woman in a letter to her aunt.[1]

Nearly sixty years later, Luly remembered the horrors of her childhood years in Missouri. "Back along the walls of time, myriads of
pictures hang," she said. "Number one of these is best faced to the
wall, for in it, I see the persecutions we were subjected to during and
at the closing of the Civil War, the awfulness of which made it easier
to bear the hardships of our journey to the West, across the plains."[2]

Atchison, on the banks of the Missouri River, was a popular starting point for wagon trains traveling west on the Santa Fe and Ore-

gon Trails. The Naves' three-generation traveling party included their eldest son, Jacob; his second wife, Mary; and their two-year-old daughter, Ellah May. Daughter Cynthia Nave and her husband, George Hale, carried three-year-old Laura and one-year-old Lucy. The group also included the Naves' unmarried youngest daughter, nineteen-year-old Lucy Ann, and twenty-seven-year-old Errendle, who somehow had managed to remain free after his prison break. (According to some family accounts, he had ventured to Colorado in the late 1850s to mine gold and haul freight before returning home to fight for the South.)

Lizzie could escape conditions in Missouri, but she could not escape her debts. A public administrator was assigned to settle David's estate and sell his land. With her limited remaining funds, Lizzie bought a wagon that she arranged to have covered with two canvases for their journey across the plains, along with one yoke of two oxen. Although slower than horses, the oxen had more endurance and could more easily navigate the rugged terrain along the trails. A relative of David's had donated a yoke of cows, which would provide the family with milk during their long journey.

Luly noticed the "many people hurrying excitedly to and fro . . . outfitting for the trip, with what little there was left after their most everything was confiscated."

The wagon train would begin its journey along the Santa Fe Trail, which led across the flat Kansas plains before it forked and joined the Oregon Trail, which headed farther north. Army captain Randolph Marcy, in *The Prairie Traveler: A Hand-book for Overland Expeditions*, offered guidelines for those planning to make such a journey, ranging from necessary supplies to handling the temperaments of fellow travelers. He did not provide advice for women but suggested that for a three-month trek, men should bring two blue or red flannel shirts, two wool undershirts, two pairs of drawers, and six pairs of socks, along with a hat, a poncho, and a coat.[3] He also recommended a belt knife and whetstone, soap, three towels, a comb and brush, two toothbrushes, and mending supplies.

Keturah Penton Belknap, who had made a similar wagon train journey to Oregon with her husband and young son in 1848, described how she planned to pack her own family's wagon:

> We will load at the hind end and shove the things in front. The first thing is a big box that will just fit in the wagon bed that will have the bacon, salt, and various other things. . . . Now we will put in the old chest that is packed with our clothes and things we will want to wear and use on the way. . . . Now there is a vacant place clear across that will be large enough to sit a chair. . . . There I will ride—on the other side will be a vacancy where little Jessie can play. . . . The next thing is a box as high as the chest that is packed with a few dishes and things we wont need till we get thru and now we will put in the long sacks of flour and other things. The sacks are made of home made linen and will hold 125 pounds—4 sacks of flour and one of corn meal. Now comes the groceries—we will make a wall of smaller sacks stood on end dried apples and peaches, beans, rice, sugar and coffee—the latter being in the green state. We will brown it in a skillet as we want to use it. . . . All we will have to do in the morning is put in the bed and make some coffee and roll out.[4]

Keturah Belknap may have been well organized, but the pioneers were aware of the countless difficulties they would encounter. Captain Marcy alerted his readers of the hazards: "There is much to interest and amuse one who is fond of picturesque scenery, and of wild life in its most primitive aspect, yet no one should attempt it without anticipating many rough knocks and much hard labor; every man must expect to do his share of duty faithfully and without a murmur."[5]

He pointed out that such a long journey could result in men becoming "irritable and ill-natured," especially when they thought they were working harder than others or were disliked by the leader of the train. He urged them to be "cheerful, slow to take up quarrels," and conciliatory, which would "contribute largely to the success and comfort of an expedition."[6]

Mary Sheehan Ronan, the nine-year-old who traveled with her

father in a wagon from St. Joseph, Missouri, to Denver, Colorado, in 1862, wrote not about the mundanities of preparing for such a long journey but of a trip filled with possibilities: "In my earliest memories I see a covered wagon halted on a dim road. It winds out of sight on a wide prairie undulating endlessly toward a vast, shadowy background of looming mountains. . . . I can recall my wonder at the bigness of the world and what the long journey might promise me."[7]

Seven-year-old Luly Martin, who had never seen a mountain, may have experienced the same sense of wonder during her journey—but mostly, she remembered her fear.

One day early in their journey, as the wagons lumbered along the rutted prairie trail, Luly spied "a long streak of dust rolling up from the earth toward us." The travelers knew that such a dust storm would most likely be stirred up by one of two things: either bison or Indians on horseback, which in Luly's naive mind was the "most dreaded of all the dangers of the plains." The group was anticipating attacks "at any and all times," she said, and all eyes were fixed nervously on the distant, roiling dust. As the cloud moved closer, the travelers realized they were watching an immense herd of buffalo—and it was heading in their direction. They faced the distinct possibility of being trampled to death. The captain ordered the men to corral the wagons and bring the oxen inside the circle. And then they waited—for hours—as the herd moved closer. When the bison were within shooting distance, no one dared to fire "for fear of causing them to stampede" and crush the wagons and passengers.

This time, their fears were not realized. The leading bison avoided the wagons, and as the end of the herd passed by, the travelers quickly took advantage of the abundance of fresh bison flesh. "We killed all we wanted from the last of the herd, then all hands that could got busy curing the meat," Luly remembered. They cut it into small pieces, salted it, strung it on cords, and smoked it over a campfire. Then they nestled the smoked meat, still attached to the cords, between the two canvas covers of their wagons to protect it from dust while it continued to dry as they moved along.[8]

Daily life during the three-month trip was not always frightening or challenging. Mary Ronan remembered, "I was nine years old and felt great satisfaction in being helpful. If we camped for the night by a stream, I jumped down from the wagon at once and ran to get a bucket of water. Then I picked up sticks to start the fire, or buffalo chips when we traveled through buffalo country."[9]

Many walked alongside their wagons to spare their oxen from hauling extra weight. Lizzie's sister Lucy Ann sewed vibrant-colored quilt squares as she walked, keeping her scissors, thimble, needle and thread, and bits of cloth handy in her large-pocketed apron.[10]

Some chores were easier than they would have been at home. Lizzie stored the cow's milk in her mother's oak churn, which effortlessly transformed it into butter as the wagon jolted along the trail. "At our night camps, we would take up the butter, making a very palatable spread," Luly recalled.[11]

There was constant stress. No one knew what the next day would bring. Would they find clean water along the route to keep themselves and the oxen healthy? Would they find animals to kill for food? Would they encounter storms, disease, or illness? And Luly, along with others, continued to worry about Indian attacks.

One day, another cloud of dust again appeared on the horizon. But this time, the travelers saw that it was raised by "some live travelers and seemingly many of them," said Luly. "Out of the dusty distance the outlines of moving forms developed into a band of Indians." She was terrified, having listened to the adults tell countless stories of violence against wagon trains. The band continued to follow the train from afar throughout the morning. As the gap began to close, the captain ordered men to corral the wagons and to place women, children, and livestock inside the ring while they rushed to build short fortifications with oxen yokes. Some of the women "stood by their men folk with rifle in hand ready to help," Luly added.

The Natives began to circle, coming closer each time, "until they could see how well we were fortified and getting some idea of our number of fighters," Luly remembered. Whatever the Natives' real intent, the pioneers came to the conclusion that when the Indians saw the immense size of the train, they "thought it best to come in friendly greeting." Luly also noted that "their only weapons then, except those captured from the whites, were bows and arrows, which could only be used at short distance; they were sorely afraid of fire arms."

The Indians moved on. "That was the nearest we came to being attacked on the trip," Luly said. "Though behind us we heard of and before us we came to burnt trains which had been first looted and the people killed, scalped and left lying around to bake in the hot sun."

Luly's perceptions were not unique. Historian John Unruh noted, "For virtually all overlanders the western Indians were akin to the buffalo in symbolizing danger and adventure.... That Indian begging and thievery were traveling nuisances cannot be denied, but it is also clear that the extent of Indian attacks on overland caravans has been greatly exaggerated." He adds that most violent confrontations "were usually prompted by emigrant insults and disdain for Indian rights, as well as by indiscriminate and injudicious chastisement meted out by the U.S. Army."[12] Another incident during the Naves' journey sheds light on Unruh's observation. At one point, the wagon train stopped to set up camp for the night near a large band of Indians who "made them feel welcome." The next day, a group of warriors rode up to the train's leaders along the trail, saying they had found a young woman in their tribe dead. They accused a member of the wagon train of her murder, asking the leaders to turn him over for retribution. The man, later described by Lucy Ann's granddaughters as "a fellow of lowly character," admitted the deed, "not believing that he would be handed over ... for killing a 'no-good Indian.'" His calculation was misguided. Choosing to protect the lives of everyone else, "the leaders of the wagon train preferred giving him up." And "a very frightened, screaming and begging young man was handed over to a fate which he richly deserved."[13]

Unruh points out that most conflicts between travelers and Indians took place west of the Rockies—the part of the journey that still lay ahead for the Naves.[14]

❧

Along the route, the pioneers stopped at forts and trading posts to freshen supplies and perhaps find a letter waiting from home. At some point during those first few months of their journey, Jacob and Mary Nave learned that both of Mary's parents were very ill back in Missouri; they returned with their daughter and remained there until Mary's parents died within one month of each other later that autumn.[15]

Three months and more than six hundred miles later, on November 5, 1863, the rest of the Nave family arrived in Denver City in the Colorado Territory. They decided to spend the winter in the tiny mining settlement of Empire City, about thirty-five miles west of Denver. Founded just a few years earlier, Empire City sat in the Clear Creek valley at the foot of a mountain that was being mined for gold. A reservoir filled by the creek provided water to many log cabin homes, and a few stores stocked provisions. These few amenities did little to soften the harshness. "We put in a very hard winter . . . physically, financially, in fact every way that was possible, seemingly," Luly remembered.[16] On December 23, 1863, matriarch Lucy Nave's mother died at the age of eighty back in Missouri—exactly a year and a day after the death of David Martin. Lizzie did not yet know that she would never again see her younger brother Jim, either.

❖

In the year after his parole, Jim Nave had become a hardened Confederate guerrilla. At about eight in the evening of December 11, 1863, while the rest of his family was in Empire City, Jim led a four-man team that stopped at a Mooresville, Missouri, store owned by a Union supporter named Shelton Brock, who recently had bought a train car of horse feed for Union troops. Jim and two of his men entered the establishment, and after briefly conversing with an employee named Jerome Bloom, Nave shot him. Brock returned fire but missed, and another guerrilla shot Brock dead. The men sacked the store, with one taking Brock's watch off his body, and left "at their leisure," stealing horses and escaping a pursuing party. They made their way to Illinois, where they would disappear for more than a year.[17]

Chapter 7

On the unprotected emigrant trails to Salmon, Boise and
Powder rivers, and to the Bannack [Montana Territory] moves,
we shall expect to hear of many murders and robberies.
—*Rocky Mountain News Weekly*, April 9, 1863

During the Naves' punishing winter in Empire City, the group selected a captain to lead the wagon train on the second half of the trip—a journey that would cover nearly seven hundred miles of vast plains, barren desert, and treacherous mountain passes.

In his guidebook for pioneers, Captain Marcy had noted the importance of selecting a male captain with "good judgment, integrity of purpose, and practical experience," because "these are indispensable to the harmony and consolidation of the association." He added, "His duty should be to direct the order of march, the time of starting and halting, to select the camps, detail and give orders to guards, and, indeed, to control and superintend all the movements of the company."[1]

The group chose as its leader a thirty-one-year-old South Carolina physician, Dr. William L. Steele, who later would become a Montana state senator, county treasurer, county coroner, county physician, and the three-time mayor of Helena.[2]

On this final leg of the journey, the group would be two-thirds smaller, with about 350 people, fifty horses, and sixty wagons. Usually, most wagons were drawn by two or three oxen, but some now had only one remaining after others had died from eating what Luly described as "poison weeds."[3]

The wagon train's smaller size may have been the result of hardships suffered during the first leg of the trip or perhaps because some members may have decided to return home, remain in Colorado, or split off to travel elsewhere. Captain Marcy advised travelers that the "company should be of sufficient magnitude to herd and guard animals, and for protection against Indians. From 50 to 70 men, properly armed and equipped, will be enough for these purposes, and any greater number only makes the movements of the party more cumbersome and tardy."

The wagon train set out from Empire City in early April 1864 and headed north to central Wyoming, where it planned to reconnect with the Oregon Trail. As the travelers continued west, they would face the choice of remaining on this widely traveled trail or veering north to the new Bozeman Trail, which offered a route to Virginia City that was nearly four hundred miles shorter and had more reliable access to water. The Bozeman Trail, so named by hunter John Bozeman after he had scouted it the previous year with fellow mountain man John Jacobs, had been used for centuries by Native tribes and later by hunters and traders. Although it offered the advantages of speed and water, following this route was much riskier. It traversed the hunting grounds of the Teton Sioux and their allies near the Powder River, who desperately were trying to protect their native land, which now was occupied by U.S. military forces.[4] Bozeman, who had been warned by the Sioux not to lead emigrants across the territory, decided against heeding their warnings. In July 1863 he was forced to turn back his wagon train after Indians threatened to attack if it crossed their land.[5]

The leaders of the Naves' wagon train chose the safer—though still exceedingly difficult—route. Each morning, the group arose at the call of the captain. The women cooked breakfast and helped their young children get dressed while the men greased and repaired wagons, tended to the oxen, and finished chores. The wagons traveled single file, gathering at night in a fortresslike circle with the fronts of the wagons turned outward and the tongues (the wooden poles that connected the wagons to the ox yokes) joined with chains. The animals were placed inside the pen, and men on horseback patrolled the corral "day and night."[6]

The travelers' fear of Indian violence was omnipresent and likely exacerbated by newspaper accounts like this one from *Rocky Mountain News Weekly*:

Our Nevada exchanges come to us filled with accounts of Indian murders and outrages in that territory and western Utah [where the Naves were heading]—Every thing indicates that the coming summer will see much trouble with the Shoshones and other tribes of the Great Basin, lying between the Rocky and Sieria [Sierra] Nevada mountains. Emigrants to the northern and western mines will doubtless fare worse than they did last year, unless they go in strong parties and prepared to defend themselves. The recent horrible massacre on the Overland Mail route . . . is a startling instance of savage ferocity.

The article went on to call for volunteers to "'pursue and destroy' red skins."[7]

✣

Before the trip was over, young Luly would witness several incidents she would never forget: "In several places we found a lone cook stove sitting in the pra[i]rie with ashes of the home blowing with the winds, while the occupants were murdered or carried off. Even though the white man has been a trespasser and an invader in the Indian lands, I have seen too much of their dastardly, cowardly doings to learn to like them."[8]

But it wasn't Indians who were responsible for inflicting tragedy on the Nave family during their trip to Virginia City. It was something much more unexpected.

Chapter 8

Yes, all over the world death comes the same
But some day God will give her back to us again.

—From a poem by Lucy Tinsley Hale

Less than one week into the second half of their cross-country journey and just eighty miles north of Denver City, the Naves' wagon train stopped for a day to rest, wash clothes, and bake bread. Near their campsite, they found an abandoned two-story cabin that seemed to offer excellent shelter for their brief stay. As the women cooked and washed, George and Cynthia Nave Hale's eighteen-month-old daughter, Lucy Elizabeth, "toddled around on the floor." Unnoticed, she crawled through a doorway and up the cabin's staircase, where the family found her sitting on the top step.

Her aunt Lucy Ann recalled, "When we found her, her little mouth was full of glass. We did our best to clean it out, hoped she had swallowed none." But soon, the toddler began to complain about her eyes, and her suffering increased by the hour. The entire wagon train decided to remain camped. More than twenty-four hours later, on April 17, she died. Luly described a scene of great "sadness and sorrow." The family was forced to disassemble part of their wagon box to build a coffin and dig a grave by the trail. Grandfather James Nave found a flat stone on which he chiseled Lucy Elizabeth's name, the dates of her birth and death, and the names of her parents. Then they had no option but to move on with the wagon train.

Later, Lucy Tinsley Hale wrote a poem about her great-aunt's heartbreaking grief, which began,

Mother told us a sad incident that happened out on the plains . . .
. . . Cynthia knelt by the little grave, her hands clasped, sorrow,
grief and woe

34

We lifted her trembling body to her feet, Come Cynthia, we must go.
We placed her in the wagon, her grief was so intense she couldn't
  speak before
As we moved on her pale lips quivered as she cried—I'll never see
  my baby's grave anymore.

They left Lucy Elizabeth's tiny body in a lone grave beside the road.

✻

Mother Nature soon offered up more dangers. The travelers had
to cross central Wyoming's North Platte River three times, which
in some cases required the men to load the wagons on a ferry with
women and children on board and swim the cattle across.

Next, the train reached a spot called Parting of the Ways, a wide,
flat, sagebrush-covered plain distinguished only by a small, sandstone
Pony Express marker inscribed with arrows pointing left and right
and the words "F. Bridger" and "S. Cut Off."[1] If the pioneers followed
the wagon wheel tracks to the left, they would continue southwest
on the Oregon Trail toward the U.S. Army's Fort Bridger, where
they could rest, stock up on supplies, and send letters to friends and
family back home. If they turned to the right, they would be choosing
the Sublette-Greenwood Cutoff, which continued west to the Bear
valley in the Idaho Territory. That route would shorten by three days
their journey to the Bear River Divide, at the intersection of Utah
and the Idaho Territory, but it also would force them to travel for fifty
miles through the bleak, desolate Red Desert. The Naves' wagon train
would follow this route, which would put the lives of their animals at
risk and test their ability to find clean drinking water.

At a spot called Barrett Springs, said Luly, "we filled our kegs and
swung them under the wagons, then filled every available container
in the train. . . . We had to limit ourselves to so much water per day."
The only other water source in the desert was the alkaline Bitter
Creek, from which the stock nearly refused to drink. "The water
was also slimy from dead carcasses that had fallen in the stream and

died," Luly said. "Some times people were forced to drink when not equipped to carry a sufficient amount along."

The wagon train next would come upon the desolate lava lands, where they would ride through ghostly rocky formations of volcanic cones.

The group arrived at the Snake River in the Idaho Territory, whose violent waters had caused French Canadian trappers to dub it *la maudite rivière enragée* (the accursed enraged river). Again, they had to ferry the wagons across. One man in the wagon train drowned as he tried to swim across with his cattle. From there, they crossed the backbone of the Rockies, winding their way up the slope toward the gold-mining town of Virginia City, which would become part of the Montana Territory on May 26, 1864.

Young Mary Sheehan Ronan and her father had taken a similar route a year earlier. Despite the hardship, she recalled the beauty of the mountain landscapes: "I can picture the golden sunsets gliding behind distant mountain peaks and flooding the valleys with magic light. . . . and the rhythm of going, going, going."[2]

❖

On April 30, 1864, just as Lizzie and her family were nearing their final destination, the authorities caught up with Jim Nave and his gang, who were continuing to hide out in Illinois. Jim's possessions included a black carpetbag containing leg-irons and two Colt Navy revolvers.[3] The fugitives were taken to jail in the town of Quincy, where one of the crew—still wearing the murder victim's watch—was found dead, hanging in their joint cell. The others were transferred back to Chillicothe, where they were indicted in May 1864 for murder and robbery and jailed in the town of St. Joseph. Along with other prisoners, they managed to escape, perhaps assisted by a jail employee. Within a month of that escape, Jim had joined another group of rebels led by a man named Clifford Holtzclaw.

On June 18, 1864, Jim and fourteen others in Holtzclaw's band of Confederate rebels raided the north-central Missouri town of Laclede.

That afternoon, "a number of the citizens of Laclede were holding a Union meeting in Earl's Hall . . . when Captain Holtzclaw, a notorious guerrilla, dashed into town . . . and surrounded the building."

Union army reports stated that Holtzclaw's men led townspeople into the public square, arrested them, and plundered stores, stealing thousands of dollars of goods. Holtzclaw "made the citizens a short speech in which he said that he visited Laclede for the purpose of hanging some abolitionists, and that if any of his Southern friends were abused, or that any of his men were hurt or killed, or that he was pursued, he would deal with them severely, killing two for one."[4]

Laclede resident David Crowder, a disabled former Union soldier, "seeing the situation, and being a brave man, took deliberate aim with his revolver, from one of the windows, and firing . . . , wounded James Nave, one of the guerrilla band, whereupon a comrade of Nave shot Mr. Crowder dead before he left the window."[5]

The guerrillas commandeered a mail hack, placed the severely wounded Jim Nave in the wagon bed, and forced its driver to head westward on a road that paralleled train tracks. During the raid, two residents had ridden to the nearby Union garrison, alerting them of the attack. Union soldiers quickly climbed into a train locomotive and steamed toward the escapees, killing one of the outlaws, wounding the innocent driver, and shooting Nave yet again.

Jim Nave died the next day, "at the house of a Mr. Stepp, near Laclede." Recorded in a Nave family Bible is this handwritten note: "Jas. Harvey Nave was brutally murdered by the enemy in Linn Co, Mo . . . aged 23 years and 8 mos. Had not a decent burial."[6] Another family Bible notes that he was "buried by strangers." An 1864 arrest report by the Union provost marshal described him, on the other hand, as a "noted bushwhacker and murderer."[7]

Chapter 9

This is a very dull, desolate looking place. . . . The houses and
stores are mostly on one street. . . . The street runs along "Virginia
Gulch" where, for a width of 500 to 1000 feet, shoveled, uplifted, &
piled, it looks as if an enormous Hog had been uprooting the soil.

—James Knox Polk Miller, writing in his 1865 diary
about Virginia City, Montana Territory

On Saturday, June 18, 1864—two and a half months after leaving
Empire City, more than a year after leaving Missouri, and on the very
day Jim Nave was mortally wounded back in Missouri—the Naves'
wagon train arrived in Virginia City. By the time the family arrived
in this newly sprung town in the one-month-old Montana Territory,
their possessions consisted of "10 cents in coin, 1 months provisions,
9 family members, 2 yoke of oxen and a wagon each and 1 milk cow,"
Luly would later recall.[1]

The family couldn't have arrived at a more electric time.[2] Nothing
more than an assemblage of miners making camp in treeless, dusty
hills less than a year before, Virginia City now was teeming with five
thousand gold seekers, entrepreneurs, and hangers-on who hoped
to profit from the riches uncovered in nearby Alder Gulch. Like the
Naves, many of these new arrivals were escaping brutal conditions
in Civil War border states like Missouri and those farther south.[3]
The presence of so much gold dust in Virginia City also brought
crime and violence by "the element . . . Robbers and road agents,"
Julia Bennett remembered her grandmother and mother telling her.
"It was a wild camp."

A few months before the Nave family's arrival, violence had
exploded. A group of men led by Henry Plummer, the town's crooked
sheriff, had terrorized residents, robbing miners of their gold and mur-

dering more than one hundred people. Fed up, a group of citizens calling themselves the Vigilantes tracked down the outlaws. Between December 20, 1863, and February 5, 1864, the Vigilantes banished eight men and hung twenty-four—including Sheriff Plummer and two of his deputies—from the gallows located in the center of town.[4] Their bodies now were lying in graves at the top of Burial Hill, which overlooked quiet valleys, grass-covered hills, and distant mountains. Although the Vigilantes had made headway in quashing the violence, Hezekiah L. Hosmer, chief justice of the Montana Territory, reported that the "revolver, however, is still there, and much too often resorted to as the umpire to settle sudden quarrels; and the terror of the vigilants has been sometimes invoked, and I fear on one or two occasions employed, when milder measures would have accomplished this same object."[5]

Nevertheless, the town was booming. On August 27, 1864, the first published issue of Virginia City's *Montana Post*—which accurately billed itself as "the only paper in the territory"—breathlessly reported,

On arriving at this place what astonishes any stranger is the size, appearance and vast amount of business, that is here beheld. Though our city is but a year old, fine and substantial buildings have been erected, and others are rapidly going up. We are safe in saying that 100 buildings are being erected each week, in Virginia City and its environs. . . . Indeed the whole appears to the stranger to be the work of magic—the vision of a drama. But Virginia City is not a myth, a paper town, but a reality. That it is a fast place none will doubt.

A young man named James Knox Polk Miller had a less enthusiastic opinion of the town. "'Everybody and his cousin' here seems to live in a log cabin and mud roof," he wrote in his diary.

This was the world Lizzie and Luly encountered after more than six months of exhausting travel across the plains and through the mountains. Lizzie's parents rented a two-room cabin, and their sons and son-in-law joined the masses mining for gold.

"It is generally supposed that the men who thus toil for gold belong exclusively to the laboring classes," said Chief Justice Hosmer. "This is not the case. I have seen lawyers, judges, clergymen, ex-members of Congress, ex-governors, merchants, even professors of the highest character in their old homes, toiling side by side with laborers from nearly all the nations of Europe. Mining is a great leveler."[6]

While the Nave men learned the workings of placer mining, which involved running their streambed diggings through rocker boxes to separate the precious gold from sand and gravel, Lizzie and her unmarried, twenty-year-old sister Lucy Ann set up a dressmaking shop in the family's two-room, shake-roofed log cabin. Having no sewing machine, they made their clothing by hand, carefully basting the fabric, then filling the gap between each stitch with an additional one to create the more sophisticated appearance of machine stitching.[7] Lucy Ann saved the scraps to use in quilts.[8]

Men vastly outnumbered women in mining camps, and there were plenty of opportunities for single women to find lucrative work. While some worked as prostitutes, others, like the Nave sisters, took respectable jobs as seamstresses and laundresses or operated boardinghouses and restaurants. They were paid in gold dust, the currency of the moment in Virginia City. The town seemed to be the perfect place for Lizzie to earn money to raise Luly and to help settle the overwhelming debts from her husband's estate.

The burgeoning town was as awash in activity as it was in gold. "It was essentially a cosmopolitan community, American in preponderance, but liberally sprinkled with people from all the nations of Europe," wrote explorer and entrepreneur Nathaniel Pitt Langford, who had arrived in the region two years earlier. "Some were going, and others coming, every day."[9]

The Montana Theatre presented plays and traveling productions. The Star bakery and saloon advertised its low prices, touting, "Here is the place to get an honest loaf, a cake or pie, and 'something to wash it down.'" Physician and surgeon H. N. Crepin, "formerly assistant in the Hospital du midi in Paris, and attached to the New York Hospital, New York—recently from Dubuque, Iowa," had just opened an office across from the hayscales on Main Street.[10]

On Sundays, other than regular church services, "there was nothing visible to remind a person in the slightest degree that it was Sunday," James Miller wrote in his diary. The Sabbath was the only day of the week miners weren't working their claims, so "every store, saloon, and dancing hall was in full blast. Hacks running, auctioneering, mining, and indeed every business, is carried on with much more zeal than on week days. It made me heartsick to see it."[11]

*

It must have taken several weeks, if not months, for the Nave family to learn of Jim Nave's death in Missouri. In her album, Luly kept a photograph of the man she called Uncle Jim, who, she wrote simply, "was killed at the close of the civil war." In the photo, he wears a beaver hat, a heavy overcoat, and a bow tie. His fresh, young face is aged slightly by a thick mustache and woolly beard that reaches to the base of his neck. Next to Jim's photo is another image, that of a serious-looking young woman in a dark dress trimmed with a high-necked lace collar and velvet ribbon. "This is Lucy Lester," Luly wrote beneath the photograph, "who he was engaged to be married."

Chapter 10

With the hardest part of the mountain winter before them, our own
citizens would do well to lay up a store of something more tangible
than pirouettes, more nutritious than the memory of varsoviennes
and more profitable than smiles and tickets as per agreement.

—*Montana Post*, January 14, 1865

The winter of 1864–65 in Virginia City was frigid, harsh, and long. It
"commenced in October and terminated in April. With the exception
of two or three warm days, the weather was uniformly cold during the
entire period."[1] Mail delivery from the States was cut off for five or six
weeks at a time, and supply trains pulled by ox teams were unable to
get through from Salt Lake City, five hundred miles away, because of
snow as deep as eighteen feet.[2] Food prices were sky-high, and flour
was so scarce that it had to be kept under lock and key. On Christmas
Eve, the *Post* reported, "The majority of [freight wagon] trains now
over-due loaded with flour and other staples have corralled and are
in winter quarters in the vicinity of Snake River. We cannot expect
them to arrive here before the latter part of February."[3]

Only meat was still readily available. In fact, many miners existed
on literally nothing else—a diet they called "beef straight."[4] As for
flour, "When a load came it was followed by a large procession to the
store," Luly reported, "where each man's five pounds was weighed
out to him at $1.25 per pound" ($20 per pound today).[5]

Virginia City residents learned how to select real, unadulterated
flour. The *Post* told its readers,

First, look at the color. If it is white, with a slight yellowish or straw-
colored tint, buy it. If it is very white, with a bush cast, or with white
specks in it, refuse it. Second, examine its adhesiveness; wet and

knead a little of it between your fingers; if it works soft and sticky, it is poor. Third, throw a little lump of dry flour against a dry, smooth, perpendicular surface; if it falls like powder, it is bad. Fourth, squeeze some of the flour between your hands; if it retains the shape given by the pressure, that too is a good sign. Flour that will stand all tests, it is safe to buy.[6]

During that difficult winter, Luly attended the first school in Virginia City, where an educated Englishman, Thomas J. Dimsdale, was her teacher.[7] "We are glad to inform our readers that Prof. Dimsdale has opened a school on Idaho Street," reported the *Montana Post* in its first issue. "Prof. Dimsdale is highly recommended by well known authorities, and we hope to see the first class school which he desires to organize and maintain, permanently established in our midst." Forced to drop out of Oxford College when his family's business failed, Dimsdale had arrived in Virginia City in 1864 after a stay in Canada. He later became editor in chief of the *Montana Post* and authored the first book published in the territory—*The Vigilantes of Montana*, which originally had been printed in serial form in his newspaper. This controversial history heralded the hangings conducted by the Vigilantes; Charles Dickens reportedly called it "the most interesting book I ever read."[8]

Lizzie used some of her earnings to send Luly to the log school; no free public schools were established in the Montana Territory until 1866. Professor Dimsdale charged tuition of $1.50 per week, and Luly attended for three months.[9] "Parents and guardians should send their children to school, even where some sacrifice of personal ease is the result," urged the *Post*.[10]

※

By the spring of 1865, the flour shortage in Virginia City had reached crisis proportions. "A few short sighted men," reported the *Post*, attempted to corner the flour market, resulting in a doubling of its price in just a few weeks—from $23 to $45 per hundred-pound sack.[11] On April 19, 1865, a group of nearly five hundred armed men, led by one on horseback waving an empty flour sack, marched through the streets of Virginia City "in an avowed determination to take all the flour in town, and divide it among those who had none," reported the newspaper a few days later. "Within five minutes of their arrival . . . they searched every store, house, cabin or cellar in which they suspected that flour was concealed."

The men did not find the three one-hundred-pound sacks of flour the Naves had carefully perched atop a roof beam of their cabin, hidden above a canvas ceiling. Nor did they find the sack that matriarch Lucy Nave had sewn inside the family feather bed.[12] Some would do nearly anything to lay their hands on the precious powdered wheat. "A miner sold his wife to another miner for two sacks of flour," Julia Bennett recalled her mother telling her many years later.

Despite the scarcity of supplies, the lure of gold kept fortune seekers coming. The Virginia City bank was buying gold dust for $30 to $34 an ounce.[13] For members of the Nave family, the boom brought the opportunity to make a good living. The *Post* noted, "Wages are high—from $6 to $12 per day [$90 to $181 in today's rates]. . . . Anything in the shape of labor commands high rates."[14] Luly remembered, "Money was no object in those days—it was plenty, and more in sight for the digging—what we needed and wanted was not in the country to buy."

In late spring 1865, supplies finally arrived, but prices were astronomical. Luly recalled that bacon and candles cost $1 per pound, coal oil was $10 per gallon, one hundred pounds of sugar cost $75, and eggs were "one dollar each when you could get them and cats were $10.00 each. We bought one."[15]

Lizzie's older brother, Jacob—who had returned to Virginia City while his wife, Mary, and daughter, Ellah, stayed in Missouri following Mary's parents' deaths—decided to take up farming, for him a more familiar way of earning a living than mining. On October 16, 1865, he wrote a long letter to his distant wife, whom he affectionately addressed as "My Dear Mollie":

It is a great Sattisfaction to me that I once more have the privilige of writing to you this morning to let you know that we are all well & doing well. . . . I have long since come to the conclusion that we had better forget past troubles as mutch as possible & live for future happiness but ones mind is of sutch a nature that it cannot be void of the power of wandering back into the vista of the past & there dwelling & commenting in moments of deep reflection.

In careful, delicate penmanship, Jacob wrote, "Times is very lively / miners generally doing well so far as I am acquainted but I am mostly interested in farming So I must tell you what I am a doing in that line." He had raised about five hundred bushels of potatoes, which would net him "something over 10 cts per lb." He added,

I must tell you Something about a little onion patch that I have / I bought two ounces of Seed & Sowed them & there was not over a half stand & they will bring me in about $400 dollars / I raised but few cabbage but I bought one half of an acre a few days ago for which I paid Seven hundred & 50 dollars / that seems to you likely to be a high price but I feel confident that I will make over twelve hundred dollars clear of all expenses.

He added a long list of other Virginia City prices, including oxen ($100 to $200 each), tea ($6 per pound), and baking soda ($0.60 per pound)—which must have sounded astoundingly high to his wife back in Missouri. "In fact," he wrote, "every thing is high & a great likelihood of being higher before there is any brought here for another year."

He then asked his wife to investigate selling their Missouri land before spring arrived, noting that he would be satisfied with any price she was able to get for it.

"Mollie you may ask & wonder why I am so anxious to Sell," he said. "Well my reason first I never expect to live in that part of the country / Second taxes will soon eat up the land. Third I want you to come to this country as soon as possible & fourth I can make $10 here to 1 in that country & lastly if you and Ellah were only here I would be well Sattisfied."

Clearly missing his family, he added a note to his daughter, Ellah, who was now five: "My dear little pet you know not how very mutch I want to see you / if you were only here what a nice time we would have a riding / I have the little pony keeping for you."

He told her to ask her mother to buy her a saddle and bridle and then added a final postscript to Mollie, asking her to send "yours and Ellahs minitures as soon as possible" and to "write often."[16]

In another letter, this one undated, he is heartbreakingly lonely, giving his wife advice on how to make the trip to join him out West. "If you have any relatives comeing out you might come with them," he wrote. "If so I can meet you Some where on the road."

He told Ellah he had enough money to buy her a "doll baby" she had asked for, and "when you and Ma comes out here I will buy you several nice things."

Then he asked Mollie to urge his friends to write, saying, "Never have I received a line from any of my once considered friends. I feel thankful that there is one who is wiling to write to me and that is you my dear Mollie for it is for you and my dear child that I care to live for / which as it is life is no enjoyment to me but I live in hope of a better day / but if that day never comes how miserable life will be."[17]

Lizzie Martin, widowed and raising a young daughter in this rough-and-tumble outback, may well have felt the same as her brother Jacob, because she and her sister Lucy Ann already had taken to the road again, also in search of a better day.

Chapter 11

The ambition of every wayfarer across the plains was
to kill a buffalo at as early a stage of the journey as he
could, and to repeat the feat as often as he could.

—Jerome C. Smiley, *History of Denver*, 1901

Lizzie and Lucy Ann weren't the only ones who had decided to leave raucous Virginia City. At about the same time, the man who would become Julia Bennett's father, a wanderer in his midthirties named Benjamin Franklin Bembrick, also moved on.

Born on October 29, 1828, Benjamin was a handsome child, with dark-brown hair, brown eyes, and a freewheeling spirit. His mother, the German-born, elegantly named Maria Magdalena Plessing, had arrived in America with her parents in 1805 at the age of twelve. Leaving on a trading ship named *Venus* from the port of Amsterdam in the Netherlands, they disembarked in Philadelphia on August 31 of that year, carrying nothing more than "three chests and one bundle."[1] Benjamin's father, Frederick William Bainbrich, was Prussian, and over the ensuing decades, public records recorded his surname as Beinbreak, Bainbrick, Baenbrick, Benbrick, and finally Bembrick. In October 1810 he married Maria in Philadelphia, and by 1820 the couple had moved to Howard County in the Missouri Territory, which was then "on the edge of the frontier." They bought eighty acres of land and started both a farm and a family. When the census taker knocked on their door in 1830, the family reported having four sons, two daughters, and one slave. Benjamin was then the youngest child.[2] When he was about twelve, the family moved to Chariton County, where Frederick purchased forty acres along Yellow Creek.[3]

In January 1847 Maria died, and two years later, the precocious Benjamin and his two older brothers were among the hundreds of Missouri Territory residents—mostly men—who decided to leave home to seek their fortunes out west.[4] Newspapers were filled with stories of the great California gold rush and the nearly unbelievable riches to be mined. Missouri's *Glasgow Weekly Times* tempted its readers with this dispatch from Monterey: "The El Dorado of fiction never prompted dreams that revelled in gold like the streams which shoot their way from the mountains of California. They roll with an exulting bound, as if conscious that their pathway was paved with gold."

The newspaper's correspondent boasted that the mineral "is found in a shape rosembling snow flakes, and is washed from the sand with great ease. . . . There is a man in Monterey who washed out five hundred dollars in six days. Every body is now going or gone to this gold region. Some thousands are on the spot, and more on the way."[5] Lured by the siren call of precious metals, the trio of Bembrick brothers set out astride mules on their two-thousand-mile adventure. If their voyage was in any way similar to that of a fellow Missourian, the Rev. Benjamin Franklin Stevens (who kept a diary of his own trip that same year), they traveled between twelve and twenty-five miles a day and argued about which route to take. They slept poorly and often were cold but at other times were overcome by heat and thirst. Before they had even crossed the Missouri border, they encountered lightning, whirlwinds, thunderstorms with gusting winds that tore apart tents, and hailstones that "whistled like bullets."[6]

They would have met and sometimes camped with fellow gold seekers since the route to California was heavy with them. The travelers encountered friendly Cheyenne, Pima, and Maricopa Indians; unfriendly Comanche, Utah, Apache, Navajo, and Snake warriors who sometimes rode with scalps dangling from their saddles; and "miserable looking Mexicans" who, according to Rev. Stevens, were "kind and hospitable."

The travelers drank coffee and ate fresh bacon, rancid bacon, bread, hard crackers, and dried apples. As they traveled farther west, they bought corn and onions from Mexicans and watermelon, salty muskmelon, and pumpkin from Indians. They learned how to eat mesquite beans from the trees; sampled prairie peas, which reportedly made good pickles; and devoured black currants as sweet as candy.

Along their trip, they came upon—and sometimes managed to shoot—buffalo, grizzly bear, wolves, deer, elk, antelope. But many found the buffalo to be old, tough, and not fit to eat.

They endured hordes of mosquitoes and were startled out of their sleep by tarantulas and centipedes. When they were lucky, they came across ash, mesquite, and acacia, which the reverend reported made "excellent and lasting firewood." Frequently, however, they did not know where to find water or wood and burned buffalo chips for fuel whenever they could find them.

They saw plants they had never before encountered—forty-foot-high saguaro cacti and sprawling prickly pears—and marveled at wild fields of scarlet, pink, and white anemones; morning glories; and asters. Their mules fed on grass, which was at times long and abundant and at other times parched and desperately scarce.

They traveled across mud, high grass, desert, swamps, fertile plains, rivers, streams, and salt lakes. They drank water that was clear and fresh, water that was sweet yet brown, and water Stevens described as "thick with mud like paint," which made them sick.

Many of the pioneers died en route to their dream—some after fights with fellow travelers and some at the hands of Indians but many more from accidents and disease. These unlucky ones were buried along the trails.

Rev. Stevens wrote, "Every grave we pass in these lonely plains casts a gloom over the mind. No one knows but it may be his turn next." The Bembrick brothers may have had the same sad thoughts at one time or another during their journey. They also may have encountered men returning home who told them that the fantastic stories of gold and riches were false. But there were others, more encouraging, who shared tales of finding "pieces of gold as large as a partridge egg."

"Every report we hear from California confirms that which we have heard before, that there is plenty of gold in California," wrote Stevens, "but indeed it is attended with a great deal of difficulty to get there."

Where the brothers set up their final camp and what they encountered there remains a mystery. They may have experienced the same mind-boggling sensations as Granville Stuart, a fellow midwesterner who arrived in California in 1849:

I felt as though I had been transplanted to another planet. There was nothing here that I had ever seen or heard of before. The great forests, the deep cañons with rivers of clear water dashing over the boulders, the azure sky with never a cloud were all new to me, and the country swarmed with game, such as elk, deer and antelope, with occasionally a grizzly bear, and in the valleys were many water fowls. Tall bearded men were digging up the ground and washing it in long toms and rockers, and on the banks by their sides was a sheet iron pan in which were various amounts of yellow gold.[7]

Did the Bembrick brothers strike it rich, or did they fail miserably? There is no record of their time in California. But four years later, in 1853, Ben, either alone or with his brothers, recrossed the plains on horseback and arrived in St. Louis, Missouri, sixty-seven days later, "thinking that he had seen enough of the world and had endured his share of hardships."[8] Later that same year, he headed back west—this time alone. His father gave him two horses—one to ride and one on which to carry his bundles. "He had a rifle and a six shooter and was an expert shot," remembered his daughter Julia. "For ten years he explored the west, hunting and trapping."[9] He met the famed mountain man Jim Bridger, who discovered the trail that led fortune seekers to the gold mines of the Montana Territory. Bridger, described by one who knew him as a born guide who had the entire West "mapped out in his mind,"[10] taught Ben how to hunt buffalo at a time when "single herds would blacken the hills and valleys as far as the eye could see. . . . The demands made upon them by the Indian population, before the white man came with his deadly rifle, had no appreciable effect in diminishing their numbers."[11] The waves of gold seekers—Ben among them—soon would contribute to their near extinction. In most cases, buffalo "were clumsy, lumbering creatures, but when wounded and brought to bay, they became dangerous customers," wrote one early western historian. "Many a hunter forfeited his life, and that of his horse to boot, to the charging fury of a wounded buffalo bull, which could gore and rip and tear with the strong stumpy horns of his shaggy head, with amazing dexterity."[12]

Ben also trapped in Shoshone country, along the Lamar River, a tributary of the Yellowstone in northwestern Wyoming.[13] Kit Carson described the hand-to-mouth existence of trappers and hunters during that time:

> Our ordinary fare consisted of fresh beaver and buffalo meat, without any salt, bread or vegetables. Once or twice a year, when supplies arrived from the States, we had flour and coffee for one or two meals, although they cost one dollar a pint. During the winter, visiting our traps twice a day, we were often compelled to break the ice, and wade in the water up to our waists. Notwithstanding these hardships, sickness was absolutely unknown among us. I lived ten years in the mountains, with from one to three hundred trappers, and I cannot remember that a single one of them died from disease.[14]

Bembrick moved on to the Kansas Territory, a desolate, mountainous region home to the Cheyenne and Arapaho. Many "declared the . . . landscape to consist of but two features—great, dreary plains of drifting sand ending at the base of impassable, appalling mountains of barren granite."[15] The Natives' homeland began to be threatened in the summer of 1858, when two miners made the first significant gold discovery in the Rockies. Over the next several years, more than one hundred thousand prospectors arrived, and new towns sprang up overnight, including one named Auraria City (today, the very heart of Denver). Perhaps attracted by the town fathers' willingness to donate a lot to anyone willing to build a house on it,[16] Ben acquired a piece of land in that four-street town. By early 1859—within just a few months of its establishment—Auraria City boasted fifty cabins, a post office, a saloon, and carpentry and blacksmith shops. By June it had grown to 250 buildings. The rapid expansion of settlers was causing increasing tension with Native tribes. One visitor to the town freely shared his virulent opinion: "The American has come to this hitherto unknown region, and the sound of the rifle and the axe, the lowing of stock and the falling of timber around the smoke columns, are sounding the death-knell of the wild beast and the wilder man of the soil—are proclaiming the fact that their restless and encroaching enemy has set himself boldly down in their midst, to scatter them like chaff, and to possess and improve the Talent they have so long had buried in the ground."[17]

These tensions may have played a part in convincing Ben to move on. Nearly one year to the day after Auraria City's incorporation, he sold one section of his lot to a baker for $200 and another portion to someone else, apparently riding away with a hefty profit.[18] He then may have headed back east for a spell, since he purchased 160 acres of rolling farmland just west of the Missouri border in Doniphan County, Kansas, on May 1, 1860, from a man named Levi Gurgonus, who had himself acquired the land from the U.S. government in payment for his service in the War of 1812.[19]

That spring, Ben was contracted by the Overland Stage Company to supply meat for those traveling on its bustling western stagecoach line. In February 1861 Cheyenne and Arapaho chiefs signed a treaty ceding more than 90 percent of their lands. That same month, an act of Congress made Colorado a free territory. The time was ripe for entrepreneurs like Bembrick. "The buffalo hunter was a businessman, the first of his class on the frontier," wrote Joseph Kinsey Howard. "Somewhere he had dug up the money to buy the rifles, several Indian horses at $10 to $20 each, hundreds of pounds of gunpowder and bar lead, tools and molds for making his ammunition, one or two 'dead-ax' wagons—at least $100 each—and a season's food. . . . His life was hard and dangerous, but it paid. . . . He had learned the country, the climate, and hardship."[20]

Known by that time as "one of the best marksmen in the west," Ben claimed a record one-day kill of twenty-five deer and seventy-five buffalo.[21] He moved fifteen miles west, to another new mining town and transportation hub for freight wagons called Golden City. The town newspaper, the *Golden Mountaineer*, observed, "Our city is now full of energetic, go-ahead men enroute to the gold mines." There, Ben wasted no time in exercising his right to vote in the first Colorado territorial election on August 19, 1861.[22]

Ben, who stood six foot three, now answered to the nickname Doc. Julia would later say that her father was given the nickname as a child, but a longtime friend said it was "due to the fact that in the early days neighbors in the community called upon him frequently for help and assistance when they were in distress."[23] Doc was cast as the hero in "War in Golden City," a tongue-in-cheek article in the *Rocky Mountain News*, written under the pseudonym A. Toughcuss and published the day after the alleged event:

THE TOWN ATTACKED BY THE ENEMY IN FORCE—GREAT
EXCITEMENT AMONG THE INHABITANTS—FURIOUS
CHARGE AND TOTAL ROUT OF THE ENEMY.

Golden City, March 20th, '62

The ordinary quiet of our dignified and peaceable city was suddenly ruffled this morning by the startling announcement that the enemy was within the corporate limits of this place . . . and about to attack the town from the west . . . and thereby cut off our retreat into the Clear Creek Can[y]on, which is so strongly recommended as a strategic position. The thrilling intelligence was immediately communicated throughout the town. When the courier, "Old Virginia," arrived with the news, Lieut. Col Cheney, by virtue of the absence of his superior officer Col Ferrell—being in command, instantly ordered out one company of cavalry under Doc. Bembrick, consisting of Doc. and another man, one company of infantry (four small boys,) and one company of artillery, and the rear brought up by Pollard and three dogs, the latter to be used as skirmishers. The enemy—a Mountain Lion—was first discovered by "Old Virginia," near the residence of Col Ferrell on the South side of the creek, but deeming his position unsafe, he seized the ferry boat and crossed over to Wall's Ranch where he gave battle to a bull dog, and was near taking a Newfoundland pup prisoner, when the bull dog was reinforced by Coleman, and the enemy repulsed. He fled to the mountains and fortified himself behind a huge rock, where he was soon invested by the forces sent out by Col. Cheney. By a brilliant charge of Bembrick's cavalry, the enemy was again routed, and eventually killed by a ball from Doc.'s rifle, which took effect in the head. The dead was triumphantly borne in by Pallard and "Old Virginia," preceded by Tige with his padlock, and deposited in front of Col Cheney's head quarters, where he was measured by the County Surveyor, and declared, officially, to be six feet in length. Col. Cheney has issued a "special order," thanking the forces under his company for their bravery, promoting Bembrick and declaring the mouth of Clear Creek in a state of blockade.

Still consumed by wanderlust and by now a seasoned adventurer, sometime in 1864 Doc Bembrick headed seven hundred miles northwest to another new mining town—Virginia City. He reached the boomtown in November—a mere five months after the arrival of Lizzie and Luly Martin. They were not yet acquainted.

Chapter 12

The scenery of the Missouri, from the point of its formation by
the forks of the Jefferson, Madison, and Gallatin, to the place
of its departure from the Territory . . . is reported by those
who have seen it, and especially by those old writers, Lewis
and Clark, to exceed any other scenery on the continent.

—Hezekiah L. Hosmer, chief justice of the Montana
Territory Supreme Court, January 1866

In the fall of 1864, after just a few months in turbulent Virginia City, Lizzie Martin's parents James and Lucy Nave, along with her sister Cynthia's family, had moved forty miles north to a new settlement, where they joined a few other pioneers who had arrived there only months before. The earlier settlers had named the spot Willow Creek, reflecting the languid trees that grew along the water's edge. Located at the edge of a fertile valley where the headwaters of the Gallatin, Jefferson, and Madison Rivers meet to form the Missouri, it must have seemed an idyllic landscape compared to the rough, treeless, and dusty Virginia City. The Naves' new home in a fertile, grass-covered valley, flanked to the west by the undulating, snowcapped Tobacco Root mountains, was not only lush and unpopulated but well suited to farming, a way of life much more familiar to them than mining.

They may have learned about the opportunity from an article published in the *Montana Post* a few months before they left Virginia City: "Many persons have the idea that our country is not adapted to agricultural purposes. This may be and we think is true of a portion, but we have seen many large potatoes, turnips, onions, etc., that have been raised in our valleys. On the Madison [River] farming is carried on quite extensively, and we are informed that the crops with the exception of corn are quite good."

The newspaper encouraged new settlers to turn to the soil: "Let a portion of our citizens turn their attention to farming and stock-raising—they will make money, and the people will receive provisions much lower. . . . We think it far better to pay the farmer at our door a good price for provisions than to purchase in the States or at Salt Lake, and pay the enormous price for freight."[1]

Along with the valley's agricultural prospects, the Naves also may have been lured by talk of the recent gold discoveries in the Willow Creek area, including the Taylor, Jefferson, Star Spangled Banner, Red White and Blue, and Willow Creek Lodes, all uncovered in July and August of 1864.

The Naves knew they had to work quickly before the early Montana winter arrived. They set up camp in tents and covered wagons while they built a small, one-window cabin with logs from alder trees, covering the roof with poles and sod and packing and leveling the dirt that would serve as its floor. They crafted a door and a tabletop from boards from their wagon and repurposed its wheel spokes as stool legs.[2]

Keeping in touch with their loved ones was difficult; letters were dropped off by the stagecoach as it passed through on its way north to the new mining town of Helena City—if it could make its way through in bad weather.[3] In his end-of-year message to the new legislative assembly of the Montana Territory, Governor Sidney Edgerton urged the development of new mail routes and a post office at Willow Creek, saying, "Our mail facilities are altogether inadequate to meet the wants of our extended and growing population."[4]

It may have taken weeks for the residents of Willow Creek to learn of the reelection of President Abraham Lincoln in November 1864. Here in the territory, they didn't have the right to vote in that election; if they had, the Nave men most likely would not have cast their vote for the Republican. The Pennsylvania newspaperman Alexander Kelly McClure, a strong supporter of the Union, encountered many former Missourians while on a speaking tour through the Montana Territory. "Thousands of them came here in the early part of the war," he told readers of his newspaper column back east, "because they were too cowardly to fight with [Confederate general Sterling] Price and too faithless to oppose him."[5] Back in the Naves' home of Livingston County, Missouri, Lincoln had defeated Democratic challenger General George B. McClellan by only 45 votes—342 to 297—although Lincoln won the state of Missouri overall with 60 percent of the vote.

❖

That winter, most of the Willow Creek settlers survived by eating wild game.[6] On Christmas Day 1864, the Naves held the community's celebration in their cabin, with the few neighboring families pitching in their meager offerings to provide the holiday meal. Rev. Lerner Stateler, a Kansas native and traveling minister of the secession-supporting Methodist Episcopal Church South who had moved west after Unionists threatened to hang him, conducted the service. The family matriarch, Lucy Nave, soon would become one of six original members of the first society of the Methodist Episcopal Church South in the Montana Territory.[7]

As the spring thaw commenced, the citizens of Willow Creek were likely unaware of the dark events occurring back in "America." They would not read in the *Montana Post* about General Lee's April 9 surrender at Appomattox until April 22. "The Best News Yet!" noted the newspaper.[8]

And just one week later, on April 29, 1865, the news of President Abraham Lincoln's April 15 assassination finally reached readers of the *Post*. "The Dark Day," read the headline. "Abraham Lincoln is basely murdered."

❖

While back east, controversy raged over the war's finale and the emancipation of slaves, in the Montana Territory the focus of discussion was on the Native population of the western territories. Territorial governor Edgerton promoted the cultivation and continuation of "amicable relations" with the "numerous Indian tribes within our borders."

He promised to punish Indian aggression but, "at the same time, hold to a strict accountability any who may trespass upon the rights of the Indian. In this way only, can peace be maintained." Yet he also called for "the extinguishment of the Indian title in this Territory, in order that our lands may be brought into market."[9]

The editor of the *Montana Post* had pointed out to his readers in August 1864, "This country belongs to the Crows who have heretofore been very hostile to the white man, but now that they are drove out themselves by the Sioux, are anxious to cede their country to the Government. This will be done this year, when we will be put in possession of one of the richest valleys west of the mountains."[10]

The journalist Alexander McClure, like many Americans at the time, also was a booster of westward expansion. He wrote that the emigrants' arrival into the Montana Territory would extend "civilization," making "a continued line of white supremacy from the Mississippi to Puget Sound. The wondrously fruitful valleys will fully supply the miners, and the savage will recede or die before this 'manifest destiny.'"[11]

This dangerous push and pull between the Natives and the recent arrivals would continue to escalate.

Chapter 13

Woman is a being to be idolized in the mountains. Her
presence inspires the roughest mountaineer with respect; and
her bravery in venturing the perilous journey there, and her
patient endurance of the privations incident to her residence,
are themes of frequent and enthusiastic admiration.

—Hezekiah L. Hosmer, chief justice of the Montana
Territory Supreme Court, January 1866

After struggling through a hard winter of their own in Virginia City, Lizzie and Luly Martin and Lucy Ann Nave decided to move on. In mid-May 1865 the trio joined a "short train of freight wagons" headed 125 miles north to the new mining boomtown of Helena City.[1] *Montana Post* correspondents had spent the last several months touting its benefits: "Everybody here is making money either in or out of pocket," wrote one. "I believe the indications of a good time coming are sufficiently reliable to justify the most cautious in planting their stakes here," reported another.[2]

Lizzie was dealing from afar with the settlement of her late husband's estate, and she desperately needed funds. She was in debt to Missouri creditors to the tune of more than $1,000 (about $16,000 in today's money).[3] The same month that the sisters headed to Helena City, the court in Livingston County, Missouri, had ordered the public administrator handling Lizzie's late husband's estate to sell thirty acres of their farm that had been rented since her departure, for the purpose of settling some of her debts.[4] She needed to earn enough money to settle the remainder, and Helena City seemed to hold promise.

❖

Helena City's initial moniker of Last Chance Gulch told its story—the miners who had discovered the site on October 30, 1864, had been ready to give up prospecting until they took a "last chance" and struck gold. The sisters may have read of the town's riches in Virginia City's *Montana Post*, which beginning in February 1865 had published breathless letters from correspondents nearly every week that described the endless nuggets to be mined and the beautiful scenery of Helena's Prickly Pear valley—much lusher than the dry and barren Virginia City.

"Doubtless this is the best timbered section in the Territory," wrote "C.H.S." in a letter headlined "A Trip through the New Mines." "The mines are so extensive that large amounts of gold will be taken out during the present season. . . . Helena, in Last Chance gulch, will doubtless be a business centre of no mean importance. It already has some 75 houses completed, and as many more commenced. . . . I spent two days at Helena, and found everything full of hope and promise."[5]

Another letter to the editor in that same paper, from a man dubbed "Tyro," touted the town's physical beauty: "Our mountains and hills are covered with yellow pine, forming the best of building material, and reaching the outskirts of the town. Besides, our hills are not barren or rugged, but covered with an abundance of bunch grass, upon which stock fatten, even in winter. . . . I will hazard my reputation as a prophet, that there will not be a livelier place within the Territory than Helena. Many of your old neighbors are already located here."

As soon Lizzie and Lucy Ann arrived, they set up business as seamstresses. The sisters rented a small cabin on Cutler Street, which was tucked up against the base of Mt. Helena in the tiny, three-block residential section of town. In addition to sewing, they served meals to the miners working Last Chance Gulch.[6] On June 29, 1865—only six weeks after leaving Virginia City—Lucy Ann wrote to their parents, "We have cleared $180.00 in four weeks. Board is $18.00 per week," adding, "We like mutch better here than there we can make more clear money."[7]

In the same letter, Lucy Ann asked her sister Cynthia to send "all

4. A studio portrait of Luly "Lulu" Martin taken in Toston, Montana Territory, circa 1866. Museum of the Rockies Photo Archive.

of my gluves and my crape shawl and all of the Delane scraps of any kind or color." She said she was using one-inch pieces of Delane, a worsted wool, to sew a quilt in the log cabin design. Lizzie added a note of her own: "May [Jacob's wife Mary?] I have sold 1 doz. of your purses for $9.00 & the rest are nearly all sold but I dont know yet for how much."

Luly was enrolled in a log cabin school for the three-month summer term. "She is learning very fast," Lucy Ann told her parents. Luly, a pretty girl with a serious countenance and chin-length, dark-brown hair swept back from her forehead, was now eight and looked older than her years.

Young Mary Sheehan, whose family also had moved to Helena City from Virginia City a few months after the Nave sisters, most likely was a classmate of Luly's. Both reported having the same teacher. "For a short time the beloved Lettie Sloss was my teacher again in a little log schoolhouse clinging to the steep side of the gulch," Mary wrote. "The distinguishing memory of this school is that on Friday afternoons we had lessons in embroidering and that Miss Sloss directed my making of some pin cushions."[8] The schoolhouse's only neighbors on the barren hill were a few miners' cabins.

When not in school, Luly also was quickly filling her piggy bank by delivering lunches to miners in the gulch, collecting a little "something extra" in tip money. Years later she recalled that she "could see the water rippling over the coarse and fine gold and being invited by the miners to help myself, which I did admiring the small nuggets most. I took those at different times until I had $150.00 in hand, when I might have had four or five times that amount had I taken the larger ones."[9]

From 1864 to 1868, $19 million in gold (the equivalent of more than $300 million today)—was mined from Last Chance Gulch.[10] Not surprisingly, Helena City was thriving. The first photograph of the town, taken the year the Nave sisters arrived, captured a bustling Main Street flanked on both sides by wood-frame stores, including the Nevada Dry Goods and Clothing Store, a grocery store, drug store, livery, tin shop, and an establishment selling pies and cakes. Canvas-covered wagons pulled by oxen lumbered up its dirt streets, along with smaller mule-led carriages. Perched on the hill above Main Street were dozens of log cabins.

Journalist Alexander McClure, who visited the town a few years later, described it to his readers: "Helena has all the vim, recklessness, extravagance, and jolly progress of a new [mining] camp."[11]

Young Mary Sheehan also fondly remembered the ramshackle town:

> I loved its setting, high in the hills of the valley of the Prickly Pear. I loved its narrow, crooked Main Street that followed the course of Last Chance Gulch a little way and broke off abruptly in a wilderness. I loved the cross streets that led up and down steep hills and ended suddenly against other steeper hillsides, in prospect holes, or in piles of tailings. It did not matter that the thoroughfares were trampled

deep with dust or churned oozy with mud by long strings of mules, oxen, or horses drawing heavy wagons. I had known life only in towns that were thus, and for that reason I was unaware of the ugliness of the hastily constructed frame and log buildings with false fronts and rickety porches. I paid no attention to the inconvenient boardwalks at different levels and only occasionally continuous. I continued, as in Virginia City, to be neither curious about Helena's vices nor interested in their blatant demonstrations. The dry, light sparkling air of the place invigorated me and gave zest to living.[12]

Luly, four years younger than Mary, played on the green hillsides covered with pine trees, wild roses, plump huckleberry bushes, and white sweet alyssum, watching the clouds make shadows on the grass. A friend gave her a honey-colored blacktail fawn as a pet, which she would lead up Mt. Helena, behind their cabin, to play. "On being spied by the town dogs, he would become frightened at their barking, rare up on his hind feet and strike me with his front feet until I would have to let him loose," she remembered. "He would be at our back door on Cutler Street by long leaps down the mountain, in a few minutes."[13]

Luly's aunt Lucy Ann also thought the new area was beautiful and reassured her parents that the town had "the best of society."[14] Montana Territory's chief justice Hezekiah Hosmer agreed, telling a New York City audience that "Virginia and Helena are favored with intelligent and interesting female society. The social virtues are cultivated by all the recognised ceremonies of civilized intercourse."[15]

When they were not working, the Nave sisters spent time socializing and taking day trips. One such trip led them to the pinnacle of Mt. Helena, a seven-mile journey. "We took our dinner with us . . . and had a nice time," Lucy wrote her parents. She went on to report on the doings of various family members and friends: "We have not heard a word from Ere [Errendle, their brother] yet and do not no where he is. . . . Uncle is working for Mr. E. Wilson he has been here twice / Mr. Warmens lives about one mile up the gulch I have been there twice and spent the day with Mrs. Wilson. They are making money like dirt."[16]

The Wilsons were fellow Missourians who had arrived in Virginia City just a few days after the Naves—in fact, they might well have been members of the same wagon train.[17] Other Nave family members also were headed to Helena City. "Aunt started for this place May 3 and if no bad lucke will bee here in six weekes," Lucy wrote.[18] However, she noted that Indians were causing trouble for settlers passing along the Oregon Trail between Denver and the Little Blue River that flowed through Kansas and Nebraska. "The whites had to fite with them," she wrote, but she had not yet heard news of the outcome.

Lucy ended the letter by apologizing for her handwriting, saying, "I hope you will excuse this cribling for my eyes are so weeke that I can hardly see to write this evening." She then added a melancholy note acknowledging the uncertainty of whether she and Lizzie would ever see their family members again: "Give our love and best wishes to all our friends and would like very much to see theme all and receive to your selves the love of your affectionate Children till Death when we all will meete again / I want you all to come and see us soon / I cannot say when we will get to go to see you all so goodby."

And Lizzie, in tiny, careful cursive handwriting, appended a note that hinted of her own homesickness: "Write to us It seems long since we heard from you. Presume Lucy has given you all the news. Good bye Lizzie."

❧

On August 8, 1865, the Missouri public administrator overseeing David Martin's estate reported to the court that he had sold Lizzie and David's farm to a man named Mr. Edgerton for $1,000. With the sale earnings, Matson paid the $300 in debts that the Martins had owed to thirteen merchants and creditors—but Lizzie still owed hundreds more.

After only five months in Helena, on October 23, 1865, the peripatetic Lizzie and Luly were once again on the move—this time, returning into the arms of their family.[19] Before leaving Helena, Lizzie paid $0.25 per foot for lumber she would use to build a primitive lean-to shelter and then arranged to have it loaded onto a freight wagon that would take them on the four-day trip south to Warm Springs Creek in the Crow Creek valley, where her parents had moved to establish a ranch and operate a stagecoach stop.[20] Along the way, their wagon paused at Crow Creek, where they gathered wood they would use for both fuel and support beams for their new home.

On October 27 the freight wagon arrived at Warm Springs Creek, where Lizzie's supplies were unloaded. The next morning, the wagon moved on, leaving mother and daughter "unloaded beside the road, and at the mercy of the Indians and wild animals the place showing fresh signs of both," Luly remembered.[21]

Chapter 14

In the Crow Creek country, at the foot of the valley, and
in Confederate Gulch, gold has been discovered, and the
prospects are as rich as in other and better known localities.
Quartz, also is to be found in the neighborhood, and many
leads have been struck, but as I am a farmer, I have more to
do with "plough in the hand," than "Quartz on the Brain."

—"Ploughshare," *Montana Post*, March 11, 1865

One hundred miles north of Virginia City lay a desolate, mountain-ringed valley through which the Missouri River twisted, turned, and extended its arms to etch a series of small creeks. The land was nearly treeless and covered with golden grasslands that spread to the foothills of the mountains. It was a fertile spot, home to the Crow (or Absarokee) Nation, and still mostly unexplored by the pioneers who were heading westward. It was there in the fall of 1865 that Julia Bennett's father, Doc Bembrick, stopped roaming, claimed sixteen acres of land, and settled down. He was thinking about entering the burgeoning cattle business.[1] The *Montana Post* had reported in its inaugural issue on August 27, 1864,

> We never saw a country more adapted to stock-raising than Montana—the grass is abundant, beautiful streams of clear sparkling water flow through rich valleys; cattle are rolling in fatness. In the valleys but little snow falls in the winter, the atmosphere being dry, and having long periods of dry weather, the grass in the winter is like the best of hay. The cattle feed on this during winter and are fat in the spring. Beef can be made here for one cent per pound, as the labor and cost of raising stock is comparatively nothing.... No country where cattle must be maintained on grain and hay can compete with us, as we will soon satisfy our Eastern boys.[2]

Doc took claim to sixteen acres of land and built a small cabin on the banks of Crow Creek, taking advantage of the Homestead Act, which the U.S. Congress had authorized three years earlier in an effort to settle the West. The act provided up to 160 acres of surveyed public land to anyone who laid claim, built a house, and raised crops on it.[3] Doc was one of only three settlers—all ranchers—living in the Crow Creek valley in the newly formed Jefferson County, but his homestead was about four miles east of the rich Leviathan and Keating lodes, which had brought a rush of prospectors to the area a year after he arrived, and a little more than two miles east of the town of Radersburg, which also had sprung up as a result of the rich discoveries.[4] To the west were the tall peaks of the Elkhorn Mountains; to the north and east, the Big Belt Mountains; and to the south, acres upon acres of golden grasslands. The prospectors would provide a healthy market for the cattle fattened on the territory's lush grass.

Journalist Alexander McClure traveled through the Crow Creek valley at about that time. "The valley is quite large and level," he wrote, "but is barely supplied with water, as Crow Creek seems to be its only source for irrigation, and that has been almost drained by the miners on the Missouri [River] side of the bluff. It has an abundance of most nutritious grass, and many fine herds were grazing on it."[5]

Although he now had a cabin, Doc still went on frequent hunting trips, often heading south toward the Yellowstone River in search of game. One Saturday in late April 1867, he was returning from a hunt in that region when he stumbled upon the noonday camp of his acquaintance John Bozeman and his business partner, Tom Cover. Bozeman (whose eponymous wagon trail had been abandoned because of attacks on travelers by Teton Sioux) and Cover had stopped by a creek to eat their noon meal on the way to Fort C. F. Smith. They did not have meat, so Doc gave them a deer and then left. About an hour later, Bozeman was shot in the chest, allegedly by a band of Blackfeet. When he heard the news, Doc figured he'd been the last person to see Bozeman and his partner before the attack.[6]

On May 12, 1868, Doc Bembrick, now forty, married Indiana-born Laura Gibson, age fifteen.[7] Within a few months after their wedding, Laura was expecting.

Doc and Laura lived about a mile from a settlement called Crow Creek City, which, with no more than half a dozen structures, appeared to be little more than a town created by wishful thinking. Meanwhile, the town of Radersburg, which had "improved more in the last three months than any other camp in the Territory," was growing rapidly. The *Montana Post* published a letter from a correspondent who wrote, "It has two first class hotels. . . . The mines are being worked advantageously. . . . Although bar rooms are very plentiful here, we have a very orderly community. Fighting and quarreling are not as frequent here as in other places of even less size. Business is flourishing. Messrs. Barrett & Mimms, and Short & Coleman have choice assortments of staple and fancy groceries, and the prices are moderate."[8]

Located about halfway between Bozeman and Virginia City, Radersburg was a convenient spot for a stage stop. The fifty-three-mile trip north from Radersburg to Helena cost $7.50 and took seven hours, which the *Montana Post* described as "quick time."[9] Nearby were the new mining camps of Beat'em, Cheat'em, Rob'em, Cinch'em, and Hog'em. McClure explained that "Hog'em was 'hogged up' by a few miners, as is alleged, and thus it won its euphonious title." Ten miles away was "the celebrated Confederate Gulch, the richest of its size ever discovered." Its name, he noted, "is a reflex of the convictions and sympathies of its discoverers."[10]

Nothing is known about Doc and Laura's time as newlyweds, but their union was distressingly brief. A year after their marriage, on June 12, 1869, Laura died after giving birth to a daughter named Adaline. Doc laid her to rest in the Radersburg cemetery, where he placed a carved gravestone chiseled with an image of a woman's right hand dressed in a ruffled cuff, her index finger pointing toward heaven.

Doc was now alone with an infant child to care for, only a handful of people living nearby, and a sixteen-acre homestead to maintain. It's not clear how he coped as a widower trying to raise an infant daughter in what was still nearly the wilderness, but two and a half years after Laura died, he would take another young bride. Her name was Luly Martin. Their union would result in four children. And more than half a century later, one of those children—Julia—would be doing some pioneering of her own.

Part II

A woman's place

Chapter 15

There will be room for adventurers here. In Montana everyone
has a quarter square mile . . . in which to stomp about and
shout, or just to lie and look up at the vibrant blue-green sky.

—Joseph Kinsey Howard, *Montana: High, Wide, and Handsome*

By the late 1920s, southwestern Montana's Madison valley was a
sparsely settled paradise. Its northwesterly neighbor, Virginia City,
was a mere shadow of its boomtown days, with just a few hundred
residents living in its run-down frontier buildings. In fact, with the
entire population of Madison County numbering little more than six
thousand, the area looked much the same as it had when the Nave
family and Julia Bennett's father, Doc Bembrick, had first traveled
through the same country more than sixty years earlier.

The valley had been home to the Shoshone and Blackfeet tribes
before a few settlers began moving into the area in the early 1860s,
eager to claim the free land offered by President Abraham Lincoln's
Homestead Act. Now most of the valley residents were ranchers or
the ranch hands and cowboys who worked for them. Huge herds
of cattle roamed the rich grasslands that stretched the length and
breadth of the valley. Towering over them were the Spanish Peaks,
part of the Madison Range, always covered with snow at their highest
points, which soared to nearly eleven thousand feet. Gently rolling
pine-covered foothills flanked the range, and the shimmering Madison River—named by Meriwether Lewis in 1805 during his explora-
tions with William Clark—rambled through the valley, giving life to
the cottonwood and willow trees that lined its banks. The river and
its streams emptied into Madison Lake, a two-and-a-half-mile-long
reservoir created by the damming of the Madison at the turn of the
twentieth century.[1] Bear, elk, antelope, mountain lions, and bobcats

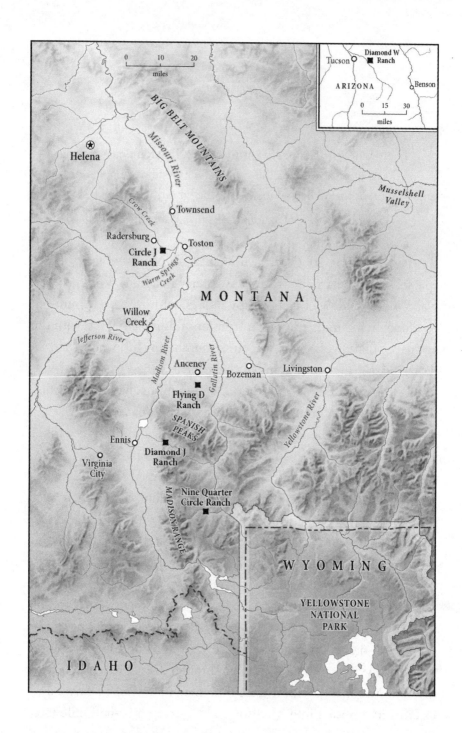

5. Map highlighting Montana and Arizona areas where the Nave, Bembrick, and Bennett families lived and traveled. Erin Greb Cartography.

6. A view from the Spanish Peaks, with the Diamond J Ranch in the valley far below, undated. Photograph by Chris Schlechten. Julia Bennett scrapbook, Sherry Merica Pepper private collection.

still roamed the mountains, and wildflowers—blue camas, pink wild geranium, purple wild aster, yellow evening primrose—blanketed the valleys and hillsides in the spring and early summer. It was an idyllically beautiful spot, rugged and wild.

In the fall of 1928, three years before she headed to New York, Julia Bennett's good friend Lee Smith—a tall, blue-eyed bachelor farmer and ranger raised in the Madison valley—had invited her to spend a few weeks in the nearby mountains hunting bear and elk. Lee moved slowly, spoke softly, treated people kindly, and had a dry sense of humor. He was seven years younger than Julia. There was no romance between the two, but they were well matched as hunting partners and had spent a month camping and shooting together three years earlier.

The unconventional pair packed up their provisions and headed on horseback into the wilderness. They planned to set up camp at an abandoned ranch in the Jack Creek Canyon, where Lee's longtime friend Art Smith (no relation) and his new wife were living. The surrounding mountains were full of elk, bear, deer, and wild game, and Julia was eager for the hunt. After having spent several summers cooking and tending to guests at the nearby Rising Sun Ranch—owned by the wealthy Butler family of Chicago, who had made their fortune in paper—she recently had rented a house in Bozeman, the largest town in neighboring Gallatin County. There her then-fourteen-year-old daughter, Marge, could attend high school and board with a family when necessary, while Julia scrambled to make a living during the winter months.

Julia and Lee rode through the valley and into the mountain foothills, wending their way into the hidden canyon. As they reached the ranch where they would set up camp, the view changed from stunning to dilapidated. Julia thought the abandoned two-story frame farmhouse was "a wreck." She saw a pile of trash in front "as high as a building," along with collapsed log cabins, mangled fences, and a ramshackle old barn. Hunters had left the place a filthy mess; they had been using the vacant house for years as a campsite. But Julia instantly was captivated by the location. Nestled in a green valley edged by two shimmering creeks, it was surrounded on three sides by pine-scented forests and capped by the Spanish Peaks to the north and by Lone Mountain and Jack Creek Lake on the east.

Julia didn't want to leave. "The country was beautiful, wild and the hunting wonderful," she wrote. She shot and killed a five-hundred-pound brown bear, which earned her a newspaper write-up. "Woman Kills Bear," proclaimed the headline in the *Helena Daily Independent*. "[Lee] Smith says Mrs. Bennett fired the shot which brought down the animal, and therefore the credit goes to the lady."[2]

"The lady" was no novice. She had been hunting since she was a child, having been taught to shoot by her marksman father, who was purported to have killed seventy-five bears in his lifetime.[3] Also like her father—who had died two years earlier at the age of ninety-seven—Julia was not intimidated by a challenge.

She took a hard look at the ranch property. Although the farmhouse was a disaster, she thought it had good bones—a rock foundation, a stone-walled cellar. There were four rooms downstairs, two small rooms upstairs, and a porch on each side of the house—large enough to make a comfortable home. She saw the potential for something else as well.

"I thought it was an ideal spot for a dude ranch," she wrote, saying that she felt like Brigham Young when he first laid eyes on the Great Salt Lake: "This is the place."

There were two major obstacles, however. Julia didn't know who owned it, and she had no money with which to buy it. Neither fact seemed to daunt her. Instead, she "got busy."

❧

After spending two weeks with Lee Smith tracking down wild game, Julia returned to Bozeman in a new pursuit. She was intent on finding both the owners of the tumbledown ranch she was determined to own and the funds to buy it. She made a visit to the bank in Virginia City, where she learned that the 160 acres with which she had fallen in love were owned by a couple named Roy and Lena Miller in Tacoma, Washington. She also discovered that the forested area surrounding the parcel was classified as national forest land, which would protect it from further development.

She managed to find the Millers and contact them about buying their property, all the while mulling over how to pay for it. She wasn't a greenhorn when it came to understanding the rigors of ranch life. She'd grown up doing chores and caring for the animals on her parents' remote 1,200-acre cattle ranch in the Jefferson valley of Montana. Her late mother, Luly—or Lulu, as she later became known—had always provided a welcoming meal and bed to travelers needing a place to rest for the night.

Julia thought she could find the money to finance a dude ranch of her own. While cooking at the Nine Quarter Circle, she met a guest from the Windy City named Mr. Murphy, who she described as a successful trader in the wheat market.[4] He told her that she ran the ranch so well she should open her own. Julia protested that she couldn't afford to. Murphy said, "Find the location, and I will finance it for you." Once she had acquired the land, she planned to track him down and ask for his help.

Nine Quarter Circle owner Julius Butler was impressed enough with Julia's talents that he called on her for yet another project. He wanted her to travel to Chicago in February 1929 to help book summer guests for the Nine Quarter Circle. It would be the first time she had ever ventured that far east, and she would be competing with other ranch owners who were visiting Chicago to promote their own places.[5] Another Montana rancher by the name of A. H. Croonquist spent three weeks in Chicago, Milwaukee, Madison, Minneapolis, and St. Paul that spring on an "advertising trip" for his Camp Senia. "The window display of the Northern Pacific offices at the corner of Jackson Boulevard and Michigan Avenue in Chicago, has brought hundreds of inquiries daily according to Mr. Croonquist," the *Billings Gazette* reported, noting that he distributed "an elaborate booklet" titled *Dude Ranching as a National Vacation*, along with a folder explaining *What People Do on Dude Ranches*. Croonquist pointed out that people especially liked railway brochures highlighting Montana's "various historical events and Indian legends."[6]

Western vacations were becoming more and more accessible in the 1920s, thanks to the national expansion of railroads and the construction of national highways catering to automobile enthusiasts. By 1930 nearly ten passenger railroads served Montana, with several offering direct routes to Yellowstone National Park in the southern part of the state and Glacier National Park in the north.[7] To ensure maximum return on their investment, railroads advertised heavily.

Dude ranches had gotten their start fifty years earlier, in the early 1880s, when Theodore Roosevelt read an article in a New York newspaper about a ranch in the Dakota Badlands called the Custer Trail Ranch, owned by brothers Alden and Howard Eaton. The adventurous Teddy, suffering following the death of his wife and his mother and eager for distraction, soon headed to the desolate territory on the Montana-Dakota border. He loved it so much that in 1883 he purchased the cattle and ponies of the nearby Maltese Cross Ranch.[8]

As more easterners began to make their way out west, the Eatons and other ranch owners began serving as hosts, charging guests for room and board. The "dude ranch" was born. The *Billings Weekly Gazette* reported in 1904,

> The dude ranch obtained its name because of the class of men who frequented it. They were the scions of wealthy New York and other eastern men, who wanted actual experience "roughing it" in the west. For a consideration the Messrs. Eaton provided them with bed and board and horses to ride. Attired like the heroes of western dramas to be seen on the cheap stage of the east, the young fellows would ride about the country and make occasional visits to the town of Medora, where they were always the center of attraction because of the gaudiness of their raiment and other unmistakable evidence of the genus tenderfoot, who wants to impress upon the genuine article that he is a b-a-ad man from away up the head of the gulch.[9]

By the 1920s the western cattle industry had hit hard times, and ranchers were struggling to support themselves. In 1926, eager to find a new source of income for himself and fellow ranchers, Ernest Miller of the Elkhorn Ranch—the first dude ranch in Montana's Gallatin valley—arranged a meeting of ranchers with the passenger traffic manager of the Northern Pacific Railroad to explore hosting vacationers at their homesteads.[10] That encounter became the first meeting of the Dude Ranchers Association, later called by its president, I. H. Larson, "one of the peppiest go-getting groups in this nation of go-getters."[11]

✳

While Julia was in Chicago learning the tricks of marketing dude ranches (whether she had any success booking guests for the Nine Quarter Circle, she never said), an unexpected opportunity presented itself. Julius Butler, whose well-to-do family was staunchly Republican, invited her to join him at president-elect Herbert Hoover's inauguration on March 4. They took the train to Washington, where Julia was Butler's guest at a farewell luncheon for the outgoing president Calvin Coolidge, who, according to a report in the *Montana Standard*, was "glad to quit office."[12] There, she reported that she "had the pleasure of shaking hands" with Coolidge and Mrs. Hoover. At Hoover's inaugural ball, she joined Butler in his box seats. She may have felt like one of Hoover's former schoolteachers—a Miss Mollie Carran of Iowa—who also attended the inauguration and reception. Carran gushed that "it was like receiving a free ticket to heaven."[13]

Still, when Julia returned to earth and headed back to Montana, she was no closer to securing the funds to buy the ranch. But as Larson, president of the Dude Ranchers Association, wrote, a rancher would "have to scramble for himself if he wanted to get along in this man's country." "Man's country" or not, Julia knew how to scramble. She had learned well from her mother, her grandmother, and her father, all of whom possessed something that Larson noted "can be found in unlimited quantities only in the west—that is a combination of character and personality."[14]

Chapter 16

As a result of the publicity and advertising which has been
done this winter by railroads, the Dude Ranchers' association,
individual ranchers and by various communities of the west, the
dude ranching idea has been made increasingly easy to sell.

—Montana ranch owner A. H. Croonquist,
Billings Gazette, April 3, 1928

In May 1929, five months before the disastrous Black Tuesday stock
market crash that would plunge the nation into its great economic
depression, Julia Bennett realized her dream of buying the ranch.
Ironically, it was the misfortune of her sister, Elizabeth, that offered
her salvation.

On May 16, 1929, Elizabeth's second husband, David Johnson,
died after three years of heart trouble. He "left her some money," Julia
noted vaguely, which Elizabeth promptly lent to her younger sister.
A mere twelve days after David's death, Julia signed the papers to
purchase for $1,200 the ranch she coveted.[1] She called her new home
the Diamond J, and she and Elizabeth (whom Julia called Diddy)
would live there together. The "Diamond" stood for a rope hitch
used to tie packs on horses, and the "J" echoed the name of the ranch
where Julia, Diddy, and their two brothers grew up—the Circle J.
Fortuitously, J also was the first letter of Julia's given name.

But she had much work to do before settling in. That summer,
Julius Butler once again asked her to manage the Nine Quarter Circle, and Marge joined her. Then Butler hired "a man in Chicago
to book and operate" his dude ranch for the following summer, so
Julia rented a house in Bozeman, where Marge would return to high
school. She and Diddy began moving into the Diamond J's run-down
farmhouse, which had stood empty for years. Lee Smith joined them

to help clean up the place. The sisters scrubbed walls, painted floors, and arranged what little furniture they had. "We had no modern conveniences," Julia said. The toilet was in an outhouse—or "chick sale," as Julia called it.[2] They burned coal in the kitchen stove and lit the house with an oil lamp.

Julia still didn't have the money to start building any cabins, with just $250 to her name. But the crew that had constructed the ranch house at the Nine Quarter Circle was out of work, so she asked them to come and start cutting logs for her lodge and cabins, confident she'd have the money to pay them by the time spring rolled around. Four men came, and she put them up in the ramshackle log cabins on the property. They began felling trees, while she and Diddy cooked their meals and Julia set to work finalizing construction plans.

"I designed the buildings," Julia wrote in her memoir, but she didn't mention that she hired the firm of Shanley, Willson, and Hugenin—Bozeman's most prominent architects and engineers—to draw up the designs. Willson, the son of Civil War general Lester S. Willson, had studied architecture at Columbia University and the École des Beaux-Arts in Paris and had worked in New York City before returning to Bozeman to open a practice in his hometown.[3] His firm drew two detailed sets of the original architectural drawings for the Diamond J that winter, one for single and double guest cabins and the other for a central lodge.[4]

The cabins, luxurious for ranch life, featured a sixteen-by-twenty-foot living room with a fireplace, along with a bathroom with bathtub and shower, toilet, and sink. The double cabins had two living rooms with a shared bathroom. The lodge, where guests would gather for meals and activities, would have a covered front porch, an expansive main room with a massive stone fireplace on one end, and an elevated dining area set off by what the architects called a "rustic rail." The building also contained a large kitchen, a walk-in icebox lined with cork to help keep the food cold, and a storeroom. In the kitchen were dish cupboards, a butcher block, a sink for washing vegetables and another for washing dishes, a range, a large cook's table, and a dining table for the help. (How much did all of this cost? The records haven't survived.)

Julius Butler, meanwhile, had decided to take advantage of the off-season to expand the Nine Quarter Circle. Over that winter, he also hired Lee Smith to head a crew to build a new lodge while he was back home in Chicago. In early February 1930 the crew stopped work because they had no windows or doors to install. Butler telephoned Julia, asking if she could head to the ranch to design them, just as she was finalizing her window and door designs for the Diamond J.

It was impossible to reach the Nine Quarter Circle Ranch by automobile in the middle of winter; the only way for Julia to get there was on horseback. She overwintered her horses at a stable in Gallatin Gateway, a tiny railroad-stop town southwest of Bozeman, so she phoned the stable owner, asking him to saddle her favorite horse and have him ready to ride by dawn the next day. Then she drove to Gallatin Gateway—where the temperature stood at a bone-chilling twenty-five degrees below zero—unhitched her horse, and headed off into the wilderness. After riding thirty miles in the snow, she reached a ranch owned by Mr. and Mrs. Lemons, acquaintances who ran the local stage stop. (The "stage" in winter was a bobsled pulled by a team of horses, which passed by just once a week.) By the time Julia reached the Lemons' ranch, the snow was twelve inches deep—high enough that she was forced to dismount and walk. She and her horse were exhausted, and it was too late in the day to move on, so Julia trudged to the house and asked Mrs. Lemons if she could spend the night in one of their guest cabins. The cabins were closed for the winter, Mrs. Lemons told her, but she invited Julia to sleep on the couch in their dining room, behind the potbellied stove, along with five cats and three puppies. The couch was the usual bed for the cats, who didn't cotton to being disturbed. Every time Julia would doze off, the cats would jump on top of her. When she awakened the next morning, she found that the dogs had scattered her clothes throughout the room. Despite a fitful sleep, she rode another twenty-five miles or so before reaching the Nine Quarter Circle. When she arrived, she didn't stop to rest. Julia and the head carpenter worked together for two days to design the doors and windows for the new lodge.

The longtime caretaker at the Nine Quarter Circle, Thomas Lincoln, was a codger. Raised in England, he had set out on a ship to America the same year Julia was born and taken up a homestead on the Madison River. He had never married, lived alone in a small cabin, and, since his arrival in Montana, had worked at various times as a sheepherder, a baker, a trapper, and a miner.[5] Known to everyone as English Tom, he preferred to spend most of this time alone. He posted a sign outside his cabin that read, "Have gone to Hell will be back in a minute." When Julia asked him what that meant, he explained that he was "just around the corner."

Julia loved people like Thomas Lincoln, whom she had known for many years. "He surely was a character," she wrote. There was no scarcity of "characters" in Montana, and she had grown up among them—men and women who had ventured into the expanses of the western territories to flee the Civil War, to avoid formal society, or to live life as they pleased. Despite Tom Lincoln's ornery personality, he and Julia loved to talk about hunting and often corresponded by mail. One year in late March, while winter continued to rage outside his modest cabin, he wrote her a letter in an ornate pen-and-ink script:

My Dear, Mrs Julia Bennett,

I received your Letter, some time ago, I have been so miserable, all through this month, snowing and blowing every day. Zero every night. . . . Snow Snow nothing but Snow, darn the Snow. . . . You mention catching a Silver Tip [grizzly bear], they are very playful little Animals. A few years ago, Myself, and old Mrs Silvertip met but not by an appointment, therefore we where [sic] both surprised by the sudden meeting, it did not, take me long, to know what to do, the first thing, I knew, I was in the upper branches, of a very Tall Tree I would have been their [sic] till now, if my Company had not moved away. Good bye.[6]

❧

7. Thomas Lincoln, Julia Bennett, and Julia's son Don Bennett, posing with the results of a hunting trip, circa early 1920s. Julia Bennett scrapbook, Sherry Merica Pepper private collection.

After Julia had finished her task at the Nine Quarter Circle, she awoke before dawn and rode through the darkness to reach the stage stop in time to catch the bobsled on its weekly passing. She tied her horse behind the sled, crawled in, buried herself under buffalo-hide robes, "and slept all the way to Gateway."

Chapter 17

What the world ought to know, is that there is no finer
hospitality anywhere in the world than that afforded upon a
western ranch, where the air is refreshing as a draught of old
wine, where the sunsets are gorgeous beyond description,
and where the mountain peaks outlined in the distance
radiate an air of tranquility good for tired nerves.

—*Great Falls Tribune*, November 24, 1929

When the spring of 1930 rolled around, Julia borrowed money—
perhaps from her friend Charlie Anceney, owner of the largest cattle ranch in Montana—to visit Mr. Murphy in Chicago, where she
planned to ask him for a loan to complete construction and pay her
workers. The stock market had crashed the previous fall, the economy
was failing, many banks had closed, and "every body was broke," as
she put it, but she was confident the wealthy Mr. Murphy would be
able to help. When she reached Chicago, she headed to his office,
where he informed her that he, too, was now broke.[1] "Six months ago
he could have given me the money," she wrote in her memoir. "Now
he couldn't give me a cent. So I returned to the ranch."

It was early April when she arrived back at the Diamond J. She
found all the logs for the cabins piled in a high stack next to the farmhouse, covered with snow. The workers had moved on to another job
in Big Timber, Montana, more than one hundred miles away.

"I had borrowed so much money that I felt I just had to build the
ranch," she wrote, so she quickly came up with another idea. She made
a trip to Bozeman, where she convinced a group of five local businessmen to finance her project, giving her five years "to work it out."

Then she "called the boys back from Big Timber and planned

the cabins." She hired more men, including expert carpenters and fireplace builders. The workers put up a tent to use for a dining hall, Julia and Diddy cooked their meals, and Lee Smith again took on the job of crew boss.

The men began the detailed process of preparing the hundreds of logs they would use to build the lodge and cabins. First, they peeled the trunks and then washed them three times. After hoisting them into place, they rewashed them with soap and water and coated them with stain, oil, and varnish.[2] The cabins were roofed with tar paper and sod, in a nod to both the romance of pioneer living and for practical purposes—the sod helped the cabins stay cool in the summer and warm in the winter.

The five cabins were tucked against the foothills and arranged in a semicircle facing the lodge, or "ranch house," as Julia called it. She named four of the cabins after wildlife her guests would see when they visited: Elk, Deer, Bear, and Antelope. A double, family-sized cabin was called Corral. Later, she would build a large barn, another single cabin, and another double cabin on a high hill overlooking the compound, which she would name Hill Top.

Julia didn't scrimp on the accommodations or the furnishings. "No dime-store stuff," she liked to say.[3] Her wealthy guests would be accustomed to first-rate accommodations, so each cabin had a private bathroom with toilet, sink, and bathtub. There was no electricity, so she provided candlesticks and candles in each cabin.

She bought high-quality twin beds, chairs, and rocking chairs, made in the Ozarks of old hickory wood and painted in vibrant colors. "Today after 33 years, that furniture is just as good as the day I bought it," she wrote.

The lodge had a rustic elegance. Its heavy wood-planked front door, studded with diamond-shaped metal embellishments to echo the name of the ranch, opened to the living room. Its massive stone fireplace was flanked on each side by small, paned windows. Above the mantel was the pièce de résistance: the brand of the Diamond J outlined with river rocks, with the J and its diamond-shaped border

8. The interior of the Diamond J lodge, undated. Julia Bennett's hunting trophies adorn the walls. Photograph by Chris Schlechten. Julia Bennett scrapbook, Sherry Merica Pepper private collection.

painted black. The fireplace andirons also were forged with her brand. On the walls, Julia hung stuffed trophies from her hunting trips: two goat heads, an elk head, and a deer head. The decor also included the hides of a bear, a horse, a calf, and two deer. Another bearskin, complete with head, was draped over the log railing that separated the six-table dining area from the living room.

To adorn the guest cabins, Julia spent more of her borrowed money on authentic Navajo rugs and Pendleton wool blankets woven with the Diamond J brand. She equipped the cook's kitchen and laundry with a Majestic cookstove and a Pella Maid washing machine. Sixty dozen specially designed white china plates, bowls, cups, and saucers arrived from Albert Pick–L. Barth Company in Chicago, each marked with the Diamond J brand in green.[4] Now Julia just needed to track down the guests who would use them.

On December 31, 1930, Julia invited Charlie Anceney's wife, Kate; their son, Charlie Jr.; and his friend Clyde Simpson to dinner. The trio spent the day ice fishing on nearby Madison Lake, and before heading back to their ranch, they stopped at the Diamond J. Charlie Sr. and their daughter, Rea, were away on a trip to Los Angeles.

After an early supper, as Julia was saying goodbye, she warned them not to drive home over the lake. The ice wasn't strong enough to hold their automobile, she told them.[5] Seventeen-year-old Charlie Jr., who stepped behind the wheel, ignored her, and the boys and Kate Anceney set off across the lake, with Kate in the back seat. Charlie followed the tracks of cars that had already crossed. About fifty feet from shore, he saw water bubbling up through the ice and stopped the car. Suddenly, the ice broke, sending the vehicle plunging into the deep lake. The boys managed to escape through windows as the car was sinking, but Kate Anceney had fainted. Twice, the boys dove back into the freezing water in an effort to save her, but "their frantic efforts to rescue Mrs. Anceney were futile," reported Butte's *Montana Standard*. The boys ran to a ranch and summoned help, and more than four dozen men rushed to help search. They cut through the ice and took a boat out on the lake, finally retrieving the car near midnight. Kate's body was still inside. She was buried the following week.[6]

A few months later, in the midst of his grief, Charlie Anceney would become Julia Bennett's savior.

Chapter 18

Is woman's place in the home? That is a question which has been
more or less heatedly debated for some years, but it seems the
women pay no attention to the conclusions of the debators. More
and more women find useful and distinguished careers outside
the home. . . . Woman's place is where she can make a place for
herself. She asks no odds and gives no quarter and the popular
belief is becoming stronger every year that in many fields of
activity she is just as qualified and just as successful as the male.

—*Bozeman Chronicle*, February 19, 1931

In the aftermath of the Anceney tragedy, Julia was facing other troubles.
"I was broke, and way in debt, so I realized I must get the ranch booked,
but how?!" she wrote. As always, she managed to devise a plan.

On a frigid evening in late February 1931, Julia announced to Diddy
that she was leaving for New York City the very next day. Diddy
replied that she was "crazy"—how in the world was she going to pay
for the trip?

Julia didn't know but refused to listen to reason. "The snow was
deep," she remembered—so deep that she wouldn't be able to maneuver
her Hudson touring car, a canvas-topped convertible, along the steep
dirt road leading out of the canyon. She asked Lee Smith to hitch up
their team of horses and help haul her car out to the main road. Then
she drove south to the market in Ennis, the nearest town, to make
credit arrangements so that Diddy and Lee could buy groceries while
she was gone. Turning north, she drove two hours to Bozeman, parked
her car at a local garage, headed to a hotel, and booked a room for the
night. But she had no cash—not even enough to buy herself dinner.
She picked up the telephone and called Charlie Anceney, who was
staying at his house in Bozeman, and asked him to stop by the hotel.

When he arrived, she asked him if he could lend her $250, explaining that she intended to head to New York the next morning on a booking trip. He handed her the bills, adding, "What are you going to do? That money won't last long."

She didn't know, Julia replied. But she had to get the ranch booked, and the only way to do that was to go to New York City. After Charlie left, she sat in her hotel room finishing the draft of the promotional brochure she would use to market the Diamond J.

"Nestled among its rugged peaks where highway ends and wilderness begins, is the Diamond J Ranch," she wrote. She rhapsodized about the mountain scenery, wildlife, trout fishing, and proximity to tourist attractions, including Yellowstone Park: "On our way to the ranch we pass Ennis, one of Montana's oldest cow towns. Here you may see the real western cow puncher. You may also visit the open range, where herds of cattle and horses graze; where wild life still enjoys freedom."

Julia stayed awake most of the night working on the brochure. The next morning, she stopped by the house where Marge stayed during the school year, to pay for a month of room and board and to say goodbye. Then she headed to the Bozeman railway station north of Main Street and bought a ticket on the Northern Pacific's new transcontinental train, the North Coast Limited. It was state-of-the-art transportation equipped with luxurious Pullman sleeping cars that had "thermostatically controlled" temperatures, "commodious wardrobes," and "box-spring beds" and with amenities that included an elegant white-tablecloth dining car, a barbershop, men's and women's showers, and a soda fountain.[1] The trip to New York would take thirty-five hours.

When the train pulled into the station at Billings, Montana, a few hours later for a brief stop, Julia walked four blocks to the printshop of the *Billings Gazette* newspaper, where she arranged to have the brochures printed and shipped to her in New York. Most of her borrowed funds were now gone. She figured she had just about enough money to last one week.

Chapter 19

Let all girls—actresses, type-setters, hoop-skirt makers,
seamstresses, sculptors, painters, or what you will—look upon
the trade they are learning as *the occupation of their lives*,
which they will always pursue, not only to support themselves
but to support or partly support their children, if they marry,
and perhaps, in sickness or other necessity, their husbands.

—Olive Logan, actress, author, and suffrage lecturer,
quoted in the *Daily Alta California*, March 14, 1869

More than six decades before Julia's journey to New York, her grand-mother and mother had begun a trip of their own, also in search of funds. Just five months after settling in Warm Springs Creek, Lizzie Martin decided to head more than one thousand miles west to San Francisco, California, where she planned to rekindle her seamstress business in what was by now the largest city in the West. It would be, by far, the largest city either she or Luly had ever seen, and she hoped it would offer many more opportunities for her to earn money to repay her debts.

They said goodbye to their family once again on March 17, 1866. Although there is no complete record of their journey, they likely were on the road for a month, traveling via stagecoach—and possibly steamboat—before finally reaching San Francisco. The most popular stage models of the 1860s, called Concord coaches, were pulled along primitive dirt roads by teams or four or six horses, mules, or oxen. Along with passengers, the coaches also often were packed with mail headed east to "America" or elsewhere in the territories, and each traveler usually was limited to twenty-five pounds of luggage. The coaches were generally either too hot or too cold, bone rattling, dusty, and dirty. If roads were bad, passengers sometimes were forced to dismount and walk, to help dig out coaches mired in mud, or to switch to open wagons, sleds, or sleighs as they crossed areas with no passable roads or covered with heavy snow or overflowing streams and rivers. Newspapers were filled with accounts of overcrowded coaches, flooded or rutted trails, road agents who held up stages at gunpoint, and accidents resulting in broken bones and sometimes death.

At one point in their trip, Lizzie, Luly, and fellow passengers were forced to pass through Oregon's Blue Mountains in twenty-five feet of snow. "At times the whole party had to get in dry goods boxes and ferry over the streams by means of ropes tied to the boxes," Luly recalled.[1]

Women traveling without male accompaniment faced another frustrating set of problems. Carrie Adell Strahorn, who chronicled her own stagecoach trip through the same region more than ten years after Lizzie and Luly, wrote about a man who told her that "women had no business traveling in such a country" and who "expressed himself in no gentle terms." She also noted that railroad officials opined that "no woman could endure the hardships that conditions of travel then required."[2]

Lizzie and Luly had no option but to endure those hardships, and when they finally reached San Francisco in April 1866, their eyes must have been wide with wonder. About 130,000 people filled its forty-two square miles, with men outnumbering women more than two to one. Luly would have been one of about thirty-five thousand children under the age of fifteen, a little more than a third of whom attended public schools.

San Francisco was prosperous, with imposing three- and four-story commercial buildings made of majestic stone and brick. The Bank of California at the corner of California and Sansom Streets, with its forty-two columns carved from Angel Island bluestone, was billed as "the most elegant and costly structure on the Pacific coast."[3] The California Market, recently completed at the cost of $200,000, boasted "elegant iron fronts" and a "solid cut granite basement."[4] A granite seawall, more than a mile and a half long and eight feet wide at its base, was under construction, designed to protect the city from the surging waters of the Pacific.[5] And a large public garden at the corner of Twelfth and Folsom Streets—described as "a fashionable resort for the cosmopolitan residents of the city"—overflowed with flowers, plants, and trees from Australia, Europe, China, Japan, and Central America.[6] Lizzie and Luly could have boarded one of the horse-drawn railcars of the Market Street Railway to run errands and visit local tourist sites.[7]

The pair took up residence in a women's boardinghouse in the heart of the bustling city. More than two hundred women—either widowed, single, or married—were making a living by operating boarding and lodging houses.[8]

Lizzie recounted the events of her day in a diary, taking care to document the first day of her menstrual period each month—discreetly referring to it as a visit from "Lady Company." She also remarked on the balmy weather, a far cry from the frigid winters in Montana. "It is not uncommon for the entire winter to pass away without bringing the thermometer down so low as the point of freezing," noted the journal *Resources of the Pacific Slope*.[9] Lizzie also recorded another relatively common San Francisco occurrence, writing that she and Luly felt two "shocks of earthquake" in the early afternoon of January 23.

She also jotted notes about her sewing projects. She wasn't alone in pursuing her occupation of seamstress; more than 122 dressmakers, nearly all of them women, were working in the city alongside her.[10] They would have had easy access to fabric. San Francisco's huge Pioneer and Mission woolen mills were churning out hundreds of thousands of yards of material, including "broadcloths, cassimeres and tweeds," and the company L. Ponton de Arce sold imported French cloth, as well as hat and cap trimmings, at its store on Sacramento Street and its "House in Paris."

Lizzie may have worked for another dressmaker; in her diary on Saturday, January 5, she wrote, "At 6 P.M. were paid off & went home to remain 2 weeks." By "home," she must have meant her boarding-house; her pay covered her rent, which she remitted a week later.

When not sewing for others, Lizzie sewed for herself—one night sitting up until midnight "beading my sacque"—or made a dress for Luly. In her free time, she explored the city and visited with women friends, including someone she called "Mrs. Day," and fellow boarders. They would go out to dinner or spend the evening chatting, playing games, or enjoying "wine and cake"; one of the women taught her to "weave hair."

Luly attended school while her mother was working. She kept a photograph album with pictures of her cousins and family friends, as well as one of a dark-haired girl wearing an elegant dark dress with a plaid taffeta bow and a lace collar: "Julia Alexander—a school mate of mine in Frisco," Luly wrote below the photo.

The photos must have been a comfort during periods of sorrow and homesickness, especially in January 1867, when it rained half the days of the month. Lizzie and Luly had missed Lucy Ann's wedding to William Tinsley, who had been a member of their wagon train heading to Montana, at Lizzie's parents' home on New Year's Day. Several fellow boarders were ill, and Lizzie was feeling low. On Sunday, January 6, she wrote, "The human family have their troubles, and I am one who tastes it often." Four days later she added that she "had troubled dreams of home," and on January 12 she recorded that she was "blue all day." (She coped better than another resident of San Francisco, John Russum of Germany, who hanged himself on October 10, 1866, with "homesickness" cited as the cause.)[11]

Later in January, on the seventeenth, Lizzie noted in her diary that she received a letter from her sister (she didn't note whether it was from Cynthia or Lucy Ann) that had been written three weeks earlier, just before Lucy Ann's wedding.

Keeping in touch with faraway family and friends was difficult. Letters came and went via stagecoach; delivery could take at least several weeks (or, depending on the state of the weather or coach robberies, several months—or not at all). San Francisco residents had access to periodicals from the States and from Europe, which arrived by steamer—a month after their publication.

In addition to sporadic letters from family, Lizzie's limited options for keeping up-to-date with news from the Montana Territory would have included reading the brief "Montana Items" article that appeared periodically in San Francisco's *Daily Alta California* newspaper. In September 1866 the *Alta* reported that new gold lodes had been discovered in Helena. In the October 7 edition, the paper noted that Luly's former teacher in Virginia City, Thomas Dimsdale, had died on September 22; that eight men had been killed by Indians on the Bozeman Trail on the way to Montana with wagons of supplies; and that Montana had endured a snowstorm on September 18. In the November 14 edition, San Francisco residents read that the "finest building in Montana" was nearly completed. The two-story stone structure in Helena City included a basement and measured fifty-five by seventy-five feet. The *Alta* reported, "Less than two years ago there was not a single cabin in Last Chance Gulch, where there are to-day probably not less than one thousand buildings and eight thousand people."

Despite her homesickness, Lizzie seemed to be doing well financially and staying busy. On February 6 she noted that she had loaned $120 to her friend Mrs. Day, the equivalent of more than $2,000 today. That same night, "a party of 8 of us went to call on the Chinaman. This being their New Year over which they have a great Jubile[e]." The Feast of the Fire Crackers, the start of the Chinese New Year, had kicked off on February 4, but the weather was unusually "cold and disagreeable, the thermometer falling to forty-one degrees" by February 7.

However, the weather was worse in the Montana Territory, where one visitor wrote to a friend, "The great drawback to this country is the climate; there are only five months in the year that a person can do anything. . . . I can't advise you or any of my friends to come here."[12] Lizzie and Luly didn't heed his advice. By March 1867 Lizzie had earned enough money to return home. She purchased a riding habit and selected a $36 saddle, which she paid for a few days later. On March 26 the weather was fine, and she noted in her diary that she was "busy getting ready to start on my journey." She went to the office of the California, Oregon, and Mexico Steamship Company, where she booked passage for herself and Luly on the *Continental*, the company's "new and favorite" masted steamship bound for Portland, Oregon. The company advertised that its ship "connected with steamers and Stages for all parts of Oregon, Idaho and Montana" (in addition to carrying "the United States Mails"). She had the option of paying $15 for a cabin in the "Upper Saloon," $10 for a cabin in the "Lower Saloon," or steerage passage for $5 (she didn't record which she chose). The 1,626-ton steamer promised prospective passengers that its accommodations were "superior to any other on the route" and that passengers could "rely on arriving in Portland sooner than by any other steamer."[13]

The *Continental* was scheduled to leave at ten o'clock on the morning of Saturday, March 30, but when Lizzie went down to breakfast that day, she found a notice announcing that the departure was delayed until the next morning. The next day, she and Luly, who had celebrated her eleventh birthday in San Francisco, headed to the Folsom Street Wharf to board the boat two hours before it was scheduled to cast off. Lizzie cryptically wrote in her diary that she "took leave of a very dear friend at 9 a.m." and then "went to my bunk sick." It was the same day that her "Lady Company" had arrived—extremely inconvenient timing for the start of a 575-mile sailing trip that would take mother and daughter on only the first part of their journey: a three-day, three-night voyage on the Pacific Ocean to the mouth of the Columbia River in Oregon.

All told, the trip back to Montana would cost Lizzie more than $300 (more than $5,000 today). They were eager to return to the place they called home after spending an entire year apart from their beloved family, but nearly five years after the death of her husband, Lizzie was still hundreds of dollars in debt.

Chapter 20

Crossed the range amidst a rain and snow
storm in an open wagon and sled.

—Lizzie Martin's diary, April 11, 1867

Lizzie lay ill in her bunk for the next two days, unable to leave her cabin. The morning of Wednesday, April 3, was clear but cold, and she managed to make it up to the deck "with a great effort while crossing the bar," as their steamer chugged past Oregon's Cape Foulweather, aptly named by Captain James Cook when he experienced "exceeding bad weather" at its point ninety years earlier.[1]

The boat entered the mouth of the Columbia River at Cape Disappointment and landed at the town of Portland, population seven thousand, at eight o'clock in the morning. By that time, Lizzie was "feeling well," so she and Luly may have found time to view the "many objects of interest to attract the eye and attention of the tourist" that a correspondent for the *Daily Alta California* noted on his steamer trip there eight months earlier. "A grand and most magnificent panoramic view of nature is the rough, high and thickly-timbered range of mountains that run in a northwest and southeast course," he wrote that preceding August, "but the most prominent features of the scenery along the Lower Columbia are the several snow peaks in the range."[2] The weather was clear, so Lizzie and Luly probably could see Mount St. Helens and Mount Rainier in the distance to the north and Mount Hood to the south.

The next day, while they were still in Portland, Luly took sick. Still, she seemed well enough to go on two walks through town with her mother. They retired to their bunks at nine in the evening and eight hours later were back on the steamer, stopping at Vancouver for breakfast and then passing through the Cascades before docking at The Dalles in Oregon in late afternoon. There Lizzie and Luly spent a very short night at Umatilla House, which advertised itself as the "best hotel west of Minneapolis and north of San Francisco."[3]

Luly had not improved by the next day, probably because she and her mother had to rise in the middle of the night to board railroad cars for the fifteen-mile journey to Celilo Falls, a magnificent waterfall flowing through a narrow cliff-banked gorge. The turbulent waters here had constituted the most dangerous leg of Lewis and Clark's cross-country journey sixty years earlier. Arriving at the falls at five in the morning, the pair boarded yet another boat, passed through the gorge successfully, and arrived in the Oregon town of Umatilla a full twelve hours later, where their ship remained overnight.

It was warm and dusty on the morning of Sunday, April 7, when they crossed over into Washington Territory and ended their seven-day steamer trip at Wallula, where they would catch the stagecoach for the eight-hour ride to the rough-and-tumble gold rush town of Walla Walla, thirty-five miles away. Luly was ill the entire trip, with the hot, dirty, and bumpy coach ride doing nothing to improve her condition. When they arrived in Walla Walla (the largest city in Washington Territory, with a population of about one thousand), they spent the night at the Oriental Hotel on Main Street, which advertised itself as "having just been elegantly furnished throughout," with "accommodations for families of the very best."[4] There they finally were able to have a full night's rest, but the next morning, Luly had not improved. Concerned, Lizzie went to the druggist to buy pills, which set her back $1.10. She paid the stagecoach agent $50 to reserve their passage on the Overland Express stage line to Boise, Idaho, and then went back to the hotel and nursed Luly, giving her medicine throughout the night. The next morning, Lizzie resorted to sponging her with vinegar in an attempt to bring down her fever, which helped ("Then she was better," she noted succinctly). She spent $2.30 on a basket and lunch for the continuation of their journey into the Oregon Territory. Luly's improvement was very good news, because the remainder of their trip would continue via stagecoach, the most uncomfortable and potentially dangerous part of their journey—and one that would last nearly three weeks. Just a few weeks earlier, a stagecoach traveling near the Snake River in Idaho Territory, where Lizzie and Luly were headed, had been attacked by Indians, its driver and two passengers killed.

There was no direct route from the Washington Territory to the Montana Territory; layers of mountain ranges stood in the way. Lizzie and Luly's voyage would take them in a huge U shape, dipping south from Washington through the Oregon Territory, crossing into southwestern Idaho, and then heading east across the entire Idaho Territory before finally turning north again and up to Montana—a trip of about 750 miles, two and a half times longer than if they had been able to travel in a straight line.

It was cloudy and windy on April 10 when Lizzie and Luly climbed into an Overland Stage Company coach. Granville Stuart, a Montana stock raiser, recorded pointed observations about an Overland stage journey he had taken a year earlier:

> Everything goes by contraries on the Overland; the climate changes so rapidly that where the sleds and sleighs are, there is no snow, and where the snow is, there you have to ride in coaches, steamboat wagons, carts, and anything else that's convenient—generally without seats, compelling you to sit on the mail and your baggage. About the time that, being utterly exhausted and worn out, (it being generally impossible to sleep unless you are in this condition) you fall into a doze and begin to dream that you are being torn in pieces by a band of wolves, or are stretched on the rack in inquisitorial halls—just about this time, the wagon gives a terrific jolt; your uncomfortable seat flies from under you and you come down souse, the side of the wagon-bed striking you under the chin, or you give a plunge and strike your unfortunate 'vis-a-vis' a telling blow in the stomach with your head.[5]

On regular stage routes, there were two types of rest stops. "Swing" stations, located every ten to fifteen miles, were small stops where the teams of horses, mules, and oxen could be fed, watered, or changed.

At larger "home" stations, about fifty miles apart, passengers would have a bed for the night (or, more likely, a floor) and a simple $1 meal, which often was barely edible.

Lizzy and Luly's stage made its way through the Blue Mountains along the newly built Thomas and Ruckel Road—one of the first in the region—and stopped for the night at a three-story log inn called Warm Springs (built near a natural hot spring). There, not surprisingly after the grueling ride, Luly again had "a chill." Lizzie, likely worried about how her daughter would fare on the uncomfortable trip ahead, brought a $3 supper to their room.

The next day brought deteriorating weather and more primitive transportation. In the middle of a rain- and snowstorm, they crossed the mountain range in an open wagon and, later, on a sled. Their vehicles tipped over twice. Despite the stormy weather and the mishaps, they managed to traverse forty-eight miles that day and to have "some good laughs" at the driver's expense with a fellow female passenger named Mrs. Goodrich, who was traveling solo. They stopped for the night at Uniontown, where Mrs. Goodrich met up with her husband.

The end of the week brought new trials. After a cold day on bad roads and a night spent in the town of Baker City, on Saturday, their wagon fell into a water hole and, Lizzie reported in her diary, "nearly drowned a horse." She noted matter-of-factly that she "had to be carried out on a man's back" and that Luly had lost her shawl in the accident—distressing news considering her recent illness and the chilly weather. The driver invited Lizzie, wet after her haul through the water, to sit next to him for the rest of the day, treating her to the best seat on the wagon.

The next day they traveled only five miles before their coach became mired in a swampy area, and the passengers waited while the driver retraced their path to find another wagon. When they finally restarted, they reached yet another swamp, and Lizzie, along with Luly, again had to be carried through the water. Then they boarded a small, flat-bottomed skiff to cross the Weiser River, which ran through the border of the Oregon and Idaho Territories. After breakfasting along the Snake River, the passengers again climbed aboard a wagon headed to Boise—another dirt-street, gold rush town, with a population of two thousand, and the new capital of the Idaho Territory—where they didn't arrive until nearly midnight.

Over the next few days, Lizzie and Luly rested in Boise at the Overland House Hotel while Lizzie waited to take delivery of a dress being shipped from California. Their trip was becoming increasingly expensive. Lizzie made detailed notes of her expenses, booking passage for the next leg for $157.60. She wrote in her diary that although the weather was lovely, she "was lonesome at the hotel." She wrote a letter to a friend in San Francisco, treated herself to a lunch of chicken, and then settled her bill of $13 to cover the "hotel and chickens."

The chicken was probably a welcome change from the other meals she and Luly had been eating at the stage stops along the route. One Idaho Territory traveler a few years earlier had complained, "Bacon, beans and bread, and bread, bacon and beans in every variety of style seems to be the favored dishes . . . and when 'mine host' is induced to come out with his apple sauce (which your correspondent never eats) he wears a very saucy air."[6]

It was fortunate that Lizzie and Luly had a layover in Boise, because the next leg of their trip, through southern Idaho Territory, was to be filled with more difficulties. Lizzie didn't detail their exact route—they could have followed the old Oregon Trail route along the Snake River or passed farther north along what was known as the Goodale Cutoff. Regardless of the path they took, one thing was certain—the Idaho Territory was desolate. Carrie Adell Strahorn wrote, "It was a land where eyes often ached with straining from horizon to horizon for the sight of a cabin, and where the heavy rattle of the stage-coach and the howling of the coyotes were the only sounds that broke the silence of the vast expanse. Yet even that great silent anthem of Nature was entrancing in its immensity."[7]

Starting their journey at four in the morning on a cool day, they found the roads to be rough and filled with swampy areas that Lizzie called sloughs or slews. They had to climb out of the coach and board leaking boats to cross high creeks and wetlands. Granville Stuart had had a similar experience the previous year:

> In Snake river valley there was a big thaw going on, and the country was covered with a shush of snow and water, every low place and ravine being full. From the crossing down to Blackfoot Butte it was perfectly awful, they having put us into a sixty-hundred freight wagon, with four little rats of mules to draw it, and as a natural consequence they "stalled" in every low place or hollow, and we were compelled to get out in snow and water up to our hips and dig the "outfit" out. I verily thought my feet and legs would freeze—but they didn't. At Blackfoot crossing station, I thought the chance of much dinner was rather slim, as there was only a 7 by 9 cabin, in which dwelt a woman and I don't know how many children. . . . To my amazement, however, she got up an excellent dinner, to which the mules "stalled" again with us before we got fifty yards from the house.

The trip was not without beautiful and dramatic scenery, if the passengers were in any mood to enjoy it. A contemporary wrote, "As the coach rolled along, I looked across the Snake River Valley to the right, where the higher elevations of the Owyhee range were alone visible, as the intervening plain and lower heights were covered with a dense fog, whose wavy surface caused the snowy mountain tops to appear like pearly isles in a purple sea." Farther east, "mountains to the North have sent down a long narrow ridge, which is crowned and embellished with blocks and columns and pinnacles of granite, arranged in the most fantastic picturesque forms."[8]

The weather was turning warmer. At eight in the morning on April 19, Lizzie and Luly boarded a boat to traverse yet another slough. Lizzie wrote, "Crossed one and the man carried it to the other til we were over then we crossed a natural bridge." The next day, a Saturday, they arrived at the Bear River in the early evening, waited there until eleven o'clock at night, and then caught an overnight stage headed north toward Virginia City. The next afternoon, they reached a stage station called Carpenter's, where they passed the night, paying $4.50 for the privilege.

Carrie Adell Strahorn noted that sleeping on floors was an accepted part of stagecoach travel: "It was a question of again rolling up in our blankets on the little store floor or sitting up out in the stagecoach and we chose the former. We chose our corner and settled ourselves as well as we could, and it was not long before there was a chorus of snores. . . . The whole scale of sounds was there."[9]

An 1864 account in the *Montana Post* described frustration that sometimes escalated into violence: "The passengers on one of Oliver & Co.'s coaches which left this town on the 17th instant had a break down, got mad, and burnt up the coach on Snake River."[10]

Lizzie and Luly's experiences in that region were not quite as dramatic. On April 22 Lizzie wrote three short sentences in her diary: "Nice day and my birthday. Passed the night at Snake River. $3.00. Lady Company." It was the second time during their trip that Lizzie would experience the inconvenience of a visit from "Lady Company." Sanitary napkins had not yet been invented, and women usually used fabric or rags saved for that specific purpose—or nothing at all. Traveling in a stagecoach would not have been the ideal circumstance during that time of the month, but that was the least of Lizzie's problems.

As they prepared to journey from the Idaho Territory into the neighboring Montana Territory, winter once again reared its head, refusing to acknowledge that spring had officially started an entire month earlier. The cold weather was on everyone's mind. "For the past two or three days we have had snow, snow, snow; and it must take a very tropical immagination [*sic*] to see anything surprisingly 'beautiful' in the 'snow,' at the present season. . . . When will spring come?" asked the *Montana Post* on April 27.

That snow made travel even more difficult. The day after Lizzie's birthday, they traveled through the dark night in a "very cold" open wagon, arriving at the Saint Louis Ranch the next morning at eight. They then climbed aboard a pack train, working their way through snow and over hills to a valley, where they sat until two in the morning. The next part of the trip would be even more rugged. To reach Virginia City, they would have to travel through a desolate mountain pass. Lizzie had no choice but to leave her valise behind, hoping it would be sent on to Virginia City, where they were scheduled to arrive a few days later. Then Lizzie, Luly, and the other passengers "piled on a sled and crossed over to the valley with two mules drawing us." Some rode, while others walked. They met the coach, and twelve of them trundled aboard. Lizzie breathed a sigh of relief, noting that they "made the last home station for supper."

They finally reached their former home, Virginia City, at four in the morning on Friday, April 26. The *Montana Post*'s regular "Arrivals and Departures" column reported the following day that "Miss Lizzie Martin" had arrived at Planter's House hotel from San Francisco. Planter's House would be a step up from most of the accommodations they had endured over the past several weeks. The hotel, the newspaper told its readers, offered a "first-class table. Comfortable rooms and beds are provided and the table is carefully furnished with the best the market and seasons afford. Passengers for the early Stage Coaches can obtain good lodgings here and be wakened at the proper hour." Being awakened at the proper hour was important since it wasn't until 1883, when transcontinental railroad travel demanded consistent timetables, that standard time zones were established. The *Idaho World* noted, "When it is 12 o'clock at Idaho City it is about twenty minutes to 3 o'clock in New York and twenty-five minutes past 11 o'clock in San Francisco."[11]

Lizzie and Luly were back home on Montana time. In Virginia City, Lizzie washed some clothes, picked up a letter from a friend in California that was awaiting her at the post office, and sold a pair of pants she had made. Two days later she "was much disappointed" that her valise, which probably contained nearly all her personal belongings, had not yet been delivered. During the layover in Virginia City, Lizzie also may have learned of the murder of Colonel John Bozeman just nine days earlier. On the same day her arrival was announced in the *Post*, Bozeman's death was reported—along with rumors of impending Indian attacks in the Gallatin valley and the plans of a pioneer militia to "drive the red devils from our doors."[12]

Lizzie and Luly still had three days of travel ahead of them to reach their family in Willow Creek, which sat north of Virginia City on the edge of the threatened Gallatin valley. Lizzie now would have to figure out how to get there. While at Planter's House, she "sent for Mr. Culver to get information of some one in the valley," perhaps to find a person who could help them safely get the rest of the way home. J. A. Culver boarded horses at his Eagle Corral and may have been a source of news from those coming from the direction of Willow Creek.

Fortunately, a neighbor of the Naves—a man named Mr. Peyton— happened to be in Virginia City. He stopped by to visit with Lizzie early that morning and told her he could transport them. At eight o'clock Culver took Lizzie and Luly to Peyton's wagon, located one mile out of town, and they set out on their way. Their journey was a safe one. On the second day, as the weather warmed up, Lizzie wrote that they "nooned" on Meadow Creek—not far from the spot that would become Julia Bennett's Diamond J Ranch sixty-five years later—and spent the night in the small town of Sterling. Finally, at six in the evening on Tuesday, April 30, 1867—exactly one month after setting off from San Francisco—they arrived at the home of Lizzie's sister Cynthia in Willow Creek. They had not seen their family in a year.

Chapter 21

In the Gallatin Valley . . . rumors regarding the Blackfeet . . .
have fanned the embers of anticipated danger into a
flame, and from credible parties we are assured that a
fearful panic prevails that will depopulate the valley in
a few days, unless something is done immediately.

—*Montana Post*, April 27, 1867

Cynthia and George Hale's household in Willow Creek was growing.
Their daughter Laura was now six, and following the death of Lucy
Elizabeth on the trail, Cynthia had given birth to two sons, one now
a two-year-old and the other born just three weeks before Lizzie and
Luly's arrival. Lizzie's other sister, Lucy Ann, and her new husband,
William Tinsley, had recently taken up a homestead in Willow Creek
as well.

Over the next few weeks, Lizzie quickly settled back into a routine with her sisters. She wrote letters to her friends in California,
took walks, and helped Cynthia with ironing. She took advantage of
the pleasant but windy May weather by washing clothes—a two-day
process thanks to the tasks of boiling water, scrubbing and rinsing by
hand, and hanging them to dry. After a man named Dan (perhaps a
hired hand) made a fruitless trip to Virginia City to collect her valise,
she dispatched a letter to the stagecoach stop in the small town of
Sterling, and he finally succeeded in fetching it there a full week
after her return.

The next day, Lizzie was off again, this time riding twenty miles
on horseback to see her parents at Warm Springs Creek. She noted
offhandedly in her diary that on the way, she "had trouble" swimming her horse across the Jefferson River and stopped for dinner at
the cabin of a woman named Mrs. Turner. When she reached her

parents' home, she "found all well," just as she had at Willow Creek, but commented no more about the homecoming.

When she returned to Willow Creek, the lovely spring weather didn't last. Over the night of May 10, three inches of snow fell, covering the garden that Lizzie had just planted.

Three weeks later, while she was doing the wash, "the men went up the gulch to bury a dead man who was found by Majers," she wrote in her diary. Two days later, on June 1, "Corporal Curtis and Company passed in pursuit of Indians."

A few months earlier, the *Montana Democrat* had reported that many residents of the nearby Gallatin valley were worried about "Indian depredations the coming season," noting that "many persons entertain the opinion, that when operations commence this spring against the Indians on the Plains, that they will take refuge in Montana."[1] The *Montana Post* was even more dramatic: "It is currently reported that hostile Indians are threatening to desolate Gallatin Valley, by massacreing [*sic*] its inhabitants, and laying waste their habitation."[2] During 1866 and 1867 the U.S. Army built five forts in the area to protect emigrants traveling on the Bozeman Trail, but still the *Democrat* opined that "no family in the Gallatin should be without firearms, and every male citizen should have in his house a good gun and such other weapons as can be procured, so that if Indians attack any portion of the country, aid can be rendered at once, and relief afforded."[3]

The mayor of Virginia City wrote to U.S. Secretary of War Edwin Stanton, asking for permission to form a defense militia. Stanton referred the request to General William Tecumseh Sherman, who sent a dispatch to the mayor saying, "Our official reports from that quarter do not justify such extreme alarm; but if the inhabitants of Gallatin valley are in such imminent danger from Indians you may organize your people and go to their relief and defense under the general direction of your Governor."[4] There was a run on arms, with the *Post* noting, "Rifles and carbines that two weeks ago were selling at from $10 to $40 are now held at $75 to $100."[5]

Soon Lizzie and Luly moved back to Warm Springs Creek, where they planned to settle and build a permanent house near Lizzie's parents. The summer season in the valley was short, and good weather was critical both for completing the house and for a harvest that would see them through the winter months. But the weather turned cold and rainy in June, so among other things, Lizzie finished a quilt for her mother and "wove Luly's hair for curls." Her brother Errendle drove by with a harvest of potatoes bound for sale in Helena, and Smith, the peddler, stopped for a two-day visit. Luly spent time with her grandmother, riding into the mountains and traveling to Crow Creek.

That summer was filled with visits from family members, as well as attempts to keep mosquitoes from eating them alive and other pests from destroying their vegetable garden. In late August, Lizzie's pony took sick, and it died a week later. The next day, the weather turned so cold that a frost killed what was left of her garden; by September 15 the nearby foothills were covered with snow; and by October 2 all the leaves had fallen from the trees. The following week brought warmer weather, and Lizzie began digging potatoes. Her house was not yet finished. The mason was still completing its chimney, and the kitchen floor had not yet been laid. She and Luly finally moved in on October 26, just two days before the ground became "white with snow." Cynthia and her children stopped over that night for a housewarming.

That same week, Lizzie received a letter from her late husband's father, informing her of the death of his wife on September 8. It had taken nearly a month to arrive from Missouri.

During that summer and fall, Lizzie received frequent visits from Enoch Wilson—"Mr. W," she called him in her diary—the fellow Missourian who had, for a time, settled with his wife and children in Helena, where Lizzie and Lucy had visited them. Now, it seems, his wife and children had returned to Missouri, where they would remain. On November 10 Lizzie wrote that Mr. W stopped by to "look after [a] cheque." The next day, he left on a trip "to the States." Nine days later she received a letter from him. Had he headed to Missouri to visit his family and make a payment on her debts? Her diary doesn't say. The following week, while suffering from a headache, she laid down in bed, where she "had a visionary visitation of a dear friend." But she did not name the friend.

�֍

Three years after Lizzie and Luly moved into their house, only 186 settler families were living in the Radersburg precinct of the Jefferson valley, and five of those households consisted of Nave parents and offspring. The U.S. Census of 1870 reported that men in the precinct outnumbered women by nearly five to one, although the *Montana Post* suggested, "The female community at Radersburg and Crow Creek is larger than any other town of like size and age in the Territory."[6] Most of the valley residents were transplanted from the States, but nearly a quarter had been born in Europe. The majority of men were miners, farmers, or tradesmen, and the women were "keeping house"—also a full-time endeavor.[7]

Fifty or so miles north of Radersburg, in Helena, Chinese immigrants were arriving to build railroad lines or work in mines. They weren't received kindly. Helena's *Daily Rocky Mountain Gazette* referred to them as, among other things, "the heathen Chinee" and "almond-eyed Celestials."[8] The newspaper also made note of "the Mongolian's 'ways that are dark.'"

Meanwhile, relations between the U.S. government and the Native residents of the Montana Territory remained tense. In 1868 the U.S. Army shut down Fort C. F. Smith, completed only a year before, and the Bozeman Trail was abandoned after the U.S. government signed a peace treaty with the Sioux. The Crow Nation, which had a friendly relationship with the U.S. Army and local settlers, signed a treaty to establish the Crow Indian Reservation in May of that same year. The Sioux, however, set fire to the remnants of Fort Smith.[9]

Chapter 22

The ride toward Radersburg on a bright May morning, when
the valleys, hills and mountains are robed in the fresh verdure of
spring, is a delightful experience and well calculated to impress
a Montanian with the grandeur of this magnificent domain, and
inspire feelings of stronger attachment to his mountain home.

—"Traveling Correspondent," *Helena Weekly Herald*, June 23, 1881

Over the next three years, Lizzie's relationship with Enoch Wilson
blossomed. He and his former wife, Cynthia, had divorced—although
no record of the dissolution exists in either Missouri or Montana—
and she and their five children had returned to live in Chillicothe,
Missouri. On May 15, 1870, Lizzie and Enoch were married at Warm
Springs. Her father and her brother-in-law, George Hale, served as
witnesses.[1] She had just turned thirty-five; he was ten years her senior.

Five months earlier—a full eight years after David Martin's death—
she had made the final payment on the remaining debts from that marriage, thanks to the sale of a parcel of land, along with rental income
from their farm and her own personal earnings. The settlement hadn't
been easy; among other things, it had required the filing of a lawsuit
against the man who had leased their farm and failed to pay his rent.[2]

When the first census of the Montana Territory was taken that
summer, Lizzie, Enoch, Luly, and a young English stock tender named
John Darrington were living on their farm, adjacent to Lizzie's parents. Enoch was building a sawmill, and Lizzie was "keeping house."
Nearby lived the families of two of her brothers (Errendle and Jacob
owned and operated a mill that extracted gold from quartz) and her
sister Cynthia, whose husband was working as a miner.

Overall, the Naves were doing very well financially—while Enoch
Wilson listed the value of his personal estate at $1,200, James Nave

and his sons Errendle and Jacob reported to the census taker that their own personal estates each were worth more than $11,000 (more than $215,000 each, in today's currency). The only other residents in the Radersburg area who were worth more were the owner of the wealthy Keating mine and a few other quartz mill owners.[3]

Also living nearby in the Radersburg precinct was Doc Bembrick, now a forty-two-year-old widower who owned farmland worth $400 and a personal estate that he valued at $6,200 (about $122,000). Sometime after the death of his wife in 1869, he had met and courted Luly. She was just fifteen (the same age at which her mother had wed David Martin), and Doc was forty-three when they married on November 13, 1871, at the home of Lizzie and Enoch Wilson. A marriage between two people of such disparate ages was hardly unique among western homesteaders. Women were scarce in these parts, and maintaining a ranch was a daily struggle. "There were darn few marriages of love out here among these early beginners," said one Montana woman. "I don't think I've ever heard a homestead wife tell how much she loved her husband. That wasn't part of it, it was survival."[4]

Doc and Luly's marriage seemed to be a good match, practically speaking. Doc was handsome, sported a dashing mustache and goatee, and stood more than a head taller than his petite new wife. He was an excellent horseman and hunter, played the violin, and loved practical jokes. Luly was independent and no stranger to hard work or adventure, and she could care for Doc's two-and-a-half-year-old daughter while he oversaw his burgeoning cattle operation.

The significant age gap may have posed some issues, however. Luly was naive, yet Doc was well acquainted with the ways of the world. But they were not unique; there were many couples like them in this country, where women were in short supply. Four days before their wedding, Helena's *Daily Rocky Mountain Gazette* had published an ad for a "Marriage Guide," which promised information on "the physiological mysteries and revelations of the sexual system, with the latest discoveries in producing and preventing offspring, preserving the complexion, &c." The ad continued, "This is an interesting work of two-hundred and twenty-four pages with numerous engravings, and contains valuable information for those who are married or contemplate marriage; still it is a book that ought to be under lock and key, and not laid carelessly about the home. . . . Fifty cents."[5]

Luly, who by this time had exchanged her childhood nickname for the more grown-up moniker Lulu, moved to Doc's cabin in the Crow Creek valley. While she tended to her new stepdaughter, Doc tended to his stock. "You raise the children and I will raise the cattle," he told her.

There was plenty of work for both of them.

Chapter 23

The number of cattle returned in Montana is 35,964. This
would give over one and three-fourths to each person of
our 20,580 people. With such an exhibit in our favor, while
we have hardly commenced cattle raising, what results
must we obtain in a few years? It proves that Montana
cannot be excelled by any country in raising stock.

—W. F. Wheeler in a report on the 1870 Montana
Census, *Helena Weekly Herald*, October 27, 1870

Doc Bembrick began to establish himself as a cattle rancher, a poten-
tially lucrative enterprise. "The best business in Montana is stock
raising," noted the *New North-West* newspaper. "Grazing is unlimited, unsurpassed and free to all. The care and cost of cattle after
purchase is merely the expense of a boy to herd them."[1]

A reporter who visited the valley in the early fall of 1871 told his
readers, "I would like to particularize and elaborate on the many
beautiful and well-fenced ranches, golden grain-fields, lowing herds,
grass rank slopes, which I could not but admire."[2]

Doc had dreams of expanding his cattle operation but didn't have
enough grazing land at Crow Creek. So every spring, he drove his
herd about one hundred miles east to the rolling hills of the Musselshell River valley, where both water and grass were abundant—and
absolutely free. Less than a decade earlier, when Bembrick and the
Naves had first arrived, the Musselshell valley (referred to by early
newspapers as the Muscle Shell) remained a vast, unknown area
to settlers,[3] although it historically had been an important buffalo
hunting ground for the Crow and Blackfeet tribes. The land now
had been stipulated as "Indian Country" by the U.S. government.
The 1867 *Pacific Coast Business Directory* noted, "This is an unor-

ganized county. . . . It is sparsely populated, and but little is known of its resources."[4] It wasn't until 1874 that Lieutenant Colonel George Custer and his men explored the area, with a number of newspapers throughout the nation reporting their discoveries: "The land was fertile and productive, well watered and well timbered. . . . General Custer thinks that there can be no doubt but there is in the locality named an almost boundless area of rich available land, that waits only the touch of the husbandman to call forth abundant harvest."[5]

It didn't take long for husbandmen like Doc to take advantage of the fertile land. In the same year as the Custer exploration, a man named James Forbes made the first shipment of Montana cattle to the eastern United States.[6] Not long after, Doc mounted his horse and drove his herd more than one hundred miles, along the creeks that ran south of the Big Belt Mountains and then to the north of the saw-toothed Crazy Mountains, until they reached the vast grasslands that bordered the Musselshell. There he set up camp near "a lonely sandstone prominence that rises above the broad, grassy valley" of the river. A cowboy accompanied him and would remain during the summer to watch over the fattening herd and protect it from cattle rustlers.[7]

Lulu remained at home, caring for Addie and maintaining their ranch with the help of a hired hand. Her days were endless: maintaining the vegetable garden, feeding chickens, sewing clothes, cooking meals, washing, and ironing. Sometimes she and Doc would head to the nearest town, Radersburg, to socialize or buy supplies.

One visitor wrote that Radersburg "has that unceremonious, *neglige* appearance which characterizes every half-mining, half-farming town in Montana." It boasted a general store, a livery stable (run by Percy Smith, "which he conducts with a care for dumb brutes that should make him patron saint of the Society for the Prevention of cruelty to animals, and with a horse-pitality which commends him to the traveling public"), a blacksmith shop, a cabinet shop, a "well-kept" hotel owned by a Colonel A. L. Parks (whose "rotundity of proportion is a standing advertisement of the digestibility and quality of the viands of the establishment"), along with two billiard saloons, a jewelry store, a tailor, a liquor store, a barbershop, a stationery and confectionery store, and a shoe shop.[8]

The village of Keatingville (named after the owner of the Keating mine) was lodged in the foothills about two miles above Radersburg, near the mine, where "hundreds of busy, brown fisted, burrowing mortals are clinking away with pick and sledge, disemboweling the golden crevices that seam with sinews of gilt the anatomy of an hundred dwarfish bills."[9]

Canadian-born John Dougherty's mercantile store was the only place relatively close to the Bembricks' cabin to buy staples like flour, sugar, coffee, and canned milk, since even milk cows were scarce.[10] Doc would stop by now and again to pick up a gallon of whiskey, a few pounds of gunshot, flypaper, or various household sundries.[11] There he and Lulu might have the opportunity to chat with their few neighbors (*neighbors*, in these parts, being a relative term). Among them were a fellow cattle rancher, David T. Williams, and his auburn-haired wife, Ann, who both hailed from Wales, and their three young children.[12] The Bembricks also were close friends with Radersburg attorney George Cowan and his wife, Emma, who was about the same age as Lulu. Radersburg was just the place for an up-and-coming territorial lawyer. In the fall of 1872 its "elegant" new frame courthouse was nearing completion, and a "horse-hotel" was planned.[13] Newspapers were filled with talk of the Northern Pacific Railroad's plans to advance through the Montana Territory, bringing additional immigrants, commerce, and a more convenient connection to the States.

The Bembricks were prospering, and they finally put to rest Lizzie's decade-long struggle to settle her family's Missouri estate. Although Lizzie had paid all the debts, Doc and Lulu had to hire a lawyer to recoup $47 that the estate's administrator owed to her.[14]

Doc became involved in the growing community's Democratic Party. At the Jefferson County Democratic Convention held in Radersburg in July 1873, he was elected to the Committee on Permanent

Organization and Order of Business.[15] Lulu's grandfather James Nave, meanwhile, petitioned to turn his homestead into valuable agricultural land.[16]

Doc and Lulu made frequent trips to Helena, which soon would become the prosperous territorial capital. They stayed at the St. Louis Hotel, on Main Street, which advertised itself as "luxuriously fitted up and . . . prepared to accommodate guests in a manner not equalled [sic] in the country."[17] They could purchase clothing and supplies at J. R. Boyce and Company, which boasted "the largest stock of dry goods in Montana,"[18] and Havana cigars at the tobacconist N. H. Webster or dine on "fresh Booth oysters" at the International restaurant on Broadway Street.[19]

The city offered a temporary respite from worries in the valley. While Doc was with his herd along the Musselshell in the summer of 1875, residents of the Missouri River valley were terrified by tales of impending Indian attacks and "stories of the depredations committed by the Sioux in revenge for their wrongs," wrote a U.S. Army captain. "Miners attempting to explore the Black Hills, Big Horn mountains, and the valley of the Yellowstone, had been murdered; the Judith Basin and Musselshell route from central Montana had been abandoned through fear of them, and now they announced their intention of making a determined effort to recover some of the many advantages they claimed to have been deprived of."[20]

In early July three soldiers were killed by Sioux in the Judith Basin, not far from the area where Doc kept his cattle. Missouri valley residents set up what they called "picket duty," with men assigned as lookouts to ensure that no Sioux breached the pass into their valley. The *Helena Weekly Herald* reported that on July 27 two of the picket men returned to town with the news that they had been chased for five miles by forty of the "red devils" and that they had last seen two other pickets surrounded by Sioux. Those pickets had disappeared, and the *Herald* continued, "Fears are entertained that they have been murdered by the Indians." Women and children were sent to shelter in nearby towns, and one resident reported to the newspaper, "I have distributed twenty stand of arms in my possession, belonging to Jefferson county. This I had no authority to do, but in the emergency I assumed this much." Meanwhile, U.S. Army scouts, led by a lieutenant named Nelson, had been alerted and, "being convinced of the immediate presence of a large body of hostile Indians . . . came down from the foothills to warn the settlers. . . . The news spread like wildfire throughout the valley."[21]

Lulu was warned to head to Radersburg with Addie. She refused. Instead, she and Addie spent the night in a patch of willows near the ranch. She had no way of knowing whether Doc was safe or exactly where he was camping in the Musselshell valley.

Meanwhile, Lieutenant Nelson and his men, along with dozens of nervous male settlers, traveled all night until they reached the location reported by the pickets. Spying what they presumed to be the Sioux camp, they surrounded and prepared to charge. But once inside, reported the *Helena Weekly Herald*, they discovered "a camp of peaceful Flatheads, composed of five bucks, two squaws and three Indian children, together with Dr. Bembrick, who it appears was camped with them on the way from his herd of cattle. So ends this Indian scare." The article continued, "This is rather a laughable and funny end of what was considered 24 hours ago a very serious matter."

Nevertheless, the newspaper opined, "The state of affairs, even though it should prove only a bad 'scare,' is truly deplorable. The farms in the beautiful Missouri valley, one of the choicest garden spots of Montana, have been abandoned—crops, horses, cattle and poultry left to take care of themselves. A few days absence of the farmers from their homes will cause a serious loss of property; and, at this season of the year, a protracted absence would materially damage the prosperity of the settlement. More troops are sorely needed in this Territory."[22]

Ever since she had first crossed the plains as a child, Lulu had harbored a deep fear of Indians. Doc, on the other hand, had spent years interacting with people from many tribes and generally was comfortable in their company. But perhaps as a result of Lulu's urging, when he returned to the ranch that fall, the family moved to a house in Radersburg. There they hosted the December 1 wedding of Doc's great-niece, Katie Twombly, to Captain James S. Smith, a miner who had arrived in Helena a week earlier with $3,500 in gold he had just discovered in the "'Jaw Bone' lead" of Upper Indian Creek.[23]

Chapter 24

The sun glowed warm, and the road was dry and dusty, the valley
free from snow, while the drifts along the foot-hills were fast
being fanned into water by the balmy breeze that came stealing
in gently from the south, as if spring had come, but the mountain-
tops lay wrapped in winter's winding-sheet of spotless white.

—R. N. Sutherlin, *Rocky Mountain Husbandman*, March 2, 1876

In late February 1876 R. N. Sutherlin, the editor of the *Rocky Mountain Husbandman* in the town of Diamond City, mounted his horse and headed about fifty miles south to the Crow Creek and Warm Springs valleys, where he noticed ranchers taking advantage of the springlike weather.

He stopped at a homestead at Warm Springs, where he "enjoyed a pleasant chat with Mr. James Nave, the proprietor." There "lies as fine a body of agricultural land as can be found in Montana," he wrote, noting that Nave's warm springs, which never froze in the winter (much like those of his grandfather in Missouri), were "valuable property." He mentioned that Nave used the water in summer for irrigation and in winter for operating a quartz mill to extract gold ore.

Later that day, he stopped at the Bembrick ranch, where he was greeted by Lulu, now eighteen years old and six months pregnant. "We called upon our friend, B. F. Bembrick, but he had gone fishing," Sutherlin wrote. "From his estimable lady, who gave us a cordial welcome, we learned that he would depart soon to see after his herd on the Muscleshell."[1]

While Doc may have had good weather for his trek to the Musselshell, by the time early June rolled around, Mother Nature was angry. A terrific rain- and snowstorm battered central Montana. Snow in the Musselshell valley reached as high as two feet. The Crow

Creek overflowed its banks and flooded Enoch Wilson's steam saw-mill, which, according to local gossip, had grossed $10,000 over the past year. The storm caused him to lose $1,000 in lumber.[2] Lulu, meanwhile, was in labor with their first child. Was Doc by her side, or was he still out camping with his herd? No record exists, but amid this turbulence, Lulu gave birth to a daughter.[3] Now Lulu would be caring for not only Addie, now seven, but for an infant of her own named Elizabeth.

✳

Later that June, about 250 miles away on the Crow Indian Reservation, Lieutenant Colonel George Custer was among the hundreds of U.S. soldiers killed during his Seventh Cavalry Regiment's attack on an encampment of Plains tribes. The news didn't reach the Bozeman newspapers until early July. A witness reported, "The battle ground looked like a slaughter-pen, as it really was, being in a narrow ravine. The dead were very much mutilated. The situation now looks serious."[4] Those living on the East Coast of the United States didn't get word until July 7, by which time the reports had grown florid, inaccurate, and sensational. "Where the Yellow-Haired Leader Lay in the Embrace of Death" and "The Savages Respect the Body of Him They Knew So Well" read the headlines in the *New York Herald*, which told its readers that the Sioux had killed Custer. Four Crow men serving as scouts for the U.S. Army also were lost in the fierce fight, which soon would become known as the Battle of the Little Bighorn.

Chapter 25

Fiendish Murders in Wonderland.

—*Rocky Mountain Husbandman*, August 30, 1877

The following August, Lulu and Doc's good friends Emma and George Cowan left their home in Radersburg for what was to be a two-week sightseeing trip in Yellowstone National Park. The couple would celebrate their second wedding anniversary during the journey, which had been planned by Emma's older brother Frank and four of his friends. Emma, twenty-four, was not keen on being the only female in the group, so she brought along her twelve-year-old sister, Ida, for companionship. The group traveled on horseback, bringing with them a carriage, a wagon full of camping equipment, and a camp cook.

It took the party a week to reach Yellowstone, which had been established by Congress five years earlier, in 1872, "as a public park or pleasuring-ground for the benefit and enjoyment of the people." The following year, Lieutenant Colonel George Custer had led an expedition to explore the region, which held a wealth of deep canyons, magical geysers, and blistering hot springs. But his expedition had not been without danger. The *Bozeman Avant Courier* told its readers,

> Observing the country for some miles in advance and on all sides, are Indian and cavalry scouts. Thus every precaution is taken on the march, and in camp to guard against Indian attacks. The orders are that Indians shall not be fired upon unless they show unmistakeable signs of hostility. Few Indians or signs of them have been seen, though the stealthy rascals have undoubtedly watched the expedition in all its course from their lurking places, and have visited the camping grounds shortly after departure of the rear guard for a square meal on the refuse of the camp and the offal of slaughtered animals.[1]

Now Custer lay buried at Little Bighorn, and as the Cowans were heading toward Yellowstone, the U.S. Army was pursuing members of the Nez Perce Tribe through the region. They had clashed in a fierce battle on the Big Hole River just a few days earlier, after several bands of the Nez Perce refused to comply with the government's order that they move to a reservation in Idaho. They were exerting their rights, agreed on in an 1855 treaty, to remain on portions their ancestral land and to hunt and fish on other land they had ceded to the government. Following the battle, the Nez Perce decided to head north toward Canada to seek assistance from the Crows. Emma Cowan and the others in her party weren't aware of any of this news as they entered the park. They found this place, promoted as "Wonderland," quite enchanting.

"Our first sight of the geysers—with columns of steam rising from innumerable vents and the smell of the inferno in the air from the numerous sulphur springs—made us simply wild with the eagerness of seeing all things at once," Emma wrote.[2] As was the custom, both women were riding sidesaddle on their ponies.[3] "My small sister and I could scarcely keep pace with the men, but we found enough to interest us, turn where we could."

The Cowans and their friends spent their days fishing, hunting, and exploring the park. On August 23 the group "encountered the first and only tourists we had seen, General [William Tecumseh] Sherman and party," Emma recalled.[4] "We also received the very unpleasant impression that we might meet the Indians before we reached home. No one seemed to know just where they were going. The scout who was with the General's party assured us we would be perfectly safe if we would remain in the [Geyser] basin, as the Indians would never come into the park. I observed, however, that his party preferred being elsewhere, as they left the basin that same night."

The next evening—the night before their wedding anniversary—the Cowan party set up camp along a creek and sat around the campfire. They were ready to start for home the next morning, as "naturally we felt somewhat depressed and worried over the news received," noted

Emma. Her brother and another member of their group, Al Oldham, sang songs, told jokes, and dressed up as pirates in an attempt to lighten the mood.

But General Sherman's scout had been wrong—some of the Nez Perce were, in fact, in Yellowstone's geyser basin. And in the darkness, they surrounded the Cowan camp. After the campfire had died down, the Cowans drifted off to sleep in their tents. At daylight Emma awoke to the sound of voices outside her tent. She thought they were the voices of Indians and peeked out of her tent to confirm her suspicions. Then she woke her husband, who went out to speak to them. "They pretended to be friendly," she later wrote, "but talked little."

The group quickly began dismantling tents and packing up to leave as the Nez Perce "devoured everything" the cook had prepared for breakfast. By this time, twenty or thirty more of their tribe had arrived. One of the Cowans' friends began giving them sugar and flour, at which point George Cowan angrily told them to leave. "Naturally they resented it," Emma wrote, "and I think this materially lessened his chances to escape."

Nervously the Cowans mounted their horses and began riding toward home, followed by what Emma now estimated was a group of forty or fifty Nez Perce. After a mile or so, the party members were ordered to halt, and more Indians, all armed with guns, emerged from the forest. They ordered the Cowan party to backtrack, "which we did, not without some protest, realizing however the utter futility," Emma said. Forced to leave their wagons and supplies behind, because fallen timber was blocking the path, they gathered warm clothing and rode ten more miles until the Nez Perce stopped and set up camp. An Indian called Poker Joe told the group, in English, that if they relinquished their horses and saddles for others, "that would be good enough to take us home, they would release us." (The Cowans would not have known that Poker Joe was a subchief who was guiding the Nez Perce north after the Battle of Little Big Hole.)

They complied and set out again on the new horses, believing they were safe. But after just a half mile, the Nez Perce returned, telling them their chief would like to speak to them again. They were led back past their earlier camp and higher into the forest. "The pallor of my husband's face told me he thought our danger great," remembered Emma. Then "suddenly, without warning, shots rang out." Emma saw her husband dismount and fall to the ground. She ran to him, later recalling, "I heard my sister's screams and called to her. She came and crouched by me, as I knelt by his side. I saw he was wounded in the leg above the knee, and by the way the blood spurted out I feared an artery had been severed. He asked for water. I dared not leave him to get it."

She saw that "every gun in the whole party of Indians was leveled at us three." One man pulled her away from her husband. Then as "another Indian stepped up, a pistol shot rang out," and her "husband's head fell back, and a red stream trickled down his face from beneath his hat." Emma promptly fainted. When she came to, her brother was at her side, telling her their young sister was safe. "The Indians had told him no further harm would befall us," she wrote. "It seemed to me the assurance had come too late. I could see nothing but my husband's dead face with the blood upon it."

Emma was forced to ride on, leaving the body of her husband lying sprawled by a pine log. Because the Nez Perce had learned that Frank was familiar with the trail, they had sent him ahead to scout the way. But Emma's sister Ida, along with the other men in their party, had disappeared.

At dusk the Nez Perce stopped at a camp, where Emma found her brother waiting. Frank told her that their sister was at another camp, along with another Yellowstone visitor captured the previous night, a man named Mr. Shively. The next morning, as Emma sat solemnly in the rain, a Nez Perce woman stopped to wrap a canvas around her wet shoulders. Soon after, she was taken to the other camp, where she was reunited with sister. "Such a forlorn child I trust I may never again see," wrote Emma. "She seemed not to be quite certain that I was alive, even though she had been told."

The journey continued. The following night the sisters, along with their brothers and Shively, watched a council of seven tribal leaders debate their fate as Poker Joe interpreted. He explained that the council had decided to let Emma and her sister leave, along with a soldier they had captured. But they would keep Frank and Mr. Shively as guides to help them reach Crow country.[5]

Emma refused to leave unless her brother was allowed to accompany them. "I had not been favorably impressed by the soldier," Emma said. "Intuition had told me he was not trustworthy." The council discussed her demand and finally agreed to let the family leave together.

The Nez Perce provided them with two broken-down horses, a tarp, a jacket for her sister, and some bedding, bread, and matches. Emma feared that the trio would be stopped again on their journey home. She told Shively as much. He, alone, was not being released. "Something tells me you will get out safely," he told her, with tears in his eyes.

Poker Joe rode with Emma, Ida, and Frank until they reached a trail along the river. He told them they must follow the path and ride "All night. All day. No sleep." If they did, he said, they would reach Bozeman in two days. They didn't trust him. As soon as he disappeared, they left the trail and headed up into the camouflage of the trees, attempting to keep both the river and trail within sight. They eventually reached a valley but were afraid to cross it in daylight, fearing they would be spotted. When darkness came, the moon was so bright that they remained in hiding, waiting until the middle of the night to move across the open valley. By the time they reached the shelter of the trees again, it was daylight. As she rode, Emma's mind raced with images of her husband lying dead on the ground, "perhaps dragged and torn by wild beasts. My own peril seemed of little consequence." With their food now gone, they ate berries and rabbits that Frank killed by throwing rocks.

Later that day, they spotted a group of horses and men in a meadow. Fearing they were Indians, Emma, Ida, and their horses hid among the trees while Frank quietly moved ahead to investigate. "He returned in a few minutes and declared them soldiers. Oh, such a feeling of relief!" Emma's intuition had not failed her—the soldiers informed them that the man with whom she had refused to leave the camp was, in fact, an army deserter whose fate now was unknown. The soldiers also told them that they had picked up the trail of the Nez Perce and were confident they were no longer in the area. Frank, Emma, and Ida were given fresh horses, and after eating supper (Emma declared herself "nearly famished"), they left with the soldiers, riding in the dark on "some of the roughest mountain trails" she had ever traveled. Near midnight they reached the park's central gathering spot, Mammoth Hot Springs, where they met two English tourists who were about to begin their tour. One of them, a doctor, cleaned and dressed their cuts and scratches.

Frank Carpenter managed to send a telegram to his brother in Helena, which was published not only in the Helena newspaper but in the *New York Times*: "Emma, Ida and myself alive; Cowan and Oldham killed. Saw Cowan and Oldham shot. Balance missing. I think all are killed, but don't know. . . . Helena party all gone except one—all missing. Indians fired into their camp."[6]

Frank was referring to a group of men from Helena who also had been ambushed in the park by the Nez Perce. The first newspaper reports indicated that a total of sixteen tourists had been killed in the two incidents.[7] One man from the Helena group, F. J. Pfiester, encountered Emma and Frank as they were escorted out of the park. "From [them] I learned the sad fate of their party," Pfiester told a reporter for the *Bozeman Times*.[8] Of his own group, he said, "I don't think the Indians intended to kill as they could easily have done so at the first volley."

Two days later, the *Bozeman Avant Courier* published an update: "Cowan was massacred in his wife's arms. He and another man are known to be dead. Others, the women think, are no doubt dead, as the Indians had them completely surrounded." The paper also urged citizens to beware: "It will be well for the settlers in the Yellowstone valley to protect themselves as much as possible, as there are not soldiers enough here to prevent the Indians from entering the valley."[9]

But the reports were not true. Emma, Ida, and Frank actually had hitched a ride to Bozeman with a man pulling a wagon and a pair of wild mules. The Englishmen and their guide also had decided to leave the park and head to Bozeman. "Wonderland had lost its attractions for the nonce," Emma said.

After spending the night at a ranch on the Yellowstone River, Emma, Frank, and Ida were met by a friend who would take them the rest of the way on the forty-mile trip to Bozeman. That night, they bunked with a large family living on Trail Creek and told their story. "To them, Indian scares were common," Emma said. "Living so close to the Crow reservation, they were always on the alert and never felt quite safe." Soon after they went to bed, a neighbor knocked on the door to alert them that Indians were near. "Several shots were exchanged, but the Indians, who were undoubtedly Crows on a horse-stealing raid, as soon as they found themselves discovered, disappeared. We retired again, but did not sleep much."

The next day, near Bozeman, the group encountered a U.S. Army lieutenant accompanied by "seventy or eighty" Crows, "on their way to intercept the Nez Perce," she wrote. "They looked rather more dangerous than any we had met."

After reaching Bozeman without further incident, Emma and Ida headed north to their parents' ranch in Townsend. Frank returned to Yellowstone, hoping to recover the bodies of his brother-in-law and his friend Albert Oldham.

The newspapers, meanwhile, began to temper their sensational statements—at least slightly—about the so-called "savages." "With all their savagery and ferocity let it be said and remembered to the credit of the Nez Perces that these ladies were treated with all respect and protected from all harm while their prisoners," opined the *New North-West*.[10] The August 28 edition of the *Helena Daily Independent* chimed in:

> The release of Frank Carpenter and his two sisters after they had been captured is the most remarkable thing that has yet occurred in this horrible Nez Perces war, and goes far to prove that these Indians

are waging their warfare on more civilized principles than those that usually obtain among savages. It was to have been expected at the very least that they would have taken the women prisoners, kept them with them, perhaps subjecting them to a worse fate than death, and under no circumstances was it to have been expected that they would spare the life of Mr. Carpenter. The release of captives is certainly a new feature of Indian warfare and goes far to mitigate the atrocities they have committed.[11]

On September 5 came a startling report from Bozeman. "COWAN ALIVE," exclaimed the *Helena Daily Independent*. "Two scouts just in from Howard's command say that Cowan is with Howard and is doing well and will recover. He is shot through the thigh and in the side and wounded in the head. . . . This news was reliable."

Lulu Bembrick, who had just learned the news, jumped on her saddle horse and rode off to Radersburg to alert Emma that George was alive.[12]

Chapter 26

Wonderland. Scenes of Bloodshed. Two Narrow
Escapes From the Clutches of the Red Devils.
The Dead Alive. Geo. F. Cowan Not Killed.

—*Bozeman Avant Courier*, September 6, 1877

George Cowan lay unconscious on the ground, left for dead. At dusk, after the rest of the Cowan party had been led away, he came to and stirred. A Nez Perce who had been watching him shot him once again, in the leg.

Cowan passed out. When he awoke again, it was daylight, and he was alone. He began to crawl back to the campsite where his group had first encountered the Nez Perce. It was ten miles away, and it took him four days. There he found an empty can, some water, and coffee beans. He built a fire to boil the coffee, but the can fell over, and the coffee spilled out. His strength sapped, he fell asleep, close to death. But the next day, he awoke and crawled a few more miles, where two U.S. Army scouts found him lying at the side of a road. The *Bozeman Avant Courier* reported:

> He was picked up by Howard about 12 miles from where he was shot, where he had crawled. He is wounded in the right leg and left hip—neither wound serious. He has also a slight wound on the back of his head. The shot that his wife and others thought killed him was in the head. The ball struck it from the front, about two inches above the root of the nose, immediately over the dividing membranes of the brain, flattened against the skull and has been removed by a surgeon. He is now in excellent health and spirits, his wounds giving him but little pain. Oldham is also with Howard's command wounded through the jaw, the bullet having carried away two of his teeth. He is doing splendidly.[1]

Emma, meanwhile, was waiting with her sister and parents for additional news about her husband. None came. Frank returned, and the two of them rode to Helena to be near the only telegraph in the area. A week went by before she received a telegram informing her that her husband would arrive in Bozeman the next day. Emma set out on the hundred-mile journey. But upon arriving in Bozeman, she learned that George had taken a turn for the worse and was being cared for at the Bottler ranch—the same place where she had spent her first night after leaving the park. She hired a carriage to take her there, where she found her husband "much better than I dared anticipate, and insistent on setting out for home with out delay."

A month and a half after their anniversary trip had started, Emma and George finally were headed home. She hired a driver and carriage and bundled him carefully in blankets and robes. Seven or eight miles outside Bozeman, on a high road along a steep hillside, a leather strap attached to the carriage's wooden steering pole broke, sending the carriage hurtling down the hill. The *Rocky Mountain Husbandman* reported, "[They] were dumped out some forty feet below the road, and the buggy continued to roll over and over, landing nearly 200 feet below. The driver says Mrs. Cowan could have jumped out when the buggy first started to upset, but preferring to stay with her husband, she shared the same fate, and was tossed upon the ground near him. Fortunately they escaped with but slight injury, Mrs. C. receiving a sprained ankle, and Mr. C. some slight bruises."[2]

Soon a man with a horse rode by, and the carriage driver headed to a nearby fort to summon an ambulance wagon. By the time it arrived and delivered the couple to Bozeman, Emma reported, "Mr. Cowan was almost exhausted, his wounds bleeding and needing attention." He was carried to a hotel. There a doctor sat down on the side of his bed to dress his wounds. The bed collapsed, sending Cowan tumbling to the floor. "This sudden and unexpected fall, in his enfeebled state, nearly finished him," Emma remembered. "A collapse followed, from which he did not rally for some time."

Despite this setback, one week later the Cowans headed home to

Radersburg. Emma sent "A Card of Thanks" to the citizens of Boz-eman via the *Bozeman Avant Courier*: "To the many friends who, in their great kindness of heart, tendered sympathy, aid and care, in my sad hour of sorrow and desolation; sympathies that did so much to alleviate the dread thought that I was forsaken by God himself, to them I return my heartfelt thanks."[3]

It took George most of that winter to recover. "A severe gunshot wound through the hip, a bullet hole in the thigh, a ball flattened on the forehead, and the head badly cut with rock. Few, indeed, are the men who could have survived so severe an ordeal," wrote his wife.

Years later Julia Bennett would relish telling the story to her grandchildren and ranch guests, who all longed to hear stories of the Wild West.

Chapter 27

This magnificent empire of the new Northwest contains
16,000,000 acres of fertile farm lands, a more extensive area
than is covered by an entire average Eastern State. It contains
38,000,000 acres of unexcelled grazing lands, a pasture-
field alone larger than the great prairie State of Illinois.

—Robert E. Strahorn, *The Resources of Montana Territory
and Attractions of Yellowstone Park,* 1879

By the mid-1870s Doc's cattle business was prospering. Newspapers
were continuing to mistake him for a medical doctor, calling "Dr. B.
F. Bembrick" a "heavy stock-grower" living in "the beautiful valley of
Crow creek where the farmers are all well to do."[1] In November 1875
he purchased 160 acres on Warm Springs Creek, three miles south of
James Nave's ranch. He'd bought the land from Lulu's uncle Jacob,
who had decided to move to the other side of the Elkhorn Mountains
to work as a prospector. The purchase ensured that the Bembricks
would have a constant source of water, since they now owned the
precious water rights to the property's spring.

In 1878 a Montana newspaper dubbed Doc "the cattle king of the
Muscleshell," also noting that "Muscleshell cattle are said to be fatter
than any others in the country."[2] The grass-rich valley was growing
in popularity and now was "the home of several hundred herdsmen
and pioneer farmers," with others talking of moving there.[3]

That May, ranchers near Radersburg were blessed with an extraordinary amount of rain, which relieved them of the need to flood their
fields in order to sprout their grain. But for the second summer in a
row, they also were battling an invasion of grasshoppers that were
"hatching out by the millions," according to Helena's *Independent
Record.* "In many places the ground is literally black with them, and

9. Benjamin "Doc" Bembrick and Lulu Bembrick, circa 1907. Sherry Merica Pepper private collection.

they are devouring everything green. We shall be satisfied if we raise half a crop."[4]

There were other, more positive, goings-on. The Bembricks' friend and neighbor, the Irish-born Hugh Galen, had just won the contract to carry mail through the valley via his stagecoach line. "His wide awake style of doing business has put new life into the people of this section, and they have ceased to growl about hard times," noted the *Independent Record* in the same article.

Meanwhile, "the Messrs. Nave"—most likely James and Errendle— were preparing to extract ore from a "very rich" vein in their mine, called the Ironclad. The correspondent reported that the Ironclad, along with the nearby Keating mine, "will give employment to a large number of men, and Radersburg will be as lively as in the good old days."

While the town had a school that operated six months a year, there was none in the valley. So Doc, along with Enoch Wilson, Errendle

Nave, and Hugh Galen, joined forces to establish one near the Naves' ranch. "It is under the management of Miss Switzer, an accomplished teacher, and withal a very agreeable lady, and popular, too, if one can judge by the number of old bachelors who make calls upon one pretense or another."[5]

Chapter 28

Everything is lovely here so far as your
correspondent is able to find out.

—"Letter from Radersburg," *Helena Daily Independent*, May 29, 1880

The weather was unsettled and chilly near Radersburg in late May 1880. But "Notwithstanding the cool weather, crops are beginning to show up green," wrote Radersburg's correspondent to the *Helena Daily Independent*.[1] The mines were coming back to life after sitting idle over the winter. The population of the Montana Territory had almost doubled since the first census, ten years earlier, and the first railroad tracks in the territory were being laid.

The Bembrick household was growing as well, having survived a severe measles outbreak that had stricken many in the town of Radersburg that winter. On May 27, 1880, Lulu gave birth to a second daughter. She and Doc named her Julia.

Sixteen months later, on September 19, 1881, Lulu delivered a son, David. He lived for only one month and seven days. The family laid him to rest in the Radersburg cemetery, an image of a seedling carved into his gravestone.

The family patriarch, James Nave, soon began fighting a futile four-month battle against kidney disease. At the age of seventy, he died in his bed at midnight on May 21, 1882, with his wife and five of his six children at his side.

"Mr. Nave was an honest, conscientious, upright man, a devoted husband and loving, affectionate father," noted an obituary.[2] "Both in Missouri and Montana he had a wide circle of friends who will learn of his death with regret."

Not long after James Nave's death, the Bembricks moved south to their land on Warm Springs Creek, three miles away from the

Nave family homestead. Dried-up buffalo wallows dotted the rolling foothills and rich grassland.

One visitor riding through the area thought it "a dreary, desolate country, fit only for the purpose of grazing and the habitation of prairie dogs and rattlesnakes."[3] But to the Bembricks, it was home. They named their new ranch, which consisted of a log cabin, a barn, and corrals, the Circle J. Lulu gave birth to another son—named Ben after his father—on December 9, 1882, and to Jim three years later. Along with Doc's daughter Addie, the family was now complete.

Chapter 29

Blue handkerchiefs, worn tightly around the neck, is the
prevailing color of the aesthetic cowboy of Montana.

—*Helena Daily Independent*, May 11, 1882

The Circle J was at its peak during Julia's childhood. In addition to
cattle, Doc was raising Morgan horses and sheep, growing wheat,
and buying up neighboring ranches. The *Helena Daily Independent*
opined, "He is now located on one of the finest farms in the Territory."[1]

He also acquired a ferry that led travelers across the Missouri
(which he leased to its previous owner to operate) and teamed up with
George Cowan, Enoch Wilson, Errendle Nave, and friend Benjamin
Townsley to buy the nearby Black Friday Mine.[2] Doc spent January
and February of 1883 serving as a representative in the territorial
legislature, following in the footsteps of Enoch Wilson, who had been
elected to serve in that same capacity in 1879 and 1881.

One fellow stock raiser called Doc one of the top-six livestock
owners in the entire region for raising cattle and sheep. Each of the
men, he said, owned between three thousand and ten thousand head.
That area, between what was known as Clark's Fork Bottom and the
Musselshell River, was still remote but expected to "be constantly
augmented with the progress of the Northern Pacific railroad."[3]

Now in his fifties, Doc continued to ride, hunt, and herd. In the
Musselshell valley he met a teenage boy who had arrived from St.
Louis a few years earlier. Young Charlie Russell was riding for the
Helena cattlemen Kaufman and Stadler, "learning to be a cowboy,
but was much more interested in painting pictures," Julia's father
told her. Charlie offered Doc a few of his paintings, but he refused,

telling Charlie that someday "he would get lots of money for them." Charlie told Doc, "Oh hell, I don't care about money."

That winter of 1886–87 was the worst any of the ranchers had ever experienced. On January 28 a blizzard with blinding snow and frigid temperatures hit the territory. By early February, temperatures had dropped to forty below zero. The grass the ranchers relied on to feed their herds iced over, and the cattle couldn't break through to reach it. Thousands of them froze to death, scattered across the ranchlands like icy statues.

When spring came, fellow rancher Granville Stuart rode through his land in the Judith Basin. He saw dead cattle "everywhere." The survivors were terribly weak, he wrote to a friend, and became "easily mired in the mud holes." Stuart added that more than half the cattle in the region had perished.[4]

There is no record of how many cattle Doc Bembrick lost that winter, but ranchers throughout Montana and other western states were hit with the realization that they couldn't rely solely on the open range to feed their herds. Young Charlie Russell painted a watercolor documenting the horrific loss, called *Waiting for a Chinook*. The image, which depicted a coyote tracking a starving cow, helped to make him one of the most famous western artists of all time.

Chapter 30

Hospitality, as proud a tradition West as South, has come down
from the days when a rancher's home was everyone's castle
and a good citizen never locked his door, knowing that a cold,
tired, and hungry rider might need to enter and cook a meal.

—Federal Writers Project of the WPA, *The WPA Guide to 1930s Montana*

Because of the Circle J's remoteness, Lulu always was prepared to
feed and entertain travelers passing through who needed a place to
sleep for the night. Doc had built a two-story white frame house that
was large enough to hold the family of seven, along with many guests.
Their new home had an air of country prosperity, with a carved balustrade and veranda above the main porch and floor-to-ceiling windows
accented with architectural flourishes. A picket fence and a sidewalk
built of wooden planks led visitors to the front door.

The five-bedroom ranch house, complete with living room and
parlor, was alive with activity; the Bembricks even looked after "broke
and homeless" cowboys who lived in a nearby cabin. The cowpunchers ate with the family and helped with the chores but, Julia said,
"mostly just played cards." Peddlers stopped by, along with neighbors
and friends and relatives from Helena, Boulder City, and other parts.
Someone was always "dropping in, so we had lots of cooking to do,"
said Julia.

Among the guests were the Cowans, who lived on the other side
of the Elkhorn Mountains. George still bore scars from his shooting
by the Nez Perce in Yellowstone a decade earlier. He had saved the
bullet that had struck his head, carrying it with him attached to his
watch chain. Julia loved to look at it. "He could lay it right in the dent
in his forehead," she said.

Along with the cowboys and various boarders, there was another permanent member of the household. When Julia was four, Lulu—fulfilling the request of a dying friend—took in Daisy Doyle, a twenty-year-old music teacher from St. Louis who had lost her sight after an eye operation. Daisy's Irish immigrant parents had passed away years earlier, and she had moved to Helena to live with her aunt. There she taught lessons in piano, organ, and guitar at her Cutler Street home (the same street, coincidentally, where Lulu had spent several months living with her mother and Aunt Lucy Ann in 1867). After her aunt died, Daisy lived with the Bembricks for sixteen years when she was not in nearby Boulder City teaching at the "Deaf, Dumb and Blind Asylum," which, according to one newspaper, housed "some thirteen of these unfortunates."[1]

Lulu sewed Daisy's clothes, read to her every day, and bought her a piano. A talented musician who could play by ear, Daisy taught all the Bembrick children to play. She also gave voice lessons to Diddy and Addie, but not to Julia, who said she "could call the pigs and chickens, but could not sing." Unlike her siblings, Julia had not inherited her father's musical ability. Doc played the violin by ear and often fiddled at dances. He "could play any piece he heard and he made up some of his own," Julia said.

Along with the other five families in the valley, the Bembricks formed a literary club, which met every two weeks. The adults gave talks on various topics, while the children performed literary readings, played the piano, and sang. Julia, for her part, remembered that mostly she loved the refreshments.

✣

Welcoming others was important to both Lulu and Doc. Julia considered her mother "very religious." Although there was no church nearby, itinerant preachers traveled through the area, and Lulu read her children Bible stories and taught them to pray. In the summer of 1888, a woman named Mrs. Havilah Heathwood arrived in Helena to introduce the new practice of Christian Science mental healing to town residents. She presented parlor talks and free lectures, explaining how its founder Mary Baker Eddy's emphasis on the power of the divine mind could successfully treat "Rheumatism, Cancer, Intemperance, Opium Habit and all kinds of diseases."[2] Whether or not Lulu actually heard Mrs. Heathwood speak, she became a believer in Christian Science's focus on submitting to faith in God's power to heal. In fact, Lulu believed that a letter she wrote to her practitioner cured Doc of a tumor on his tongue. Julia said, "I can remember the day we were eating and he got up and coughed, and it came out."[3]

Doc, on the other hand, was not a believer in organized religion. He "did not read the Bible but had a religion of his own," said Julia. "He lived by the Golden Rule and was generous to a fault. His word was as good as gold."

Despite their religious differences, Doc and Lulu had a playful relationship. He called her "Miss Lou," except when he was angry with her, when he called her "Madame." He loved to tease her, and when saying grace at dinner, he would add, "God Almighty make us able to eat all Miss Lou put on the table."

Lulu had her own quiet way of getting even. Once, after reminding him countless times to fill the woodbox so she could stoke her kitchen stove, she came up with a plan she thought might be more effective than words. At noon, when Doc came in for dinner, he sat down to find slices of raw meat, raw potatoes, and raw green beans laid out on the table. Lulu sat in the kitchen, "patiently awaiting the torrent of expletives for which Doc was famous," but heard nothing "but the clatter of silverware." Peeking around the kitchen door, she found Doc silently eating his dinner.[4]

Chapter 31

I can still see it as I did that morning long ago.

—Julia Bennett, memoir

The Circle J was almost entirely self-sufficient. Lulu rose each morning before everyone else to begin the chores. Along with maintaining the household, she kept the ranch's books. Although Lulu's last formal schooling had been in San Francisco, Julia said her mother "wrote a good hand, was a good reader, and could spell any word given her."

Lulu had learned to sew from her mother and grandmother, and she and Lizzie made clothes for the entire family from patterns of their design. Emptied flour sacks became underwear; hand-me-downs were transformed into new petticoats. Not until she was twelve did Julia own a dress made from new fabric, a luxury. "It was plaid and I was proud of it," she wrote.

Lulu tanned deer and antelope skins to make buckskin gloves, moccasins, hunting pants, shirts, and coats for the entire family. The weeks-long process included an initial bath of acid (lime, lye, alum, arsenic, or lead) to remove the hair, a soak in chicken manure to soften the hide, and finally, perhaps a mixture of tree bark and water to convert the hide to leather. By the time Lulu removed the skins from the final tub, "they were snow white and soft," remembered Julia. Lulu learned to bead and sew buckskin from a Native woman. She also made quilts, including woolen ones called sugans—plain squares of fabric sewn together with the sole purpose of keeping people warm.[1] Cowboys used them when camping out on the range; Doc probably used them on his hunting trips; and the children most certainly bundled up in them, perhaps along with a few buffalo robes, when riding to school in a sleigh.

Laundry, too, was considered women's work, and it wasn't a job for the dainty. Lulu and the girls hauled buckets of water from the creek, heated it in a large boiler, scrubbed the clothes on a washboard with homemade soap, and used the only "modern" device—a wringer—to squeeze out excess water. As the youngest, Julia was assigned the responsibility of washing the socks and stockings. She had to stand on a box to reach the washtub. And she remembered, "Every Saturday night we took baths in tubs whether we needed it or not."

The Bembricks raised all their food except flour and sugar, which they bought from the mercantile store in hundred-pound sacks, and twenty-pound bags of green coffee, which they parched and ground by hand. The large pond on the ranch was stocked with German carp, supplied free of charge by the government.[2] Vegetables came from their large garden. They hauled cabbages, potatoes, carrots, and squash to the root cellar and canned the fruit, making jellies and jams and many varieties of pickles, along with vinegar. Their orchard burst with berries, apples, and plums. In May, when its five hundred plum trees were in bloom, Doc said the landscape resembled "a vast stretch of white, fleecy clouds."[3]

❖

Every fall, Doc and a friend drove a four-horse team on a 120-mile hunting trip to Henry's Lake, a trout-laden alpine pool near the Montana-Idaho Territory border, to gather enough meat, game, and fowl to last the winter. They returned with a massive load of elk, deer, bear, mountain sheep, ducks, geese, and fish. Doc butchered thirty hogs each fall as well, which the family preserved in the smokehouse or cured into hams, ground into sausage, pickled into pigs' feet, rendered into lard, or boiled until it became gelatinous head cheese. Lulu may have used a recipe like this one from a nineteenth-century Montana cookbook: "Boil a pig's head and four feet until the bones drop out. When still warm chop fine and season highly with pepper and salt. Return to a kettle with one tea-cup of the liquor to every quart of meat. Cook a few minutes, turn into deep dishes, set in a cool place and when cold cut into slices."[4]

They shared their food with others, including Native visitors. When Julia was seven, a band of Indians set up camp near the ranch. The Native tribes that Lulu earlier had feared now were starving. The bison herds that had sustained them had nearly disappeared thanks to indiscriminate slaughter by sportsmen, settlers, and the frontier U.S. Army.[5] In addition, the U.S. government had forced them to give up their land.

"They always came in begging for food. Dad always gave it to them," Julia remembered. Sometimes, he would butcher one of his cows and give it to them. While he butchered, the Indians ate the cow's entrails and drank its blood. Julia was transfixed by these encounters. "We never missed [them] although it made us sick," she said.

The family's dairy cows supplied milk, which Lulu churned into butter, as well as ice cream, which Doc would offer to the Indian visitors. When the frozen concoction gave them sudden headaches, he would spread it on bread for them to eat—an event the children also loved to watch.[6]

Doc and Lulu brought along a milk cow when they went on weeks-long camping trips near the Yellowstone River. In a letter to her niece from the Pine Lodge Camp, she wrote, "We are reveling in cream. I churned 3 lbs of butter, have nearly another churning saved." They stored the butter in stone crocks to overwinter. An icehouse and springhouse on the ranch helped keep food fresh over the hot summer months. They devised other, more innovative ways to ensure that there was enough in the larder to keep themselves fed in the winter. A pond on the ranch, in the path of migrating ducks and geese, often served as a rest stop for the birds. Doc soaked corn in whiskey and left it at the pond for them to eat. One morning, at the break of dawn, Lulu, already up and hard at work, heard something hit the house. "She ran out and a whole flock of ducks were on the ground," Julia recalled. "She picked up seven in her apron before they came to."

Chapter 32

Backward, turn backward, O Time, in your flight.
Make me a child again just for tonight!

—Julia Bennett, quoting poet Elizabeth Akers Allen, 1832–1911

Despite the endless ranch chores, Julia remembered her childhood as "the happy carefree years." She wasn't interested in cooking, like her sisters, Addie and Diddy—she preferred to work outside, pruning trees in the orchard, rising early to pick berries with her mother, and milking cows with Ben. She fed the chickens, took care of the orphaned calves and pigs, and adopted a Jersey cow and a female calf as pets.

From an early age, Julia seemed to share a special language with animals. When she was four, ten-year-old Diddy declared to their father that "it was about time" Julia learned to ride. Diddy climbed on the back of Bill, a gentle white gelding that lived in their yard, and Doc lifted Julia behind her. The two girls set off alone on a journey to visit the Galens, who lived on a ranch four miles away. At some point during the trip, Julia pushed Diddy, who began to fall off the horse headfirst. Julia grabbed Diddy's foot, and then both dropped to the ground. Bill stopped, but Julia recalled that Diddy "was so mad she made me walk the rest of the way. So I learned to ride."

The first horse Julia called her very own was a golden-brown, part-Thoroughbred colt that could "run with the wind and jump anything." She named him Flash. Lulu wouldn't let the children use a saddle, so Julia learned to ride bareback and rode with the cowboys when they went to gather wild horses. She loved to ride like them, at full speed—or, as western wranglers liked to call it, "burning the breeze." Diddy wasn't as fond of riding as Julia, but they often joined up to herd cattle. However, they weren't always diligent about their duties—"Many times we spent [the] whole day getting two range bulls together and watch[ing] them fight."

When Julia was twelve, her grandmother Lizzie bought her a side-saddle. That fall, Doc let her ride her cutting horse to the roundup, where she helped the wranglers separate cattle and drive them back to the ranch.[1]

Julia taught her calf to play hide-and-seek, showing her how to stick her head in a haystack and "hide." The Jersey served as her protector. It once mowed down her younger brother Ben when he pushed Julia to the ground and rubbed her face in manure. "After that all I had to do was cry out and she came on the run," Julia said. "So he stopped."

The Bembrick children were fearless. The girls would lead their horse Bill to stand under a high swing and then leap from it onto his back. After Lulu took them to a traveling circus, they pretended they were circus riders, jumping off their horses onto their pet sow. "We worked her hard," Julia said, "but she never got cross." One spring, when Doc was fattening more than one hundred calves and pigs for market, Diddy, Julia, and their cousin Della would tiptoe out of the house on moonlit nights and ride them. An Indian woman who worked at the ranch would bring them a pail of warm water to wash up before they headed back to bed. "We never got caught," said Julia, but "Dad wondered why his animals were so wild."

High in the hills about twenty miles north of the Circle J was a mining camp called Hassel, where Della and her family lived. Julia and Della loved to pass the time calling mountain lions that lived nearby. "They would answer and come nearer," Julia said, and "when they sounded close we ran for the cabin."

One day, Lulu gave Julia and Della permission to go on a picnic in the mountains near Hassel. They mounted an old horse and rode up into the hills. When it was time for lunch, they stopped to sit on a large fallen log. Three rattlesnakes slithered out from beneath it. The girls tried to bludgeon them, but the snakes retreated. Then they decided to set the log on fire, which sparked what would soon become

10. Julia Bembrick at about age fifteen, circa 1895 (*top*), and Elizabeth "Diddy" Bembrick at about age nineteen, circa 1889 (*bottom*). Museum of the Rockies Photo Archive.

a blaze. "We had to race back and get the miners to put it out. That ended the picnics for us."

Lulu was the designated disciplinarian. Doc loved to tell stories and tease his children. "He very seldom corrected us," remembered Julia. Once, however, he angrily barred her from riding a horse named Fanny after she lost control of her while riding in a funeral procession, causing the horses carrying the cart with the coffin to bolt. Lulu was tough but never resorted to spanking. "She talked to us and said she would settle with us later," Julia said, "and believe me, she never forgot a settlement."

Julia and Diddy rode eighteen miles every Saturday to pick up the family's mail at the Toston post office, a trip that required them to ford the Missouri. They wrapped the skirts of their riding habits around their waist as their horses swam across. "Later we had a ferry, but it wasn't half as much fun," Julia said. She may have thought it was fun, but river drownings and other accidents weren't uncommon. People in the valley drowned while crossing the river, died after being struck by lightning, and were maimed in mining accidents. An eight-year-old boy was killed when he fell from a boxcar, and a two-year-old girl, her legs pierced by prickly pear thorns, was found dead in a mining ditch.[2] The bones and blue bonnet of another toddler, carried away from her home by a mountain lion, were found months later in a cave.

"We were never sick or had a doctor," Julia recalled. "I can't remember that we ever took any medicine. If we did not feel good Mother put us to bed for a couple of days." They were lucky. Fatal illnesses were common. Infants died of measles, scarlet fever, and other diseases. Julia's older cousin Ellah May Nave died while attending a girls' academy in Helena at the age of thirteen. The Bembricks' friends David and Ann Williams lost three of their children, with their three-year-old daughter and ten-year-old son succumbing to diphtheria within two days of each other just before Christmas. Although Julia remembered her childhood with fondness, life in the valley was not particularly bucolic.

Lulu was insistent that her children have a good education, but the only schoolhouse in the valley—a one-room wooden building that held one teacher and about thirty students in eight different grades—was six miles away. Each spring and fall, Diddy, being the eldest, drove Julia and the boys to school on a buckboard led by a team of mules. "The mules ran away at the least excuse. So we hung on," remembered Julia. In winter the trip was especially difficult. Lulu rose at four in the morning, heated rocks, and placed them in a bobsled. The children climbed aboard and huddled under buffalo robes while the hired man drove them through deep snow to the schoolhouse. "Although it was only six miles it took him five hours," Julia said. When they arrived— some walked, some rode horses—the children circled the school's potbellied stove in an attempt to thaw out. The hired man waited at a nearby ranch until dismissal time, then drove the children back home.

"All this worked such hardship on everyone," said Julia, so in 1888, when Julia was eight, Lulu turned an upstairs bedroom of the ranch house into a classroom. She hired a teacher named Samuel Penrod, who taught the four Bembrick children and their cousin Della, along with three other children who lived in the valley.

The attempt at homeschooling was not a success. "We didn't do so good," remembered Julia, and her cousin Della returned to her family in Hassel. Perhaps all the activity at the ranch had made it difficult for Mr. Penrod to keep order. All was not lost, however. He married nineteen-year-old Addie Bembrick at the ranch house on September 26 of that year, and the next season, the children returned to the valley schoolhouse.

In addition to the regular school year, the Bembrick children also spent six weeks of the summer going to school in a cabin on an abandoned homestead. They and the children of two other families walked three miles each day to reach the cabin. The teacher boarded with the Bembricks. "She was an old maid and cranky," Julia said. "She was sweet around Mother but cross at school and we did not like her." Doc was not fond of her either. One day, he was working near the school and decided to stop by to pick up his children. Seeing the teacher writing on the blackboard, he crawled through the door behind her and grabbed her ankle. "She screamed, upset the board and was very mad," Julia said. "She dismissed school." Another time, believing Doc was a physician, she asked him for advice about how to cure her toothache. He told her to fill her mouth with cold water and sit on the stove until it boiled. That was the end of their conversations.

Julia was a good student. Unlike her mother, she continued her studies through high school. When she was seventeen, her teacher at the Valley School presented her with a "Card of Honor" and "One Hundred Tokens of Merit" for "Good Deportment and Perfect Lessons."

In 1894 she, along with Diddy and Lulu, took classes at the Helena Business College, which described itself as an "institution [that] offers to young men and women a course of instruction tending directly to prepare them for business pursuits . . . which will be found useful in every OCCUPATION OF LIFE."[3]

But what Julia really loved was hunting. "It's not about killing, it's about the chase," she said.[4] She and her friends donned double-breasted blazers, high-necked white blouses, thin neckties, and ground-length A-line skirts for their all-girl hunting parties. Along with their rifles, they wore brimmed hats perched precariously atop their Gibson girl pompadours.

Chapter 33

In view of the recent agitation in favor of woman's suffrage
in the United States, it may be of interest to know that
in nearly all the countries of the globe women have had
some form of suffrage for years. We of the United States
are somewhat slow in extending to them this privilege.

—*Neihart* (MT) *Herald*, November 2, 1895

One Sunday in April 1889, Miss Anna Kline, the new traveling correspondent for the *Rocky Mountain Husbandman*, rode her horse through the Missouri valley, where only the Bembricks and five other families were living. Her publisher had dispatched her to take a tour of the territory on horseback, telling his readers that Miss Kline would ambitiously "endeavor to visit every farmer, stockgrower and fine stock breeder in Montana." She also was charged with selling them subscriptions to the newspaper.[1]

After a tiring first week on the job, Kline and her horse, Bar, stopped to spend the night at the Bembricks' ranch. Although she offered them money for her stay, they wouldn't accept it. She arose the next morning and rode south to Warm Springs Creek, where she stopped to visit Lulu's mother. "Called on Mrs. Lizzie Wilson who gave me a very cordial welcome and showed me around the springs," the thirty-year-old Kline, a petite woman with a haircut as short as a man's, reported. "She is preparing to raise carp, and an excellent place it is for that business. Mrs. Wilson means progress when she undertakes anything, and like Samantha Allen has got a 'firm mean [mien] by her.'"[2]

Kline was comparing Lizzie's determined mien to that of a character created by Marietta Holley, one of the era's best-selling comic authors, whose satirical books humorously commented on current issues of American society, including the burgeoning women's rights movement. Holley's plainspoken character Samantha Allen made no bones about her feelings on equality of the sexes: "Give a woman as many fields to work in as men have, and as good wages, and let it be thought jest as respectable for 'em to earn their livin' as for a man to, and that is enough."[3]

The issue of women's suffrage had slowly been gaining strength since 1887, when the territorial legislature granted female citizens the right to vote for school trustees in their district.[4] The same year as Kline's visit with Lizzie, two petitions for "equal suffrage" were presented at the territory's constitutional convention, one of them by a representative from Jefferson County. A reporter for the *Helena Daily Independent* submitted that he did not "assume that women are not qualified to intelligently exercise the electoral privilege," because, in fact, "unquestionably they equal men in intelligence and probity," but he believed that the matter should be left to a vote of citizens, not to the legislature.[5]

By now, Enoch, nearly sixty, had completed three terms as a Democratic territorial legislator representing Jefferson County. Three years earlier, "having accumulated sufficiently of this world's goods," he had sold his "fine farm near Radersburg" for $5,000.[6] He recently had returned from another long trip to Missouri, probably to visit his children.[7]

Lizzie, who soon would celebrate her fifty-fourth birthday, continued her hardworking ways. For several years, she had been tending to her mother, who had moved in with them after being widowed. Lucinda Nave had died the year before, on July 2, 1888, of "paralysis of the brain" at age eighty-three. "Her declining years were made pleasant at their beautiful home, surrounded by relatives and warm friends and in the enjoyment of all comforts of life," noted her obituary.[8]

Just six years later Lizzie would follow her mother to the grave. On September 7, 1894, the *Townsend Messenger* reported that "Dr. Gilham went to Crow creek, this morning, to administer to the wants of Mrs. E. Wilson, who has been very sick of late." Ten days later she

11. Julia Bembrick (*seated*), along with her sister Elizabeth "Diddy" (*far right*), cousins, and friends, dressed for a hunt, circa early 1900s. Julia Bennett scrapbook, Sherry Merica Pepper private collection.

died at the age of fifty-nine, after "a long suffering of cancer of the stomach." She was buried in the Radersburg cemetery alongside her mother and father, and a Townsend newspaper remarked that her "circle of friends was large and cosmopolitan."[9]

Lizzie's obituary garnered only a brief mention, but over the next several weeks, Townsend newspapers saw fit to publish Enoch's letter to a local merchant extolling the virtues of the Sulky plow he had purchased, a mention of his visit to town, and his candidacy for a fourth term on the territorial legislature.[10] In early November he was spotted in Townsend after having "been on the sick list for some time."[11]

The newspaper also reported that a "large force of Native Americans, horses, dogs, squaws and lodge poles" had passed through town. The correspondent could not identify their tribe, because, it said, "they could, or would not 'cumtuck Chinook wa wa,'" which meant they did not respond to the settler–Indian trade language called Chinook. He went on to note unsympathetically that "they had nine wagons or Sioux carts, a large band of cayuses [horses], and possessed the usual vagabond appearance of a roving band of Indians."[12]

That autumn, poles were placed for a new telegraph line between the town and Warm Springs. "Before many days," one newspaper reported, "messages will flash along these wires."[13]

Two years later Doc would take a Northern Pacific train to Chicago—the city where more meat was processed than anywhere else in the world—to sell his cattle at the Union Stock Yards.[14]

And on November 8, 1889, Montana—whose population had nearly tripled during the past decade—became the forty-first state in the Union. "Hurrah for Statehood! Hurrah! The State of Montana! That sounds good!" proclaimed the *Helena Weekly Herald*. "It marks the termination of our Territorial vassalage, the beginning of our grand career as a sovereign State. For the first time the people of Montana become endowed with a full and equal right to choose the President of the United States and the signal right to participate in national legislation."[15]

The *men* of Montana, that is.

Chapter 34

The years passed swiftly by and all at once we found
ourselves grown up. Gone were the happy carefree years.

—Julia Bennett, memoir

Nearing seventy, Doc was still capable of raising a ruckus. In the fall
of 1889 a Presbyterian preacher from Helena named Rev. Pool was
riding his bicycle along a dirt road when he confronted Doc, who
was hauling a load of wood on a large wagon. The reverend, irked by
what he saw as Doc's refusal to yield, "in elegant diction but without
mincing matters a bit, expressed his opinion of 'road hogs' then and
there," a newspaper reported. Irritated by the tongue-lashing, Doc
jumped down from his wagon and "proceeded to wipe the ground
with the preacher," who reported him to the sheriff, who in turn
promptly charged Doc with assault.[1]

Doc hired his friend, the attorney George Cowan, to defend him.
Cowan successfully requested a change of venue to Broadwater
County, where Doc was acquitted. Rev. Pool refused to back down.
He filed a $5,000 lawsuit against Doc for damages, saying he had
been made "sore, sick and disabled" from the assault.[2] Doc told the
newspaper "that he has informed the reverend gentleman that he can
appeal his case to the supreme court, if he likes, and he, Bembrick, will
defeat him there. If he is not satisfied with this, says Mr. Bembrick,
there is only one other place where the case can be heard and the
preacher may get a decision there as the defendant expects to go to
a country where the climate is not so warm."[3]

Rev. Pool lost that case as well, and Doc's reputation apparently
remained untarnished. Voters elected him in 1900 to the post of Broadwater County commissioner, "free from entangling promises and
ready to honestly serve the county," noted the *Townsend Messenger*.[4]

The town's competing newspaper, for its part, dubbed him "the sage of Warm Springs Creek."[5]

The "sage" told the census taker that summer that he was ten years younger than he truly was. He was still farming, assisted by three hired hands—two to help with the farm and another with mining. Daisy Doyle, now thirty-six, continued to board at the Circle J, as did a Scottish miner. But the household was getting smaller. In November 1899 Diddy married a carriage painter from New York named Arthur Huntley. The couple lived at the Circle J for a time but then moved to the nearby town of Toston. Addie, her husband, and their two young children had moved north to the tiny town of Choteau, where Samuel worked as a building contractor.

Julia, now twenty, no longer had her companions nearby, and she was incredibly lonely.

❖

On February 26, 1901, at the age of thirty-one, Addie died at home in Butte, where her family had recently moved.[6] Her husband brought her body back to the Circle J for her funeral. "She was beloved of all who knew her, being possessed of a kind and loving disposition," wrote a friend.[7] Their two children, ten-year-old Frank and six-year-old Lulu, returned to live with Doc and Lulu, who cared for them over the next ten years until their father remarried.

The following February, seventy-seven-year-old Enoch Wilson died in Missouri, where he had moved two years earlier to live with a daughter—the only one of his five children still alive. Those reading his obituary in the *Chillicothe Constitution* would find only a mention of his first wife, Cynthia. Lizzie's name was nowhere to be found.[8]

Chapter 35

The ideal marriage is just as rare as the ideal anything else. . . .
The only trying time of an unmarried woman's life, and which
she might avoid if she chose, is the bad quarter of an hour before
she quite abandons hope and reconciles herself to the inevitable.

—Dorothy Dix, in the *Butte* (MT) *Miner*, October 21, 1902

Already seven years older than her mother had been when she married, the solitary Julia was nearing what folks called "spinsterhood." She lamented the fact that by the age of sixteen, she had never been kissed. There were few opportunities for romance, because there were few young men living in the valley. Then a friend introduced her to Anson Bennett, the blue-eyed, brown-haired son of a neighboring sheep rancher. His parents, Willard and Elizabeth, had moved to Montana from their native Canada when Anson was a boy and had raised him, his sister, and his two brothers on the ranch.[1] Julia found Anson "very handsome." She herself was lovely, wearing her blondish-brown hair piled atop her head and carrying herself in a self-assured, stately manner.

Lulu thought Anson would make an excellent husband. So she "made the match," Julia said. The couple, both twenty-two at the time of their engagement, spent the month before their wedding socializing, chaperoned by Lulu. They attended the Thanksgiving ball in Townsend and visited friends and relatives in Helena.[2] Their wedding was held in that city on Monday, December 29, 1902, with Julia's brother Jim and cousin Ben Smith serving as witnesses. Then the newlyweds set off on an "extended wedding tour"—in the middle of winter—to Oregon, Washington, and California.[3]

There was a problem, however. "We were not in love," Julia said. As the couple started their life together, Anson leased the Circle

J from his new father-in-law, and Julia kept house. They spent their free time doing the same things Julia had always loved to do: taking long camping trips with their parents at nearby Dry Creek Falls, hopping on the train to Helena for shopping trips, and visiting relatives.

A mere eleven months after the wedding, Julia was expecting. Never one to confine herself to bed, she went camping with her family at Dry Creek barely a month before giving birth, and she also took a forty-mile trip to Belgrade to visit her married sister. Donald Brooks Bennett was born on September 4, 1904. Soon after, she posed with him for a formal photograph, cradling him in her arms with a tender smile. Donald wears a long white christening dress, and Julia looks elegant in a beaded dress, her hair in a pompadour and ringlets framing her face.

But by the time of Donald's birth, Anson already had grown tired of ranching—the start of what would become a continuing pattern of dissatisfaction with work. Trying to find a trade that would appeal to him, Doc and Lulu bought a small mercantile store in the town of Toston, about eighteen miles to the east of the Circle J, that they asked Anson to run. When Don was three months old, Anson and Julia leased a two-bedroom frame house behind the store and moved in. "It had running water, [and a] bath, which was the first one I ever had," Julia said. She brought along furniture from the ranch, cooked on a woodstove, kept their food cool in a wooden icebox on the porch, and did her laundry out in the yard with a pail and washboard. She declared that she was very pleased with that "beautiful yard with tall cottonwood trees."

There were very few trees of any kind in Toston, nor were there any paved streets—only a wide dirt road that stretched southward to Bozeman and northward to Helena, lined by a handful of buildings. No more than fifty families—mostly hired hands, miners, railroad employees, and shopkeepers—populated this tiny burg on the east bank of the Missouri River. Nevertheless, Toston was prospering as a transportation hub in this lonely landscape. Ranchers and miners brought their bounty from the valley for shipment via the Northern Pacific, whose tracks and station bordered the river. The town boasted a post office, a hotel, a pair of saloons and grocery stores, a jail, a butcher, an Odd Fellows Hall, a new school with about forty students, and a livery stable.[4] A church service was held twice a month, but Lulu's fellow Christian Scientists met every Sunday in the schoolhouse.[5]

"Toston is booming," reported the neighboring *Townsend Star*. "We hear some talk of a large company embarking in business soon. The more the better."[6] The editor of another Townsend newspaper visited as well, opining, "Those people have a wide-awake little village filled and surrounded with up-to-date progressive people."[7]

Anson's new store stood on the town's dusty, nearly empty Main Street, which ran along the railroad tracks. He excavated a cellar, and by July 1905 A. B. Bennett Mercantile had opened its doors. That fall, he added a "roomy" coal shed to his business, and in December the shop was preparing for Christmas sales. "The children can all but hear the jingle of Santa Claus' bells at Bennett's store," the *Townsend Star* reported.[8] Near the end of the year, he also acquired an ornate wrought iron cash register with the words "amount purchased" boldly painted on its top, along with a finger pointing to the total—an enhancement considered important enough to be published in the newspaper.[9]

12. A. B. Bennett Mercantile, Main Street, Toston, circa 1907. Julia Bennett scrapbook, Sherry Merica Pepper private collection.

13. Lulu Bembrick (*center, wearing coat with striped border*) in A. B. Bennett Mercantile, Toston, circa 1907. Julia Bennett scrapbook, Sherry Merica Pepper private collection.

Chapter 36

Where once you rode circle and I night wrangled, a gopher
couldn't graze now. The boosters say it's a better country than
it ever was but it looks like hell to me I liked it better when it
belonged to God it was sure his country when we knew it.

—Charlie Russell, March 1913, quoted in Joseph Kinsey
Howard, *Montana: High, Wide, and Handsome*

Doc, now in his seventies, decided to retire from active ranching, and
in late 1904 he and Lulu moved to Toston to be closer their grown
children, all of whom now lived nearby.[1] They sold most of their
more than 1,150 acres of land at Warm Springs Creek, although Lulu
"proved up" an eighty-acre tract in that area (which might originally
have been her mother's) and became its owner.[2] The Bembricks purchased a large, two-story log house built by the manager of a large
smelting plant that had closed its doors a few years earlier. Their
new home was purported to be "one of the quaintest and prettiest
log houses to be found in the west"; its new owner was heralded in
the newspaper as "the oldest pioneer of Broadwater County."[3] The
house featured the latest amenities: hardwood floors, running water,
and gas lighting. It also had five bedrooms, three fireplaces, and three
bathrooms, and it wasn't long before the bedrooms were full. Despite
Lulu's belief that "divorce was a disgrace," Diddy's husband of three
years, now an alcoholic, left her. Only six months earlier, she had
given birth to a son named Bruce.[4] Diddy moved back in with her
parents, where she cared for both her infant and Addie's two children
while Lulu assisted shoppers at A. B. Bennett Mercantile.

With the Bembrick clan once again intact, the house—filled with
Oriental rugs, china, ornate wallpaper, a Victrola, Doc's hunting
trophies, and a massive porch—became the frequent site of parties.

14. Bembrick family portrait, circa 1905. *Left to right*: unidentified, Doc Bembrick, Julia Bennett with baby Donald, Anson Bennett, Elizabeth "Diddy" Bembrick Huntley with son Bruce, Ben Bembrick Jr., unidentified, Jim Bembrick, Lulu Bembrick. Julia Bennett scrapbook, Sherry Merica Pepper private collection.

Lulu had not tired of entertaining. In her early forties now, she was plump, with a round face and broad smile, and had boundless energy and enthusiasm. She hosted parties of the popular card game whist, holiday dinners, and the town's "prettiest social event of the season" that winter.[5] The Bembricks even provided board for the local school-teacher, Miss McRae, "that she may be near her school and avoid the cold walk or ride."[6] During the same week in March 1905 that Lulu served a "delicious" lunch at a social dance held at the town hall, Anson and Julia's milk cow wandered onto the railroad tracks and was killed by a passing train.[7]

Now that he no longer had a large ranch to maintain, Doc, who for decades had been active in the state Democratic Party, decided to run for election to the Montana House of Representatives. He won

15. Anson and Donald
Bennett, circa 1907.
Julia Bennett scrapbook,
Sherry Merica Pepper
private collection.

16. Myrna Williams,
granddaughter of the
Bembricks' friends and
neighbors David and Ann
Williams, circa 1909.
Myrna would grow up
to become the movie star
Myrna Loy. Lulu Bembrick
scrapbook, Sherry Merica
Pepper private collection.

and spent two months at the capitol in Helena when the legislature convened in January 1905, returning home by train on weekends.

Julia continued to stay in touch with her friends in the valley, including Della Williams, who had married just two months after Julia and Anson and who in August 1905 gave birth to a daughter named Myrna.[8] Just a year younger than Don, Myrna was a beautiful baby, with a headful of curly red ringlets and a button nose—features that two decades later would send her to Hollywood as Myrna Loy. More of Julia's friends moved to Toston. George Carpenter was the town's photographer. A few years earlier, he had married the Bembricks' former ward, the blind music teacher Daisy Doyle. Carpenter also was a musician, and he and Daisy often entertained at parties and dances throughout the valley, where "their symphonious strains are appreciated," the *Crow Creek Journal* noted.[9] Like many men in small Montana towns, Carpenter had multiple responsibilities; he also served as the town's judge.

By 1907 A. B. Bennett Mercantile was doing $100,000 worth of business annually, employed seven people, and had expanded to two buildings—one offering general merchandise and the other, next door, featuring farm machinery, supplies, and coal. "This store is in fact the only general department store in the county," noted the *Townsend Star* on May 11 of that year, and "is reputed to carry the largest stock and do the largest general merchandise business in Broadwater County. No verification of this claim is necessary further than a visit to the store, where there is constant hum of activity and business."[10]

The newspaper, in what seemed to be an excess of local boosterism (or perhaps as a result of the fact that A. B. Bennett and Company had purchased a full-page ad in that same issue), continued, "In all they have a stock of twenty-five thousand dollars which comprises groceries, men's furnishings, shoes, dry goods, ladies' and children's furnishings, hardware, farm implements, harness, wagons and buggies, and has the exclusive agency for the McCormick's mowers. They carry the noted make of Lisk tin and granite ware; together with this they have their own lumber and coal yards, this they buy in car load lots, and the customers are fortunate enough to be able to buy their lumber and coal cheaper than in the larger towns."

Although the store was owned by his in-laws, the newspaper described Anson as "the enterprising spirit of this company":

> From the very first his business grew as if by magic and it was not long before he had to have larger quarters, and to-day he has one store covering an area of thirty-five hundred square feet, with two ware houses and a storage for hay and grain, and yet has not room to transact the enormous business he is doing. It is the intention of the company to erect this spring, a two story building warehouse and elevator. In connection with the different business houses that they occupy they have their own electric light plant, which also lights Mr. Bennett's residence.

Lulu, unmentioned in the article even though she helped to run the store, also had her own millinery business, making large, dramatic hats in the style of the day. In 1905 she had purchased eighty acres of land at Warm Springs Creek in her name. Perhaps now that her husband was nearing his eighties, they were planning ahead to avoid the financial trials both she and her widowed mother had endured. But by late August 1907 she was suffering from what must have been a rather serious health issue, because she and her son Jim headed to the bustling mining city of Butte, where, the *Crow Creek Journal* reported, she would "remain for some time to take treatment from a physician."[11]

The following month, Julia, Anson, and his parents and relatives took a two-week hunting and fishing trip to Dry Creek Falls, bringing along "tents, cots, camp stools, a cook tent and even," the newspaper pointed out, "a colored chef."[12] The trip would prove Julia's hunting prowess—a talent, the paper noted, that would challenge "not only the members of her own sex, but also the masculine followers of the rod and gun." Late one afternoon at the start of their trip, the women were "lounging around camp, waiting for the men to come in from their day's hunt," when Julia's mother-in-law spotted a three-antlered buck "calmly reviewing the newly pitched tents." Julia went for her rifle but could only find one shell. "Drawing down on the deer as calmly as though shooting at a target she pressed the trigger," the *Journal* recounted. "The buck leaped in the air, ran a few feet and fell, the bullet having gone directly through its heart." Observing that Julia had "long been known as a clever shot with both rifle and shot gun," the reporter congratulated her for her marksmanship, noting, "For with but one shell to shoot at the first deer would be apt to make almost anyone nervous."[13]

❖

Anson was growing restless. The mercantile business was changing. He took out a newspaper ad telling his customers he would no longer accept the sale of merchandise on credit and urging them to "buy local" instead of ordering supplies through Sears Roebuck and other catalogs. The new mail-order business was growing rapidly in the West, thanks to the expanding railroad, and it was apparently challenging Anson's market. Eventually, he sold his shares in the store and, with the proceeds, purchased shares in the Black Friday Mine, now owned by his father and his uncle Albert Galen, who held the prestigious position of Montana's attorney general. One East Coast newspaper called the Black Friday "one of the most promising mines of the Radersburg district."[14] Hidden away in the barren, treeless foothills of the Elkhorn Mountains, it was miles away from Radersburg. Nevertheless, Anson decided to move to a cabin in this desolate spot, where he would manage the mine and its thirty-five employees. Julia and Don went along, and the entire family lived in a one-room cabin. Their only source of water was a nearby stream, and they had to haul drinking and washing water to the cabin in a barrel.

The new venture quickly turned sour. "Anson had trouble with one of the miners and fired him," Julia recalled. "The man refused to leave and threatened to kill us. I didn't dare let Don out of the cabin. I kept my gun ready and told him if he molested us I would kill him."

Anson gave up the mine, and the family moved back to Toston. In the spring of 1909 he won a contract to oversee the construction of a branch railroad called the Gilmore and Pittsburgh, which would run from Armstead, Montana, along the Red Rock River near the Idaho border, to Salmon, Idaho. Although it was more than one hundred miles from Toston, Doc, Lulu, Julia, and Don frequently joined him. Armstead was a primitive town in the middle of nowhere. Founded only two years earlier, it consisted of a few cabins and a post office surrounded by mountains, along with a large number of rattlesnakes and timber wolves. The location held historical significance as Camp Fortunate, the spot where members of the Lewis and Clark expedition had camped in August 1805 and secured from the Shoshones the horses that allowed them to continue their journey west. Armstead soon would sprout a railroad depot and restaurant for hungry travelers, but lodgings were sparse. The Bennetts and Bembricks set up camp on a stream called Bloody Dick (ostensibly named for an Englishman who had lived there in the 1860s). Julia called it "the best fishing stream I have ever seen." Although the fishing was indeed excellent, other wildlife was not as benign. One day, as Julia sat next to the stream with her fishing pole, she was startled by a noise. A timber wolf stood ten feet away, poised to attack her. She screamed; the wolf retreated. Although she wasn't hurt, the incident made enough of an impact for her to record it in her memoir decades later.

Anson spent most of his time in Armstead, and Julia was alone with young Don in Toston in the fall of 1909, when crime was picking up in the town. "Things got pretty rough," Julia recalled, when more than one hundred temporary laborers—nearly all from Italy and Japan—took up residence in local boardinghouses while they built a railroad branch line.[15] One evening in October a brawl broke out between two feuding groups of Italian railroad workers at the nearby saloon run by Julia's brother Jim.[16] As one man was shot dead and two more were stabbed, Jim dodged bullets by hiding under a table. He then managed to run two doors down to warn Julia at home, telling her to turn out the lights and get her gun. "I sat up the rest of the night," Julia said. "I could hear them fighting and running over the porch.

Living alone as I did most of the time I always had my gun handy. I was not afraid."

Julia *was* frightened, once. Returning alone from a trip to Helena, she arrived in Toston at one o'clock in the morning. The train station was empty and completely dark, as were the streets. She walked the two blocks to her house; when she arrived, she entered and turned on the gas lamp. As she walked back to lock the door, she saw its handle turning. Dashing to secure it, she turned out the light and grabbed her shotgun. She heard the rattling sounds of someone trying to open every single window and door. Was it a drunk from Jim's saloon? An itinerant railroad worker? A business enemy of Anson's? She knew Jim loved to play tricks on her, but it was clear it wasn't him. Julia sat up all night, shotgun by her side. She never would learn who was hunting her down.

❧

Once Anson's work in Armstead was done, he drifted from job to job and "could not seem to find what he wanted," Julia said. He decided to go on the road, selling machinery, so the Bembricks sold the mercantile store. Julia hired help to manage the household, which also included a "companion," Mable Lipard, and a twenty-three-year-old servant whose name, according to the census, was Eathel Walker.[17] Anson won contracts in the spring of 1912 to build both a road and a railroad spur, which again kept him away from home for several months. The following spring, he and a friend named Dick O'Hearn started a business with the intent of building railroads and bridges, which they probably viewed as a lucrative prospect during those years of frantic railroad construction in the state. Julia also was listed in the articles of incorporation of the so-called Bennett Construction Company. Although its prospects may have been promising, it was not well funded. "It is capitalized at $50,000, of which $30 has been subscribed," noted a local newspaper.[18]

Despite the growing distance between them—both physically and emotionally—Julia conceived twice during those years. In the earlier pregnancy, a daughter died while in her womb and had to be forcibly removed. The trauma caused Julia's hair to fall out, and she nearly died. She never talked about the pain it caused her.[19] That event may have been the reason the *Townsend Star* reported her to be "on the sick list" in February 1910.[20] Two years later, in March 1912, at the age of thirty-one, she was hospitalized at Johnstone Hospital, a ten-room private clinic forty miles away in Belgrade, where Anson brought seven-year-old Don on the train to visit her.[21] Although the physician likely knew at the time that the child she was carrying was no longer alive, he sent her home to give birth naturally, as was the practice. On April 6, back in Toston, Julia delivered an unnamed son, stillborn, who was buried that day.

On January 13, 1914, she finally gave birth in Belgrade to a healthy, "beautiful baby girl named Marjorie." Don was now nine, and Julia reported that she was "very happy with the children."

She remained very close to her family, seeing her parents and brothers frequently. Her brother Ben Jr. was what the neighbors might have called a "character." Now married to a woman named Vera, he kept a collection of animals that included eagles, two wolves, and defanged rattlesnakes. Periodically, he would walk up into the nearby hills with his wolves on a leash and howl along with them.[22] He also had two pet monkeys, which he turned loose at Julia's house. They stayed on to live in the cottonwood trees in the yard, where she fed them, and they engaged in what Julia described as "mischief." "They tore the shingles off the roof looking for spiders and pulled clothes off of [the] clothes line and stuffed them down the chimney," she said. "Whenever I washed clothes I had to sit in the yard until they dried." They also opened the icebox on the porch, broke the eggs that were inside, and threw the food all over the yard. The icebox soon gained a lock.

Brother Jim, now married to a teacher named Sayde, was known for his practical jokes and tricks, many of which occurred during his frequent bouts of drunkenness. Once, Julia hosted a dinner party for a visiting preacher with whom her unmarried cousin Martha was "very impressed." She planned an elegant six-course meal for fourteen guests. Her cook prepared the dinner, she hired a local girl to serve, and the table was set with her best china and silver. She hoped her father would not learn about the dinner, aware that he might find the affair entirely too highfalutin. But Jim couldn't keep his mouth shut and told him. The evening of the dinner, Doc showed up at the dining table just as the first course was being served. "Jesus Christ," he announced to the server. "You can't do all this alone." And he started to carry in all the courses at once. "Everyone looked shocked," Julia said. "Then the young minister burst out laughing. So Dad sat down with us and we all enjoyed the dinner. I never tried again to outdo my neighbors."

Among Jim's other pranks, he stole a prize turkey from her neighbor and then plucked it in Julia's yard. The furious neighbor recognized the feathers, and Julia had to pay for the bird. When she was entertaining women from the Ladies' Aid Society, Jim somehow managed to get the cook drunk and steal the roast turkey that was to be the main course. At another dinner party, featuring a roast pig, Jim again got the cook drunk, and Julia had to finish cooking dinner. But she didn't judge. "[Even] with all the tricks, I loved him. We had good times together."

Julia didn't feel as kindly toward her husband. She was fed up with his inability to settle in a job. He also was drinking too much and, whether she knew it or not at the time, sleeping with other women. She made up her mind to leave him. However, because Lulu disapproved of divorce, they decided to separate. But circumstances conspired to keep them living together. "We stayed together and worked for the children."

❖

Julia continued to fish and hunt, but in Toston, she also took on a few of what were considered traditional women's roles. She was an active member of the town's Ladies' Aid Society, hosting fundraising luncheons and lawn socials to raise money for charity projects. In the summer of 1914 Lulu, now nearly sixty, and Doc, in his mideighties, headed on horseback to their favorite campsite, the Pine Lodge Camp north of Yellowstone National Park, where they would spend a few months "roughing it."

There's no record of how Julia or her mother felt about women's suffrage, although, like Lizzie, they certainly had spent much of their lives being self-sufficient. They would have had the opportunity to hear Mrs. Annie Dean Young, a suffragist speaker who visited Toston a few weeks before November 3, 1914, when Montana men went to ·the polls to cast ballots on the question of whether women should have the right to vote.[23] The day before the election, tucked in among the serious articles in Helena's *Suffrage Daily News* was this ad for Hughes Millinery: "Ladies: You may not believe in suffrage, but you all believe in wearing the best hats for the least money."[24]

It took three days for the men's votes to be counted. "Female Suffrage Has Carried the Treasure State," read the November 6 headline in the *Daily Missoulian*.[25] The men in Julia and Lulu's own Broadwater County had been among those voting in favor of suffrage, 51 to 49 percent, the measure winning approval by a mere 28 votes out of 938 cast.[26] A few days after the election, on November 10, the *Townsend Star* boasted that the newspaper "did not add to, or detract from, the chances of women at the polls. Personally, the editor was not in favor of the movement—we have too much regard for women to plunge them into the whirlpool of strife and political avarice incident to every campaign. We do not doubt for one moment woman's ability to vote properly, but we still maintain that she has a loftier mission to perform."[27]

Despite that editor's opinion, a slight majority of Montana men had felt otherwise, and now women in eleven states—all of them in the West—could vote in elections.[28] It wasn't until the national election two years later that Montana women actually cast those votes, and Jeannette Rankin, who had led the suffragettes' charge in the state, was elected as the first female U.S. representative. She became "the first woman to earn a seat on any elected body in the world."[29]

Chapter 37

There had been no general rain over the
state for the entire crop season.

—*Missoulian*, July 12, 1918

The year 1918 was not a good one for Montana. After two years of
record wheat harvests, drought—or "drouth," as most Montanans
called it—struck the state in 1917, and the following year brought no
relief. An influenza epidemic was killing thousands, and a world war
was raging in Europe, where, proportionally, more Montana men were
fighting and dying than any other state in the nation.[1] The Bennetts
and Bembricks were spared personal tragedies caused by war and
influenza, but Julia and Anson had other troubles to contend with—
money troubles. Anson needed work.

He came up with yet another in a long line of plans. Despite the
drought, "wheat was bringing a big price," Julia said. In fact, the price
had doubled in just four years. As a result of the war, it now was
higher than $2 a bushel, and Montana was expecting "its greatest
wheat crop in its history."[2] Anson decided to become a wheat farmer.
He bought a new eight-cylinder Oldsmobile and leased land in Big
Horn County, near the site of the Battle of Little Bighorn.[3] Along
with the property, Anson acquired a white frame farmhouse with
running water and a bathroom that sat among the nearly treeless,
rolling grasslands. Julia, Anson, and the children packed up and
moved. Lulu and Doc joined them from time to time. Julia was up
before dawn to cook and serve breakfast to the farm crews at four in
the morning. She baked eleven loaves of bread every day. Using a
hand plow, she, Anson, and Doc, wearing wide-brimmed straw hats to
protect themselves from the hot sun, planted a garden with peanuts,
cantaloupe, and watermelon. They bought chickens, turkeys, and

17. Donald and Marjorie
Bennett, circa 1915.
Julia Bennett scrapbook,
Sherry Merica Pepper
private collection.

pigs to raise. Julia was constantly confronted with farm crises. One
of the sows, which broke out of her pen and destroyed the garden,
was "the meanest animal" she had ever seen. "She had 13 pigs and
ate all of them." A huge bull snake was eating the chicken eggs, and
Julia had to kill it.

Don, now thirteen, was old enough to help with the chores, and
four-year-old Marge, a beautiful child with dark bobbed hair, played
with her dolls and baby carriage on the front porch of the farmhouse or
in the hammock with their dog and cat. Their cousin Bruce Huntley,
who had just graduated from eighth grade, also joined them for part
of the summer.[4]

Although the weather was hot and dry (the temperature reached
one hundred degrees or more in June, July, and August, without "a
drop of rain"), the wheat was thriving and nearly ready for harvest.[5]

All at once, the locusts came, clouds and clouds of them, eating everything in sight. "We could hear them working," Julia recalled. They "sounded like a machine. We had to keep windows and doors closed to keep them out." Within just a few days, they destroyed the Bennetts' entire wheat crop.

"We were completely wiped out. All we had left was our car." Julia sold the chickens, turkeys, and pigs, and the family headed back to Toston—with nothing. It was time for her to start over yet again. Anson would soon be gone, and she had no money to her name.

Chapter 38

Out of a study of wages in thirteen states today came a report from
the women's bureau that "many thousands" of full time women
workers earned less than a bare living wage from 1920 to 1925.
—*Bozeman Daily Chronicle*, June 11, 1931

Julia's marriage now was held together by nothing more than a thread.
The Anson Bennett of autumn 1918 was a far cry from the handsome
young man she had married—balding and potbellied, unwilling to
hold a steady job, and having a taste for liquor and loose women. That
September, Don turned fourteen and was ready for high school, while
Marge was not yet six. Since Toston had no high school, Julia decided
to move to Bozeman—a relative metropolis, with a high school, a college, and a population of more than six thousand. She needed income,
so she rented a two-story house with six unfurnished bedrooms and
a large basement and placed an ad in the paper for boarders. Four
male students at Montana State College moved in.[1] She borrowed
money to buy a stove and a washing machine—a ponderous appliance
consisting of a large tub with a heater underneath and a handwringer
clamped to the top. Doc and Lulu soon joined her, while Diddy stayed
in Toston with her new husband. Now forty-one, Diddy had married
a forty-four-year-old bachelor rancher named Dave Johnson in May.

Meanwhile, Anson was back living with his parents in Helena,
where he had spent the winter nursing what Julia described as a "running sore" on his leg. His mother telephoned her, saying he had been
offered a summer job herding two thousand sheep at the immense
Biering and Cunningham ranch in the Gallatin valley, near Bozeman.
She asked if Julia would be willing to go along to help him, because
the sore prevented him from riding. Julia's income from the college
boarders would dry up in the summer, so she agreed. When the school

year ended, she sent Don off to a summer job at Yellowstone National Park, where he worked with a fellow Montanan named Gary Cooper, who a few years later would head to Hollywood to become a stunt rider and then a movie star. Doc and Lulu returned to Toston for the summer, taking Marge with them.

The state's economy that summer was reeling from an agricultural emergency caused by the continuing drought—June 1919 set a record as "the driest month in the recorded history of the state."[2] Julia didn't talk about her summer herding sheep with Anson, but the adventure clearly didn't lead to a reconciliation. "I helped Anson until fall and then I left and never saw him again," she wrote. In fact, Julia noted many years later that she had divorced him when Don turned sixteen, but although she may have "divorced" him in mind and body, she actually wouldn't file for divorce until more than ten years later.

Now truly on her own, she returned to Bozeman in the fall of 1919 so that Don and Marge could attend school. Julia moved the family to a smaller rental house, and her parents once again arrived from Toston. She needed work. A friend suggested that she start her own business, telling her that an unfurnished hotel was available for lease in the tiny railroad-stop town of Wyola on the Crow Reservation in Big Horn County—the same county where she had spent the summer of 1918 with Anson. "It sounded like a good idea," she thought, so she rented the hotel, taking along all her furniture, fine china, and silver. She must have believed that the increasing railroad traffic would bring business, since the population of the town, located in the middle of nowhere, numbered only 513. The vast majority of its residents were farmers and laborers, including a fair number of Japanese immigrant farmers. Once again, her parents came along, and Julia cooked all the meals for the few guests who arrived. "The whole thing was a complete failure," she wrote. "There was no business and I couldn't pay the rent." The building's owner confiscated her entire stock of furniture, china, and silver as payment. "It was like Custer's Last Stand," she joked.

While in Big Horn County, Julia became friends with Plenty Coups, a survivor of the Battle of Little Bighorn and the last surviving hereditary chief of the Crow Nation. Now in his seventies, the chief had encouraged the tribe's young men to fight for the United States in World War I, although it would not be until 1924 that Congress would pass the Indian Citizenship Act that granted them the rights of U.S. citizens. Plenty Coups owned a general store on the reservation, "forever counseling his customers to be friendly with the white men whose encroachments were maddening to his people," wrote a historian who interviewed him. Plenty Coups continued to mourn the loss of the bison. "When the buffalo went away the hearts of my people fell to the ground," he said, "and they could not lift them up again."[3]

*

Julia knew there were no business opportunities for a woman living in Toston, so she sold the house and bought herself a Ford coupe. She applied for a job with the Fuller Brush Company as a door-to-door saleswoman, even though such positions were listed in the employment section of the newspaper under the category of "Help Wanted—Male." One such ad read, "WANTED—Several energetic, neat appearing young men for salesmen. Montana territory. Experience not essential as we train you. Small capital or bond required."[4]

Although she was not a man, she certainly fit Fuller Brush Company's description of "energetic" and "neat appearing." She may have been attracted by the job's supposedly lucrative potential. "A Fuller man makes good money," noted one ad. "Can save and is able to give his family its rightful advantages. He is virtually in business for himself with all the possibilities that lie in such a situation."[5] Despite her gender, Julia was hired and assigned a breathtakingly vast sales territory that included all of Gallatin County and Yellowstone National Park. Bozeman was in Gallatin County, but the rest of the region was sparsely populated and required driving long distances on mostly primitive roads. Julia didn't find the opportunity lucrative. "I tried it all summer but couldn't make my salt," she said. "It did one thing for me and that was cure all foolish pride."

She sold her car and took several jobs cooking for people. When ski parties visited the Butler family's Nine Quarter Circle Ranch near Bozeman, she headed up to prepare the place for guests and fix their meals.

In November 1921 the entire Bembrick family gathered in Toston to celebrate Doc and Lulu's fiftieth wedding anniversary. He was ninety-three, and she was sixty-five. "Famous Pioneer Celebrates Half Century of Domestic Felicity," read the headline in one Montana newspaper. "Both Mr. and Mrs. Bembrick hold their age remarkably well. Mr. Bembrick . . . takes his daily walk down town. He has never used a cane in his life. . . . His eyesight cannot be surpassed for a man of his age, but his hearing is slightly impaired."[6]

Anson was back living in Toston as well. His running sore had worsened, and around Thanksgiving the following year, his foot was amputated at the hospital in Butte. "This amputation was necessary due to blood poisoning, resulting from an infection," noted the *Toston Times*.[7] Julia was far from Butte at the time, hunting with her nephew Bruce Huntley at the Nine Quarter Circle, where he bagged an elk.

She had only Marge to care for, since Don was enrolled at Montana State College in Bozeman. Julia took Marge to stay with Doc and Lulu in Toston, and in January 1923 she headed to the state capitol in Helena to work as a stenographer for the legislature, earning $5 a day. Her earlier training at the Helena Business College wasn't helpful. "I wasn't very good," she recalled, "but did the job." She needed the money not only to survive but because she, Anson, and Lulu were named in a lawsuit filed by the receiver of the land office in Bozeman, presumably for a debt they owed on a property note. In April 1924 they were ordered to pay $472.18.[8]

*

On May 14, 1925, Doc Bembrick died of heart failure at ninety-seven, vibrant until the final few months of his life. An obituary in the *Helena Daily Independent* called him "one of the most picturesque figures of pioneer days . . . one of the oldest men in Montana and one of the earliest settlers." Doc had requested that his eulogy be written and presented by Albert Galen, who was now an associate justice of the Montana Supreme Court and whose wife, Ethelene, was Anson's sister. Doc had once claimed that Galen was the only Republican he had ever voted for. At the service, Galen spoke of the "splendid character of the old patriarch, his friendly and wholesome life," and "how in the early days his hospitality was noted throughout the whole territory." He also highlighted Doc's stellar marksmanship and his "many very narrow escapes from death or injury."[9] After the interment in the Radersburg cemetery on the day after Doc's death, Galen sent a letter to the secretary of the Montana Historical Society asking that Doc's biography be preserved in the state's archives. "His death ended a most remarkable career," he wrote.[10]

*

The next few years continued to be difficult ones for Julia. Lulu, now alone, moved into the house Julia had rented in Bozeman.[11] Don graduated from Montana State College in the spring of 1927; a few months later, he married Kansas-born Violet Marshall, the daughter of a Bozeman furniture salesman, and moved to Seattle.[12] On October 29 of that year—her late husband's birthday—Lulu died of heart disease in the middle of the night at home. She was buried two days later next to Doc. Julia described herself as "really heartbroken."

Chapter 39

We are in the midst of a nation-wide industrial and
economic depression, the baneful effects of which are
halting our progress and impairing our prosperity.

—Gov. John Erickson, address to the Montana
State Legislature, January 1931

The dude rancher's stock in trade is solid. It doesn't
fluctuate—despite what the stock market may be doing.

—I. H. Larson, president of Dude Ranchers
Association, *Montana Wildlife*, February 1931

In mid-May 1931 Julia Bennett's train pulled into the Bozeman station,
just about a month before she planned to open the Diamond J for its
first season. She had been pounding the pavement in New York City
for a full three months. As she walked through town, she ran into her
friend Charlie Anceney. "He asked how I made out," she said. "I told
him fine and paid him back the money I owed him."

Charlie was taken aback. "My God, don't you know what has happened?" he asked. "They have attached your ranch and won't let you
open it."

Julia was unaware that while she was gone, the Madison County
sheriff had delivered a summons to the Diamond J. That legal document informed her that H. B. McCay, a hardware merchant and vice
president of Bozeman's Gallatin Trust and Savings Bank, was suing
her for $13,474.01 on behalf of eleven creditors. McCay also asked the
judge to assess 8 percent interest on the amount she allegedly owed. In
addition, he requested that a "keeper or keepers [be assigned] to care
for and hold" her property and livestock until she settled the debts.

Julia remembered it this way: "The creditors had gotten together and decided to sell the ranch although they had promised me five years to pay them back. There I made my mistake—[I] did not have them sign [a] contract." She had taken her lenders at their word, but now—in the midst of the greatest economic catastrophe the nation had ever seen—they apparently had decided that a single woman with a bullheaded dream of opening a dude ranch would not be able to repay her debts.

McCay alleged that Julia owed money for labor, painting, plumbing, and decorating buildings on the ranch; for hardware, lumber, and other merchandise; for animal feed and groceries; and for a fire insurance policy premium. He was operating like a collection agency, convincing the creditors to sign over their debts to him, then returning either all or part of their money if he won the lawsuit. The creditors probably were having just as hard a time as Julia was. That same year, more than two thousand banks across the country would close their doors.

Julia, typically, refused to be cowed: "They told me I could not open unless I paid them in full. They knew I couldn't do this. I made up my mind they could not stop me, so I went to the ranch to open up." Meanwhile, the sheriff sent one of his men to the ranch to keep an eye on her and to attach all her property—including twenty thousand feet of peeled logs, seven cabins, two Jersey cows, and one sorrel gelding.[1]

Her first guests would arrive in just a few days. Julia climbed into her Ford pickup truck, drove back to Bozeman to hire a cook, and then headed to the grocery store with a long shopping list. When she walked back to her truck, she found that the sheriff had just attached it as well.

Julia was frantic. Once again, she tracked down Charlie. She found him in Bozeman, and he told her to take his car. She drove back to the ranch in it. And now, while setting up for the guests, she also had to find a lawyer. She hired an attorney in Bozeman named Ernest Peterson, who went to work preparing a response to McCay's complaint. At the same time—perhaps because she now had an attorney—she finally filed for divorce from Anson. That story, too, was picked up by the press. "Woman Married for 29 Years Seeking Divorce," read the headline in Butte's *Montana Standard*, which stated, "She charges that her husband has wilfully failed to provide for her for the past five years."[2] Julia requested custody of Marge. Anson didn't even bother to show up in court, and the divorce was granted.

❖

On June 7, the day Julia's first guests were scheduled to arrive in Bozeman aboard the North Coast Limited, she stopped to pick up the Hudson touring car she had stored at a local garage.[3] She intended to drive it to the station to pick up her guests. She hadn't yet paid its storage costs—or an $85 gasoline bill. The owner refused to let her take the car unless she paid him on the spot. Julia told him she had a $5,000 booking arriving in just twenty minutes and could pay her bill the following week. He refused her offer.

The only recourse Julia could think of was to find Charlie Anceney once again. Making a few calls, she learned that he was now a patient at Bozeman's Deaconess Hospital, just a few blocks from the station. She ran to his room and told him her predicament. "Take my car," he told her, but then he changed his mind, "NO, get my wallet out of the dresser." He handed her a $100 bill and added, "Now go pay that son of a bitch and don't ever go there again!"

Julia ran back to the garage, settled the bill, got in her car, and made it to the station in time to meet the train. She warmly greeted her first wealthy East Coast guests. They didn't have an inkling of what had just happened, nor did they have a clue that only three and a half years earlier the 190-acre Diamond J ranch might have generously been called a "dump."

However, if they read the local newspapers, they soon might have learned Julia was being sued. In mid-June articles about the lawsuit were published in newspapers throughout the state. (In Butte's *Montana Standard* the news was on the same page as a bulletin that gangster Al Capone, "alias Snorky," had been indicted by a Chicago grand jury for tax evasion.)[4]

"Dude Ranches Finding It Tough These Times," noted the sympathetic headline in the *Helena Daily Independent*. Julia's wasn't the only ranch in trouble—McCay was suing the wealthy Butler brothers, co-owners of the Rising Sun Ranch, along with their partner M. S. Cunningham, for $16,659.57. McCay also was seeking custody of twenty-eight of the men's buffalo—buffalo that President Herbert Hoover himself had granted them permission to buy.[5]

Chapter 40

The Diamond J invites you to this land of shining
mountains, rich in romance of the old west, to spend
an unforgettable vacation in its great out-of-doors.

—Diamond J brochure, 1931

There were only nine ranch guests that entire summer, but Julia came
up with a long list of western activities to keep them entertained. They
could go horseback riding (Charlie Anceney had loaned her "a fine
string of saddle horses" for the season), trout fishing, or hiking. She
offered to drive them to Yellowstone National Park, seventy miles
away, or take them to Ennis, the "typical cow-town" mentioned in
her brochure. They could visit Anceney's half-million acre Flying
D Ranch and watch his cowboys brand cattle. They could ride far
up into the Spanish Peaks—with Julia leading the way—and camp
in tents, reveling in the pine-scented forests and icy mountain lakes.

If they weren't interested in camping, they could relax at the ranch.
Julia's brochure described the accommodations: "The log cabins are
all newly built with the purpose of giving the guests every comfort
of home—private bath and shower in each cabin, dressing room, old
hickory furnishings, twin beds with Simmons springs and mattresses
and Pendleton blankets." She did embellish a bit: "The Diamond
J maintains its own dairy and poultry plant." Actually, the "plant"
consisted of one Jersey cow, a cream separator, and a chicken coop.

Soon the guests were affectionately calling Julia "Boss," just as her
wranglers did. Diddy prepared delicious meals, including the angel
food cake for which she was famous. And even though Prohibition was
in full swing, guests were invited to bring their own bottle of liquor to
the lodge and enjoy a drink before a hearty dinner of steak or chicken

18. Diamond J Ranch and cabins, circa 1930s. Julia Bennett
scrapbook, Sherry Merica Pepper private collection.

and potatoes. At night they sat around the campfire, listening to Julia
tell stories about growing up in the West, or sang cowboy tunes, as a
boy rode a burro to their cabins to light the oil lamps.[1]

While Julia kept her guests busy, she also kept her lawyer hopping. On June 18 Ernest Peterson filed a response to H. B. McCay's
complaint, arguing that it failed to include sufficient details to result
in a legal ruling. Unfortunately, the strategy didn't work. Instead of
dismissing the case, the judge ordered Julia to respond. What's more,
the day after the judge's order, McCay filed a second suit against Julia.
This time, he claimed that she owed $2,389 to four other creditors—
including $1,000 to her old friend Tom Lincoln—and asked that her
already-attached 159.98 acres of ranchland be attached yet again to
cover these new debts.

In July Julia's attorney filed responses to both cases, denying "each
and every allegation," asking that McCay receive "nothing" and reim-
burse Julia's legal costs as well.

"The creditors made life very difficult all summer," said Julia. The sheriff's man continued to stay at the ranch to watch her. Nonetheless, she proclaimed her first season a success.

Eventually, the lawsuits against Julia and the Butlers were dismissed, although no court records exist to explain why. Did Charlie loan her money or pay off her debts? Or did a judge rule that H. B. McCay didn't have the right to sue? The reason remains a mystery. But the struggle hadn't ended. Julia now had to spend all her time preparing for her second summer season, and she was no further along than she had been for her first.

Part III

SELLING *the* WEST

Chapter 41

Plenty of women are finding out that they can combine business
and pleasure very profitably by running ranches of their own
for the benefit of wide-open-space-hungry Easterners.

—*New York Evening Post*, April 18, 1931

Those dining in the restaurant of Manhattan's fashionable, 1,100-room
Roosevelt Hotel in the winter of 1932 must have been surprised by the
looks of the trio sitting nearby. The middle-aged woman at the table
appeared to have stepped straight out of a Western film. She wore a
cowhide vest, a silk neckerchief, and a black felt bolero. Joining her
were a distinguished-looking gentleman wearing a Scottish kilt and
an American Indian chief whose head was framed by a feathered
war bonnet.[1] "We made quite a sight," said Julia Bennett, who was
on her second booking trip to New York City.

Although her room at the Roosevelt was the perfect location from
which to hunt guests, much like the previous year, she could not
afford to be staying or eating there and continued to permit herself
only one meal a day. She had, however, refined her marketing strategy.
If she could find clients willing to part with a substantial deposit to
reserve their spot to spend the summer at her ranch, she would be able
to pay her hotel bill. I. H. Larson, president of the Dude Ranchers
Association, told readers of *Montana Wildlife* magazine that a dude
ranch vacation was a good investment. "When the dude invests in
a vacation on a Wyoming or Montana dude ranch," he wrote, "he's
placing his money in something that will bring him an incomparable
amount of health and recreation just as sure as Old Faithful will fling
a stemming, snow-white jet into the air every sixty minutes."[2]

Julia's luncheon companions that day were two chiefs from vastly
different parts of the globe. Seumas, chief of the Clanfhearghuis of

Strachur, Scotland, was an explorer and cartographer who once had walked across the Sahara Desert. Now he was staying at New York's Explorers Club, founded at the turn of the century by a group of adventurers promoting scientific exploration. He was "the most famous Scot in New York," Julia noted, and "a direct descendant of Macbeth" (which may or may not have been true). She had met the middle-aged bachelor, who was writing a book, at the Explorers Club, and she found him "very handsome." With his sleek, pomaded hair, fine features, and well-groomed mustache, he looked a bit like the movie star John Gilbert, who recently had had a scandalous on-and-off-screen romance with the glamorous actress Greta Garbo.

Chief Max Big Man, "a towering Indian" who later that month would visit the White House to pay a call of respect on President Herbert Hoover, had stopped in New York while touring the country.[3] The Crow elder wore his chest-length hair in black braids secured with rabbit-skin cords. Julia already knew Chief Big Man, having met him when she managed the small railroad hotel on the Crow reservation more than a decade earlier. He had stopped by the Roosevelt to pay her a visit, and a few minutes after his arrival, she received a phone call from the Scottish chief. She immediately invited both to dine with her. When they finished their lunch, a photographer asked Julia and Chief Big Man to head to the roof of the hotel to pose in their western regalia.

On the rooftop, the luxurious new Waldorf Astoria hotel loomed behind them. Together they held the buffalo robe Julia had brought from Montana, and in one photo, Chief Big Man held one hand atop the other, making the Crow sign that meant "buffalo all gone."

It was true; most of the buffalo in Montana were gone. Eastern "dudes" were taking their place, and Julia wanted to give them a taste of the Old West. "No, I don't wear this stuff much out there on the range," Julia told a reporter from the *New York World Telegram*, gesturing at her fringed buckskin jacket, black leather breeches, and bead-banded hat. "But it goes big here in Manhattan."[4]

The *World Telegram* found Julia intriguing enough to publish a half-page feature story about her. It included a photo of Julia gazing confidently at the camera, clad in her western duds. "I told them the facts," she said, "but the write-up was exaggerated beyond belief." Indeed, it was more fiction than fact—even claiming that Julia owned Charlie Anceney's cattle ranch:

> Julia Bennett, blonde and youthful despite her tale of a grown daughter, is that strange phenomenon—the only woman dude rancher extant. She thinks she was born in the saddle. Her earliest memories include riding to the round-up with her dad, cutting cattle, wearing a ten-gallon hat and the shaggiest chaps they could locate in Bozeman.
>
> Her own Diamond J ranch is "only 10,000 acres," she blushes in disparagement of those meagre holdings. And so, to keep her hand in, she manages the Nine Quarter Circle, too. It covers 25,000 acres and is forty miles away from the Diamond J. Mrs. Bennett commutes between the two.

ROUGHING IT IN LUXURY

> Bored brokers and their wives like to leave their pet Pekes and Spaniels at Manhattan kennels in the middle of a dull summer and hurry West to "rough it" on Mrs. Bennett's guest ranch. They "rough it" in brand new, spotless, heated "cabins" that sport showers, private baths, fireplaces with elk head over the mantel, electric lights, hot and cold water, expensive old hickory furnishings, twin beds and Pendleton blankets.
>
> "We do have thousands of cattle," she says, "and the round-up, the usual cattle ranch activity, isn't phoney. The Park Avenuites go on long pack trips, they fish, swim, hunt and hike. And just because we throw in a dash of comfort, we shouldn't be scored."

The article was snatched up by wire services and sent to newspapers and radio stations throughout the country. Before she knew it, the tall tale appeared in newspapers including the *Pittsburgh Press* and the *Tennessean* and on the front pages of the *Sandusky Register* and the *San Bernardino County Sun*. It even made its way to the other side of the world. As a result, Julia received a booking from China, one from Norway, and even a long-distance marriage proposal from a man in San Antonio, Texas. Charlie Anceney happened to be in San Antonio buying cattle when he was approached by a man carrying the newspaper clipping. Aware that Charlie was from Montana, the man asked him if it was true that Julia "owned all that land and cattle." Playing along, Charlie told him it was. The suitor sent Julia his photo and several letters, one of which contained a marriage proposal. She did not reply but joked that she was "sorry I did not frame his letter."

Chapter 42

Montana is a remote hinterland about as well known to the
average eastern seaboard citizen as East or West Africa.

—Joseph Kinsey Howard, *Montana: High, Wide, and Handsome*

While preparing for her second booking trip to New York, Julia had
packed up a trunk with a buffalo skin and skull, sagebrush, saddles,
chaps, silver-mounted spurs and bridles, and a six-shooter. She wanted
to use the iconic western paraphernalia in a marketing display—one
she hoped the manager of the Northern Pacific Railroad would feature
in the window of its booking office at 560 Fifth Avenue.

Since the railroad's completion in 1883, the Northern Pacific had
ferried passengers westward from Chicago, Milwaukee, and St. Paul
to cities and towns in North Dakota, Montana, and Washington.
But the ever-worsening Depression was affecting railroad compa-
nies, which reckoned with a dwindling number of people who could
afford to take vacations. The national unemployment rate now stood
at nearly 25 percent; those who still had jobs were forced to take wage
cuts of up to 30 percent.

The difficulties led the railroads and dude ranchers to expand
their joint efforts to attract passengers and guests. The railroads published "vacation albums" promoting, among other western sites, dude
ranches and Yellowstone National Park. "*It's big medicine!*" one ad
exclaimed. "The clean electric ozone of the high country gives your
lungs a new lease on life; your internal machinery gets to hitting on
all eight. *Big medicine, indeed!*"[1]

When Julia arrived in Manhattan, she headed to the Northern
Pacific Office and asked the assistant general passenger agent, a man
named Howard Fletcher, if he would feature her display. "It was a
good one," she thought, and Fletcher agreed. He let her place it in the

front window facing Fifth Avenue. "It surely attracted much attention," Julia said. "At night a great crowd would gather around and talk about it." Sometimes, she stood among the crowd and listened to what they had to say.

One day, Julia walked by the office and saw that her display had been removed and "stuffed in a side window." She went inside to find out why. Fletcher explained that the display had become so popular that two other Montana dude ranchers who also were in town to book guests thought she was "getting too much publicity," so they "demanded it be removed."

"Pack it up," Julia ordered Fletcher, "because I have several places on Madison Avenue that want it." She told him she would stop by the next day to collect her items. When she did, she found the display back in the Fifth Avenue window. Fletcher had reconsidered. It was "the best exhibit they ever had," he told her. In fact, it was attracting so much attention that it was benefitting other dude ranchers as well. "One day they called me from the office and said that I had better come down and do some booking," she said. "The other ranchers were getting a lot of business from my exhibit. I said, 'Fine, I put it there to sell the West anyway.'"

Her generosity was remarkable, especially since she hadn't yet managed to book any guests of her own. But it wouldn't take long before her display began to prove its worth. "A lady stopped in the office one day and they [other ranchers] tried to book her," Julia said. "She told them no, she wanted to see the lady that had brought the exhibit to New York and owned the Diamond J Ranch."

That lady was Florence McMahon, an unmarried, forty-year-old New Yorker whose sister had wed one of the wealthiest men in Manhattan. Julia knew nothing about her or her background. The Northern Pacific office sent Miss McMahon to the Roosevelt Hotel, where she met Julia and immediately confirmed a two-month booking at the Diamond J for herself and two teenaged nieces who attended Foxcroft, an exclusive girls' boarding school in Virginia.

Not long after, Julia received a call out of the blue from a gentleman

19. Diamond J brochure cover, circa 1930s. Sherry
Merica Pepper private collection.

named Herbert Stursberg, a friend of Miss McMahon. "He said he
could not pass the exhibit window without stopping" and made a
booking for five people. He did not, however, give her a deposit. She
was "desperately in need of money." She now was overdue on her
hotel bill and still surviving on one meal a day.

After her display had been at the Northern Pacific Railway Office
for two weeks, she arranged to have it featured for two more weeks
at another prime location: the window of a Madison Avenue bank.
And two weeks after meeting Herbert Stursberg, he called to invite
her to dinner, where he handed her a $1,000 deposit check. "This
saved my life," she said.

Julia would board a Northern Pacific train headed for home, with
that check from Stursberg, one of the wealthiest men in New Jersey,
tucked safely in her pocketbook. Little did she know that the booking would bring an indelible change in the life of her breathtakingly
beautiful eighteen-year-old daughter, Marge.

Chapter 43

There is the urge inherent in many a stuffed up metropolitanite,
to get away from the turmoil of battling for money and
existence and to become lost in the west where health,
happiness and friendship count more than money.

—Kirby Kittoe, *Mineral Independent*, May 11, 1939

Julia was scrambling—traveling to New York City, cleaning up the ranch, and driving back and forth between Bozeman and the Diamond J to buy supplies. She was, she simply noted, "very busy trying to survive."[1] As a result, Marge was spending much of her senior year of high school away from her mother. Julia arranged for Marge to board with a family in Bozeman while attending Gallatin County High School. This wasn't an unusual arrangement; many Montana ranch families who lived far from a school brought their children to town during the school year. Marge was a shy girl, unaware of her remarkable beauty despite the attention she received from boys. One weekend, she accepted invitations for three dates and then canceled all of them. Charlie Anceney's son, Charlie Jr., who was in love with her from afar, described her as a "lovely, innocent, sweet" young woman who "took my breath away."[2]

After Julia returned from New York, she accepted an invitation from Don and his new wife, Violet, for Marge to come live with them in Seattle. Marge would finish her senior year at Broadway High School—an immense institution with more than two thousand students, located in the heart of the city. It was cosmopolitan—a far cry from Gallatin County High School and its few hundred students. She thrived academically, though, graduating with honors in June 1932, and then briefly attended the Cornish School, which focused on the arts.[3]

Marge returned from Seattle just in time to meet the young man who would alter the course of her life.

✤

At the stroke of midnight on June 26, 1932, a railroad car pulled out of New York City's Pennsylvania Station. Settling into sleeper cars headed for a three-month stay at the Diamond J were Herbert Stursberg; his wife, Marie Louise; and their fourteen-year-old daughter, Louise.[4]

Also joining them was Herbert's favorite nephew, nineteen-year-old Edward Stursberg, known to all as Pete. He would begin his freshman year at Yale University that fall, following in the footsteps of his millionaire father, Albert Stursberg, and his older brother Laird. Five foot eight, with a full head of dark, wavy hair and piercing dark eyes, Pete was strikingly handsome, devilishly charming, and a bit of a rabble-rouser. He and his two older brothers had attended Choate, an exclusive boys' college-preparatory boarding school in Wallingford, Connecticut, where Pete was a member of the junior football and wrestling teams, served on the board of the school newspaper, and went by the nickname Zip.[5] He was not a particularly good student, in part because of his penchant for having fun rather than studying. At the end of his senior year at Choate, the school's headmaster, George St. John, had written a letter to Pete's parents. "I hold my breath as Pete enters the College Board examinations in German and Physics," he told them. "I am awfully afraid he can't pass these two—especially the German. Pete has been a delightful member. Humanly, he has enriched our life. Academically, he still worries us an awful lot."[6]

Pete wasn't worried about his College Board exams. He was fixated on his trip out west. This wouldn't be his first stay at a dude ranch with his forty-year-old uncle Herbert, whom he affectionately called Unk. The pair had spent an earlier summer at a ranch in Wyoming, where Pete had fallen in love with the wide-open landscape.[7] It was a far cry from his upbringing in a stone mansion at 16 East Eightieth Street in Manhattan—one block from the Metropolitan Museum of

20. Edward "Pete" Stursberg in 1932, the year he first visited the Diamond J. Stursberg 1932 scrapbook, Sherry Merica Pepper private collection.

Art—and at Stonehyrst, his family's 108-acre English Tudor–style summer estate in the Somerset Hills of Bernardsville, New Jersey.

Pete had yearned to spend another summer in the West but didn't think he'd have another opportunity before he headed off to Yale. However, a few months earlier, he'd received a playful letter from his Unk. He'd pasted it in his scrapbook under the handwritten headline "Unk puts new hope into approaching summer." Unk's letter informed Pete that a trip out west was back on, thanks to his chance encounter with Julia Bennett's display window in New York. In a feeble attempt at speaking "cowboy," Unk had written, "We got introduced to a Dude wrangler from Montan and it sure looks like we was going to have to go places and see things again. In fact we have had her up here for dinner a couple of times and she brought some movies with her and so we know all about the country and the ranch and everything and the womin is all sold."[8]

He then added a particularly enticing detail: "The best thing about the pictures was the lady's daughter and I'm thinkin that a certain pair of black chaps that I know of is going to get the greatest brushing they ever saw. . . . I sort of have a feelin that there's romance in them thar hills."

*

Late in the afternoon of June 26, the Stursbergs' westward-bound train stopped at Union Station in Chicago. There the travelers had supper in the elegant, columned dining room, where they were served by waiters wearing tuxedos. Such luxury was de rigueur for the Stursbergs. Pete, along with his two older brothers and two younger sisters, were the children of Albert Stursberg, a partner in his family's New York City commercial banking company as well as its prosperous second-generation woolen manufacturing company.[9] Albert and his brother—Pete's "Unk" Herbert—each had inherited a portion of their father's million-dollar estate upon his death in December 1929.

In Manhattan the Stursberg family's roster of five servants included a governess and two nurses.[10] At Stonehyrst Pete had a chauffeur and his own maid. At the Diamond J he would sleep in a log cabin with a sod roof and no electricity. But he couldn't wait for his summer adventure to begin.

In Chicago the Stursberg party transferred to the Northern Pacific line for the second leg of their journey. Their train pulled into Bozeman the next evening, where they spent the night at the Hotel Baxter, the fanciest lodging in town. The next day, Julia picked them up and drove them to the Diamond J. "Here's where it begins," Pete wrote in his scrapbook below a photo of the ranch. "To the end of the Cañyon—after 2 years waiting."

When the Stursbergs arrived that afternoon, Julia introduced them to Button, the ranch dog; Dickie, a wrangler; and Marge. Pete was immediately smitten.

Julia took the clan to watch a polo match at the nearby Jumping Horse Ranch, owned by a wealthy East Coast businessman named Wetmore Hodges. She also led them on an outing to Virginia City, where they drove along the Vigilante Trail and visited Robber's Roost, an inn and stage station that had been built just before Lizzie Nave Martin's return to the Montana Territory from San Francisco in 1867. Julia liked to tell her guests that when the Nave family had first arrived in Virginia City, her mother stood on a street corner and watched as the wife of Joseph Slade—who was set to be hung by the Vigilantes— galloped through town on her black stallion "with bridle reins in her teeth and six shooter in each hand" in a futile attempt to save her husband's life. The problem with that story is that the Naves didn't arrive in Virginia City until a year after that event took place. Had Julia misheard her mother's story, had Lulu told her that tale, or had Julia created her own western legend—one that that her eastern guests eagerly lapped up?

❖

Meanwhile, Marge was becoming infatuated with the handsome Pete Stursberg. He was an artist and a bit of a romantic. On the first page of his scrapbook that year, he pasted this newspaper clipping: "We ought to say: As life goes I have maybe ten, fifteen, or, at the most, thirty years. Therefore, I ought to quit thinking, 'How much money can I pile up?' and begin thinking, 'How can I be sure to do all the things I want to do, see all the places I want to see, and leave behind me a reputation for having been a reasonably good and generous individual?'"[11]

A week after he arrived at the Diamond J, Pete celebrated his twentieth birthday. It fell on July 3, right in the middle of the famous Livingston Roundup, a three-day event in the town of seven thousand that sat on the other side of the Bozeman Pass. Julia made sure her guests had the opportunity to attend the rodeo, which had "a national reputation for being one of the foremost exhibitions of cowboy sports in America," according to one newspaper, which touted, "Here you will see a clear and intimate view of the actual living cowboy as he rides and plays on the vast ranges of Montana."[12] It added that a "motley group" of thousands attended the annual event: "Among their number may be found cowboys from plains and hills, sun burned to a brick red; flappers from the east, westernized over night at some nearby dude ranch; Canadians, Mexicans, Indians in native regalia camping in nearby tepees; hard riding horsemen from the ranges and 'dudes' out for a fortnight of fun and a good time."

"The air is charged with romance," noted the paper, presciently in the case of Pete, who wrote in his scrapbook that it was at the Livingston Roundup where he "fell harder for M!" He and Marge went to a dance that weekend at the Woodman Hall in Ennis, where she told him, "You're certainly sure of yourself!"

Only one week later, he would declare in his scrapbook that he was in love with Marge:

> Love makes the World go round,
> Love is beauty song and sound
> Love makes the stars and moon revolve
> Love is God's one great resolve
> Love is life, and Life to me
> Is to be all in love with thee.

Marge felt the same way. She had to go out of town for a few days and left him the following note:

> Dear Petie;
>
> I felt too kind-hearted to call you this morning. You really need the sleep—and the longer you stay out of mischief!
>
> I'm going to miss you terribly—if only for two days—so please don't let the moon or the atmosphere get the best of you. May I again assure you the promise is well under control.
>
> See you Tuesday—or sooner if I find an airplane.
>
> All my love, Marge[13]

In July teenaged sisters Victoria and Genevieve Brady, also of New York City and Somerset Hills, New Jersey, joined the Stursbergs as guests at the Diamond J. They were chaperoned by their aunt Florence McMahon, who had first introduced Herbert to Julia's New

York display. The two young heiresses owned inheritances worth more than $10 million each.

Someone snapped their photos and placed them in the Diamond J guest book. Victoria, who had returned a few months earlier from a trip to France, would celebrate her seventeenth birthday at the ranch. She stands scowling in front of the barn, arms crossed, wearing a tailored, double-breasted suit. Fifteen-year-old Gene, as she called herself, smiles broadly in a western getup of cowhide vest, jeans, and cowboy boots.

Victoria and Gene had grown up in New York City a few blocks from the Stursbergs in a five-story limestone mansion maintained by thirteen servants. They spent their summers near the Stursbergs at the family estate called Hamilton Farms in Gladstone, New Jersey, called by the *New York Times* "one of the show places of Somerset Hills." And just a week after her departure from the Diamond J, Victoria would appear at her New York City debutante ball, where guests included the governor of New Jersey and the former governor of New York.

The girls' father, James Cox Brady, had died of pneumonia five years earlier, leaving his third wife and his four children an estate worth $55 million. His second wife—the girls' mother—was Lady Victoria May Pery, who had died in the influenza epidemic of 1918 and whose grandfather, the Earl of Limerick, had served as lord-in-waiting to Queen Victoria.[14]

Another guest at the ranch that summer was Miss Anna Depew Paulding of Manhattan, age thirty-seven, who two years earlier had inherited one-sixth of her cousin Chauncey Depew Jr.'s multimillion-dollar estate.[15] Depew, a bachelor, had himself inherited $4.3 million from the estate of his own father, a U.S. senator and chairman of the board and president of the New York Central Railroad.

When Julia Bennett met these people, she did not have an inkling about their backgrounds, other than the fact that they could afford to spend two months at her ranch in the midst of the country's great economic depression. If she *had* known, it would have made no difference to her. While her guests were at the Diamond J, whoever they were, Julia would do her best to make sure they had a grand time.

✤

Julia's sister, Diddy, was usually at the ranch helping tend to guests. In late August, however, she headed up to Helena for a short visit with her friends Roy and Claudia Sieger. Early in the afternoon of Friday, August 26, all three were heading back to the Diamond J, along with James Cumming, the fifteen-year-old son of another friend who was seriously ill. Roy Sieger was at the wheel, six miles from Toston, when the rear tire of the car blew, flipping it three times and sending it hurtling over a fifteen-foot embankment. All four passengers were thrown from the car, and Roy Sieger and James Cumming were severely injured. Diddy and Claudia Sieger tried to flag down passing automobiles, but "cars whizzed past . . . without extending aid," a Helena newspaper reported. "The injured lay near the car for two hours before aid arrived."[16] One of the first to stop was Diddy and Julia's brother Ben, who just happened to be driving by. Sieger died in an ambulance on the way to the Helena hospital. Diddy was treated for bruises, lacerations, and internal injuries. She recovered but would suffer physical impairments for the rest of her life.

✤

While Julia worried about her sister, she continued to entertain her guests—who were nearing the end of their stay—in grand style. Florence McMahon wrote, "Magnificent country / Splendid table / Lively hostess!" in the Diamond J guest book before she departed, while "Unk" Herbert Stursberg penned a lengthy, handwritten poem that included these stanzas:

> Here's to the Boss of the Diamond J
> Who makes us wish we could always stay,
> At her lovely spread in the canyon cool,—
> But "Unk" has to work, and the kids have school . . .

So once you've rode from the "Diamond J,"
Late in the night or at break of day—
You'll want to return and live in the West
Where folks *is folks* and you are their Guest.

In fact, Herbert Stursberg was so enamored with the Diamond J that he would spend August 30—his family's final day at the ranch—offering Julia the opportunity to ensure its survival. But could she meet his stringent terms?

Chapter 44

Diamond J is owned and run as a dude ranch by Mrs. Julia
Bennett, an amazing woman whose energy is of the quiet
kind and whose serenity is equal to that of the mountains.

—Betty Cass, Diamond J guest, *Wisconsin State Journal*, August 16, 1939

Sometime during his family's stay at the Diamond J, Herbert Stursberg had learned about Julia's money troubles. Her debts were overwhelming—they now totaled about $40,000 (more than three-quarters of a million dollars today). Diddy had taken out a second mortgage on the property, and Julia still hadn't resolved the outstanding loans that nearly had resulted in her losing the ranch in 1931. Creditors continued their threats to shut down her business if she did not pay up.

Because Stursberg had grown fond of both Julia and the Diamond J, he wanted to help. So he offered her a deal: he would give her a total of $10,000 to pay her creditors *if* she could convince them to settle for about a quarter of the amount she owed them. In other words, they would have to agree to accept a payment worth about twenty-five cents on the dollar. To receive the $10,000, Julia also would have to sign over to Stursberg all her personal property and equipment, along with the land—with the option of repurchasing everything from him within five years, at 6 percent interest. If she couldn't attract enough paying guests to cover the costs of running the ranch, Stursberg and his family would have the right to stay there privately, and he would assume the expenses involved in the upkeep. In either case, he would pay her salary of $2,000 a year to manage the ranch.

There was yet another risky component of the offer. If Julia couldn't get her creditors to accept the reduced payment terms within one month—by October 1—Stursberg's proposal would be off the table.

With the sad realities of the American economy, Julia didn't have an alternative. She signed the deal on the day the Stursberg family headed back to New York.[1]

✻

Although she never wrote about it, Julia apparently succeeded in convincing her creditors to settle, because the deal with Stursberg was finalized in mid-October.[2] And in the early months of 1933 she returned to New York City in her third quest to drum up business. This time economic prospects were even more dire than the two previous years. The Great Depression had entered its most serious phase. Unemployment stood at nearly 24 percent, and the average American income per capita had dipped to $5,133—a decline of more than 28 percent from four years earlier.[3] To top it off, the tax rate for the wealthiest Americans—those most likely to still be able to afford her dude ranch—had recently more than doubled, from 25 to 63 percent.[4] "People were just not taking vacations," Julia said.[5]

Nevertheless, she booked a room at the Roosevelt again, taking up residence on the sixteenth floor, where she would have a bird's-eye view of Manhattan. In a lucky break, she met a "wonderful" doctor—she did not say where or how—who provided her with a letter of introduction to fourteen other "important" Manhattan doctors. She telephoned the first physician on the list and, "being very honest," told the receptionist that she wanted to speak with the doctor about booking her ranch for the summer. The secretary told her he was too busy to meet with her.

Undeterred, she devised a new strategy. Calling the next doctor's office on her list, she told the receptionist, "I do not know what my trouble is, but Doctor So and So said I must see Doctor ——; Dr. Millet told me to be sure to see a big Doctor at Medical Center."[6] When she arrived for her appointment, the receptionist "asked my business," she recalled. "I said 'I do not know—but must see [the] doctor.'" The receptionist ("She was very nasty," Julia noted) left her sitting in the waiting room all day long. She returned the next day and once again waited the entire day without seeing the doctor. On the third day, she showed up again. Finally, the doctor himself called her into his office and asked why she was there.

She showed him the letter of introduction and explained that she wanted to tell him about the Diamond J. "He laughed," she said. "I showed him pictures and we were busy hunting [and] fishing when [the receptionist] came in and said, 'Doctor, you have many patients waiting.'" He replied, "Oh, to hell with it. I wouldn't have missed seeing this girl for anything."

"I spent the two months seeing those doctors and almost starved," Julia wrote, "but did get some good bookings."

She also managed to get some excellent publicity in the "smart" publications. A June 1933 issue of the *New Yorker* magazine, in an article on western dude ranches, highlighted the Diamond J as "one of the very best, with particularly good food." That good food added to her costs, as did the fact that she chose to feed her help virtually the same meals she served her dudes.[7]

❖

Julia's warmth and lack of pretense were clearly appealing to many of those she encountered. As were her manners. "She is finishing school polished and university educated," said one guest, "and in her city clothes she could be anyone's socially prominent mother."[8]

Someone—perhaps the Scottish chieftain she had met the previous year—once again invited Julia to the famed Explorers Club. The club was housed in a stately Gothic-style brick building whose wood-paneled walls were adorned with dozens of exotic preserved animal heads, tusks, and skins. Although membership was open only to men, women were permitted to visit as guests.

At the club, Julia was introduced to Guthrie Y. Barber, a clothing manufacturer's representative and a handsome widower just a few years older than she was. Dark haired with a rugged, cleft chin, Barber owned a several-hundred-acre camp in upstate New York's Adirondack Mountains called Camp GY-BA-JK, where he kept an impressive collection of valuable western memorabilia. "Mr. Barber also loved the Indians," Julia wrote. In fact, she noted that the year before she met him, he had become "one of the few white men adopted in the Pauni [Pawnee] Tribe" and given the name Sim-Ko-La Shar. He soon would become a good friend.

Julia had promised Marge that she could spend a few months in New York and see Pete, who was now in his second semester at Yale. The romance that blossomed in the summer of 1932 continued to flower, despite the distance. Marge had sent Pete a photograph of herself standing in the snow holding cross-country skis, which Pete had pasted in his scrapbook and marked with an "xo." He also included a portion of her letter: "Another P.S.—I almost forgot to tell you that I still *love* you and can't possibly change my mind for the next million years—."

At Yale, Pete already was a top member of the wrestling team but appeared to be spending more time making mischief and having fun than studying. "Went swimming instead of taking exams," he wrote in his 1933 scrapbook. In an invitation to the Yale prom that he sent to his sister Babs, he reported that fifteen of his former Choate classmates had been put on probation. "Smocking [smoking], drinking, necking, or what?" she replied in a letter. "I was most flabber ghasted to hear that you, my own flesh and blood, were not one of their number."[9]

Pete also was working as a promoter, encouraging his fellow Yalies to spend their summer at the Diamond J. An ad in the student newspaper touted unique opportunities to experience the real cowboy life:

This Summer The Diamond J. Ranch, Ennis, Montana, offers you a chance to see a real 500,000 acre cattle ranch in action. This is not a dude ranch proposition, but an invitation to one of the largest cow outfits in the West. Also pack trips, hunting, fishing, punching and rodeos. See our display of equipment in Fitzgerald's window at 992 Chapel Street. Mr. Fitzgerald has literature for distribution, or see E. A. Stursberg, 1125 Bingham Hall. (First five men to sign up, get a discount of $25 on the R. R. Fare.)[10]

Pete and Julia were both aware that the promise of a visit to Charlie Anceney's immense cattle ranch was a much more enticing draw for young men than the Diamond J alone.

Pete wined and dined Marge in Manhattan. He came into the city from New Haven on weekends and bought Saturday night orchestra-seat tickets to see the Broadway musical revue *Strike Me Pink* featuring vaudeville star Jimmy Durante and the fiery actress Lupe Vélez, "the Mexican Spitfire."[11] He then left for a weeklong Easter vacation trip, driving to Savannah, Georgia, with his friend Charles "Chiz" Miller (shown in a photo in Pete's scrapbook wearing a top hat and tails, a cigarette dangling from his lips).

On April 7 Pete documented with a newspaper headline in his scrapbook what he must have considered significant news: "Beer Floods Nation at Midnight; Brew Trucks Roll Here at 6 A.M.; 6,000 Get City Licenses First Day." Congress had declared that 3.2 percent beer was "non-intoxicating" and could be sold once again, despite the continuing prohibition on the sale of other alcohol. Not that it wasn't still available—New York City was estimated to have one hundred thousand speakeasies. And Pete was spending as much time living the high life as he was studying. "Gee but you're a lucky devil to get every week-end off and just sort of amble down to New York; pretty soft I calls it!" teased his sister.[12] Ambling, he was. On a Sunday in April, he was back in Manhattan, taking Marge to the Astor Theatre to see Helen Hayes and Clark Gable in the movie *White Sister*, a romantic tale about a woman who becomes a nun after she mistakenly learns that her lover was killed in battle. "The SUPREME ROMANTIC THRILL of all time comes at last to the TALKING SCREEN!" the film poster proclaimed.[13]

The handsome and charming Pete had a way with the ladies, and despite his devotion to Marge, he was not eschewing other coeducational activities. One weekend in May, he went to Troy, New York, with two friends to attend his sister's spring dance at Emma Willard, a posh private girls' boarding school. Pete's dance card showed that he had partners for all fourteen dances—only three of them with his sister—and then he went skating on Sunday. On Monday he was briefly back at Yale but returned to the city to bid farewell to Marge. Oddly, their last meeting was at the Regent Nursing Home on East Sixty-First Street, where the noted banker Joseph Harriman, an old family friend charged with bank fraud, had been institutionalized before attempting to take his life that very day. It was news that made all the New York newspapers. "Met Marge here on this day. It was our last date in New York. . . . At the Crossroads Once More," he noted sadly in his scrapbook on May 20.

❖

Meanwhile, Guthrie Barber and Julia had hit it off, not surprisingly for a man who loved everything western and a woman whose family history personified the West. Barber also was a huge circus fan, having been a circus roustabout in his earlier years. He was a member of the all-male Circus Saints and Sinners Club, "an organization composed chiefly of 'circus fans,'" noted the New York Times.[14] Every spring when the Ringling Brothers and Barnum and Bailey circus performed at Madison Square Garden, Barber hosted a luncheon for its star performers at the Roosevelt Hotel. He asked Julia to decorate the party room with her western regalia. She placed a stuffed coyote in the middle of the main table. "Much to my surprise the toastmaster asked me to make a speech," she said. She told the crowd about her childhood desire to be a circus performer and how she and Diddy had "trained" their pet sow in the Circle J corral.

Barber also invited Julia and Marge to attend one of the premier events of the New York social season: the annual spring Circus Ball, which attracted more than three thousand "members of society and the artistic world" to the grand ballroom of the Waldorf Astoria in April.[15] Three dance orchestras performed at the charity event, including one conducted by George Gershwin. Dozens of celebrities— including Jimmy Durante, Fanny Brice, Noel Coward, and members of the Broadway cast of Strike Me Pink, which Marge and Pete had seen a month earlier—entertained the crowd with a costume parade and show that kicked off at midnight.

Most of the costumed guests "garbed themselves as clowns, bareback riders, trapeze athletes, snake charmers, freaks, lion tamers, country bumpkins and fire eaters," reported the *Times*.[16] Julia and Marge, of course, wore their western attire. Seeing an excellent opportunity to meet New Yorkers ripe for summer vacation opportunities, Julia hosted a "side-show" booth featuring her western paraphernalia that earlier had proven so popular in display windows. She also provided entertainment. "I had three Indians dancing for me, [and] gave a trophy to be sold. Marge looked very beautiful in her western clothes," Julia said. In the wee hours of the morning, as the event was winding down and Julia was packing up to leave, an acquaintance walked by in his evening clothes and tall silk hat, hoisted her saddle onto his shoulder, and carried it through the ballroom, drunk.

Julia and Marge had quickly captivated New York society. Guthrie Barber invited them to dine at his East Thirtieth Street apartment and to visit his camp in the Adirondacks before they headed back to Montana. Soon after Marge's final date with Pete, she and her mother boarded a train that took them north of Albany, where they disembarked at the tiny Stony Creek station. Julia reported that it consisted of nothing but a boxcar and "chick sales" (her term for an outhouse). "A cowboy met us in a buckboard—we drove over the roughest road I have ever seen. I had gone on many wild rides in buckboards but this was the wildest; we hung on for dear life."

Chapter 45

My life has been devoted to picturizing the West.
—William Henry Jackson, radio interview, April 3, 1941

William Henry Jackson was ninety years old in May 1933 when he first laid eyes on Julia Bennett. Jackson was an American icon, the man who had scaled mountains and descended into canyons six decades earlier to take the now-famous photographs of the land that would become Yellowstone National Park. Since that time, he had documented thousands of miles of western landscape, the 1893 Chicago World's Fair, and hundreds of exotic sites in twenty-four countries. Now, at ninety, Jackson remained exceptionally spry and vibrant although somewhat hard of hearing. A distinguished, professorial-looking man who wore round, wire-rimmed spectacles, he still possessed a full head of white hair and sported a well-trimmed mustache and goatee. Having outlived two wives, he lived alone at the Latham Hotel in New York City and stayed busy drawing and painting, writing articles, and documenting his life's accomplishments, all of which had come about because he had headed out west in the spring of 1866, at the age of twenty-two, after a heated argument with his then fiancée.

In 1871 Jackson had been the first photographer to bring the Yellowstone region to the attention of the nation. His images were largely responsible for turning the geological wonderland into the nation's first national park. Early explorers and guides, including John Colter and Jim Bridger, had told stories of the region's bubbling cauldrons, dramatic canyons, and steaming geysers, but their tales were so fantastical that most people thought they were making them up. Nathaniel Langford and Henry Washburn had led an expedition to the area in 1870, and Langford published an article about the trip in *Scribner's Magazine*. But no photographs of the landscape had ever been taken.

Then, in 1871, Congress approved $40,000 in funding for a United States Geological Survey expedition to document the Yellowstone landscape. Its leader was a man with the impressive name of Dr. Ferdinand Vandiveer Hayden, a geology professor at the University of Pennsylvania. He recruited a band of thirty-two assistants—among them a meteorologist, an entomologist, a botanist, a zoologist, an ornithologist, and an artist—to accompany him on the three-month summer trek. He selected Jackson to be the mission's photographer.

A native New Yorker and budding artist, Jackson had survived a stint in the Union army and headed west after breaking off his engagement because of an argument over something he couldn't remember. His westward journey was far from unique. He noted in his autobiography, "When times were hard in the East—when there were too many children to share the New England farm—when you left the Army after serving through a war and were restless and footloose—when you had a broken heart, or too much ambition for your own good—there was always the West. Horace Greeley's advice was far too obvious to be startling. Go west? Of course go west. Where else?"[1]

And so just two years after the Nave family had headed out on their journey, Jackson became, with no previous experience, a bullwhacker—one of a team of twenty-five men who drove wagon trains of oxen that freighted goods across the plains. Like the Naves, he had planned to head to Virginia City in the Montana Territory, but instead he bought a camera and secured a job photographing the construction of the Union Pacific Railroad as it extended its tracks into Wyoming, where he first met Dr. Hayden.

Following the Yellowstone expedition and the publication of the first photos documenting Mammoth Springs, the Grand Canyon of the Yellowstone, and other natural curiosities, Jackson went on to produce more than eighty thousand photographs and paintings of the West, as well as of sites he witnessed on a seventeen-month trip around the world in 1892. He had become an American icon, and in 1932 he was invited to the White House to meet President Herbert Hoover.[2]

On April 4, 1933, the Explorers Club of New York had hosted a celebration in honor of Jackson's ninetieth birthday. And now, in late May, he was spending the week at his friend Guthrie Barber's camp in the Adirondacks. As Barber conducted an American-flag-raising ceremony one Thursday afternoon to inaugurate his immense new banner, Jackson gazed over the horizon. He spied a buckboard headed their way, carrying two women. Barber, an enthusiastic amateur filmmaker, filmed them with his hand-cranked Ciné-Kodak as they approached.[3] Jackson noted in his diary that Barber "had them alight and join our group around the flag pole while the photographing went on," and being a frugal man who meticulously documented every expense, Jackson remarked on the large amount of film Barber was using to do so.[4]

Julia and Marge were surprised to find that Camp GY-BA-JK looked much like a Montana ranch, albeit without the snowcapped mountains. "The camp was in a beautiful spot with [a] fishing stream running thru it," Julia wrote, and it featured a two-story log building designed to look like a western lodge. Among Barber's vast collection of memorabilia were an original covered wagon that had crossed the plains, buckboards, a Concord stagecoach similar to the one in which Julia's grandmother had traveled, and a tepee. "His camp was more western than my ranch," Julia proclaimed.

That evening, the group sat on stones encircling a hillside campfire, "toasting 'weiners' and bread sandwiches," as Jackson described the curiosities. He also wrote in his diary about his new acquaintances: "Mrs. Bennett runs a splendid 'dude ranch' on the upper Madison in Montana—judging from her photographs of which she has several very fine ones, both as to subject and technically—She is much interested in the work I did in her locality as to the early days of the U.S.G.S. [United States Geological Survey]—I must send her photos of Virginia City and Mystic Lake [in the Beartooth Mountains of Montana]. Her father was a pioneer of that region and she was born out there."

Barber, Jackson, and the Bennetts had plenty in common, and they hit it off immediately. Julia reported that the group spent a "delightful" week fishing, pitching a tepee, and filming mock stagecoach hold-ups—an activity she soon would introduce at the Diamond J. Jackson described the goings-on: "The chief business of the day was the photographing (with Ciné Kodak) of the 'Hold up' and of the various guests in combination with the old Concord Coach. . . . The whole proceedings immensely enjoyed by all, particularly Mrs. Bennett and daughter, who come from the country of real holdups. I was the 'Camera Man' for most of the picture making."[5]

The next day, two men on Barber's staff drove Jackson, Julia, and Marge to the boxcar train station, first through the woods in the bone-rattling buckboard, then switching to a Buick roadster. The trio boarded the train and rode together until they reached Albany, where Jackson left them with a promise that he would make a visit to the Diamond J Ranch that summer.[6]

✤

Meanwhile, Pete Stursberg was looking forward to another summer at the Diamond J, but it wasn't to be. He was required to attend summer school in Princeton and was summoned to appear in court in Massachusetts on a traffic violation. Worst of all, his father succumbed to pneumonia on July 14 after an illness of several months. Pete was heartbroken. He dedicated a page to his father's memory in his scrapbook with a poem that read in part,

> Dad, are you watching and
> Guarding me now?
> Are you still saying
> Are you showing me how?
> Oh! I know you are, Dad!

Marge sent him a telegram: "All my love and sympathy."

Just nine days after his father's death, Pete celebrated his birthday.

"I woke up this morning to find I was 21 years young," he wrote in his scrapbook. "I am now a Man! So what!!"

Unk was helping to manage the disposition of his brother's nearly million-dollar estate, which would be divided among his wife and five children. Pete's father's death would leave him with an inheritance of almost $175,000 (the equivalent of about $3.5 million today).[7] In an August 13 letter to Pete discussing finances, Unk invoked the memory of Julia and the Diamond J while explaining that he had been very busy with estate matters: "I feel like you look when you were juggling those eggs—or rather aaags as our Julia would say—at the picnic. So far I haven't dropped any yet but—I'm getting cross eyed!" He urged Pete to be strong: "You sound a bit discouraged, but youve [sic] got a job to do like all the rest of us and its [sic] every bit as important although I know that it doesn't look that way. . . . I'm in a bad jam—my old bronc is acting mean and the trail is steep and rough. . . . Keep your cinches tight and stay with him."

Unk said he would send Pete a check for $200 that would cover his bills and leave him "$132.04 to last you til Christmas!" (an amount equivalent to more than $2,600 today and about half the average U.S. per capita annual income at the time).

Julia, on the other hand, was still broke.

Chapter 46

In making the new kind of ranching her profession, Mrs.
Bennett is living the only life in which she is ever completely
happy. Climbing mountain trails, fishing mountain streams,
spending long days in the saddle, hunting deer or bear—
several of the bear rugs in the main cabin at the ranch
show what a good shot she is—for everything that has
to do with the outdoors she has an ardent passion.

—*New York Evening Post*, April 18, 1931

The summer of 1933 would turn out to be a productive one after
all, because William Henry Jackson made good on his promise to
visit the Diamond J. A few weeks after she returned to Montana,
Julia sent a letter encouraging him to visit. She included an invitation from the Livingston Chamber of Commerce to be its guest at
the Diamond Jubilee on the Fourth of July, an event highlighted by
the rodeo that had enchanted Pete.[1] Jackson arranged to make the
stop during a planned visit to Colorado (where he would reconnect
with his fellow 1871 survey partner, the artist Thomas Moran) and
Yellowstone National Park. There he would spend time with his
friend Jack Haynes, the official park photographer, and Haynes's wife,
Isabel, who managed the park's stores, before heading to Livingston,
where he planned to meet Julia at the rodeo.

On the morning of the Fourth of July, the Haynes' chauffeur drove
Jackson and Isabel Haynes north toward Livingston through the stunning Paradise Valley, where Jackson noted that he "failed to recognize
some of the points from which I made my 1871 photographs." They
arrived at the "fine appearing little city" just before noon, where a
large crowd had gathered to celebrate the nation's birthday and the
town's fiftieth anniversary. Because of the throng, they had a hard

time tracking down Julia but finally found her and Marge at the Park Hotel, where they were eating lunch. Jackson was impressed with what he called Julia's "cowboy costume," which he found noteworthy enough to detail in his diary: "Black fringed buckskin skirt, fancy vest embroidered with beads on back, black wide-brimmed hat and short cowboy boots. Quite attractive costume which she wears on all occasions away from house out here."

At the rodeo, Jackson and a handful of other honored guests were invited to come to the front of the grandstand to be introduced, "our various titles to fame announced by the loud speaker"—an unexpected event that Jackson seemed to find somewhat awkward. Following the festivities, Julia put her persuasive powers to work. She convinced him to return with her to the Diamond J, "altho I had no toilet articles or change of clothing. We . . . started out at once for Bozeman for supper."

Jackson was surprised to find that Bozeman had changed significantly from "the scraggly little frontier town" he had last seen in 1871. He thought it a "prosperous looking little city," and Julia cemented that impression by registering him at the finest hotel in town, the Baxter, where she had greeted the Stursbergs a year earlier. Jackson described it as "a modern 6 story building" that would be "a credit to any city," though he lamented that "Mrs. B. is insisting on paying every cent of expenses which I find to be somewhat embarrassing." He was unaware that Julia's cash supply was quite limited since no other guests were due to arrive at the ranch until later in the month.

That evening, Julia took Jackson to yet another rodeo, this one at a nearby hot spring. He didn't arrive back at the hotel until midnight and didn't have much opportunity to rest the next day either. While Julia attended to business in town, he bought a toothbrush and a shirt for his stay at the ranch, was invited to lunch at the local Rotary Club, and met Charlie Anceney. Jackson described Anceney in his diary as the "owner of the 500,000 acre Flying D Ranch—an alert, vigorous man of 70." Late that afternoon, Julia drove him to the Diamond J along a road paralleling the Madison River and then into the canyon, where he found the ranch "beautifully situated in a nook of the mountains." Jackson thought the six guest cabins were "about the last word in log home construction and furnishings." Since there were no other guests, Julia invited him to dine with Diddy, Marge, and her in the large kitchen, which he thought had "fine up to date equipment." But he found the meal, prepared by Mrs. Baker, who was the cook that summer, to be "the only thing that is not first class."

After dinner, Julia escorted him on a long walk. She pointed out the ongoing construction of a new building, along with a "Pioneer Wading Pool" and playhouse she was having built for guests' children. Jackson noted the "evidence of considerable outlay—half a dozen men about the grounds." When he returned to his cabin for the night, he found the oil lamp in his room already lit and a "generous" blaze in the fireplace.

The next morning at seven, he joined Julia and the family at breakfast and, after a discussion, decided to remain at the Diamond J until the end of the week, when she would drive him back to Yellowstone. That morning, he was left to his "own devices until noon—wandering about the grounds." In the midafternoon, Julia and Marge, accompanied by two local girls and a ranch waiter, drove south toward Virginia City as storm clouds gathered over the divide. Jackson had not seen the town since his visit with the Geological Survey sixty-two years earlier. "I had been given the impression that this old frontier city was in a sad decline," he wrote, "but was surprised to see it looking better than of '71 although with not as many inhabitants as in prosperous mining days."

There the group met a man named Mr. Peale at the Virginia Hotel, located near the spot where the Vigilantes had taken the law into their hands and hanged criminals in 1864. Peale, a lifelong resident who told them he was born in the city in 1869, "invited us to a bottle of beer over the same old bar room counter that we boys of the Survey of '71 patronized," Jackson recalled in his diary on July 6. Julia then led the group, accompanied by Peale, to visit the graveyard where the Vigilantes had buried their hanging victims and on to Nevada City and the old Masonic Hall, "where the Vigilantes organized . . . still standing." At Alder Gulch they visited the monument marking the spot where gold was discovered in 1863. Jackson thought the Virginia City museum was "rather good . . . better than in some much larger cities." Then the group headed back to Ennis, where he was "amused by the cow herd coming in thro' the town" as the group waited an hour for the mail delivery to arrive. Julia had squeezed all those sites into a trip that lasted only five hours or so, and then she drove the group back to the ranch, where a "cheerful" hearth fire greeted Jackson in his cabin.

The next day, a sunny one, Julia had promised Jackson a horseback ride, but he spent his day wandering about the ranch and writing letters, since "we did not get off until 4 o-clock. I was given a good old gray. Mrs. B. had a fine bay and one of the horse wranglers who went along was also well mounted."

Julia led her nonagenarian guest across Jack Creek and up steep trails to a horse pasture in the foothills and then circled back to camp along the creek—"a splendid two hour ride," Jackson proclaimed. "Only effect a little stiffness in the knees that soon passed off."[2]

That evening, Julia invited her neighbors at a nearby ranch, Bert and Lucy Maynard, to dinner, telling Jackson that Mr. Maynard's father was "said to be [the] oldest pioneer in Ennis."[3] Ethyl Augustus Maynard, now ninety-one, had arrived in Virginia City from Michigan in 1864, at about the same time as the Naves. He was reportedly the first pioneer to sow grain in the Madison valley, which Julia's mother and grandmother had crossed in 1867.[4]

That July, George and Emma Cowan's eldest son, Fred, also made a visit to the Diamond J. Julia took Fred to Yellowstone Park, where she snapped a photo of him standing in front of the historical marker that told the story of the group known as "the Cowan Party." She commemorated his visit by pasting the photo in the Diamond J guest book.

❖

The rest of the week passed quietly. Jackson watched a blacksmith at work shoeing Julia's more than thirty horses and sat for photographs, this time with Marge as the photographer. On the day of his departure, he arose before dawn to prepare for his return to Yellowstone. He was joined on the drive by the cook, Mrs. Baker, who was making her first visit to the national park. Jackson remarked on the "splendid scenery up the Canyon but not what I expect to see regarding my experience in the Gallatin in '72." After a long day, Julia dropped off Jackson at his lodgings and continued on the long drive up to Bozeman to spend the night.

The following day, Jackson worked on a thank-you gift for Julia. The noted artist was painting a picture for her guest book, "the first part of the work being discouragingly difficult on account of poor surface of paper for water color and also that I have none of the colored pencils and pastels to help out with." The next day, he completed it, commenting in his diary that it "turned out fairly satisfactorily after all."[5]

Jackson made another summer visit to the Diamond J in 1934, where he took a walk around the ranch to see the latest improvements, remarking that "everything [is] done in an orderly efficient way." He noticed that "among the people here it is difficult to tell the guests from the employees. The older guests seem to have left their young people here while they are off somewhere else."[6] Julia once again hosted an old-timers' dinner in his honor, inviting a dozen or so friends whose families had been among the first settlers in the Madison valley. And Jackson took photos with his Kodak camera, adding images of the Diamond J to his world-famous collection.

Julia would treasure the painting he made for her for the rest of her life, and Jackson, who always referred to her as Mrs. Bennett, would remain her friend until his death eight years later at the age of ninety-nine.

Chapter 47

Tucson: The Metropolis of Southern Arizona.
Summer Rays on Winter Days.

—*Tucson City Directory*, 1934

The Diamond J was one of only a few dude ranches in the Madison valley of Montana when it welcomed its first guests in 1931. By the mid-1930s, the competition was growing; Montana soon would have more than one hundred.[1] And while Julia's first four seasons at the Diamond J had been successful, she was learning that she couldn't make ends meet year-round with a guest season that lasted only a few months.

She also was still beholden to Herbert Stursberg. At the end of the 1934 summer season, the two had renegotiated their agreement. Their new contract gave her full rights to operate the ranch until the end of the 1939 season, but he would continue to own the land. While he would no longer pay her a salary, he would offer her operating funds of up to $5,000 over the five-year period, if she needed them. He also would relinquish his right to reserve cabins for his family and would pay the full rate to stay at the Diamond J. Julia also would have the option to buy back the land from him at any time.

She still needed to find a way to make ends meet in order to keep the Diamond J. She didn't have many options, because the state's winters were too harsh for hosting guests. Audaciously, she hatched a new plan—she would open a dude ranch in a warmer climate to cater to guests from November through April.

Following the close of the 1934 season at the Diamond J, Julia drove 1,200 miles south to Tucson, Arizona, hoping to find a ranch to lease for the winter. Times were "not good," she wrote. The nation's economic depression continued, and the unemployment rate stood at nearly 22 percent. Nevertheless, the Santa Fe Railroad was promoting vacation travel to Tucson, calling it "Star Land, Sun Land, Rope, Spur and Gun Land" and a place "where cacti stand like statues."[2]

Tucson was the second largest city in a state with a population even smaller than that of Montana.[3] Because of its dry desert air, mild winter days, and brilliant sunshine, it had become a destination not only for vacationers but for those seeking cures for tuberculosis and other respiratory ailments, including many veterans whose lungs had been scarred by mustard gas during World War I. The city of about fifty thousand housed twenty-two hospitals and sanitariums; a health-food store; and a bathhouse that advertised massage and hydrotherapy, colonic irrigations, infrared treatments, and "alcoholic treatments."[4]

Tucson also had a number of tourist courts, and a few ranches served guests in the area. But Julia struck out in her attempt to find a place to lease. She drove back to Montana with nothing to show for her trip. She would have to rely on the summer guests at the Diamond J—at least for the time being—to stay afloat.

❖

Near the very end of the Diamond J's 1935 season, fate would lend a hand. On October 4 Mrs. George Westinghouse III arrived for a three-week stay, along with her two teenaged daughters. Violet's husband was the only child of George Westinghouse Jr., the famed inventor of the railway air brake and manufacturer of alternating-current electrical products. The wealthy Westinghouse family was always on the move, bouncing among their five houses: three in the United States, one in Canada, and one in the Bahamas.[5] Since the notorious kidnapping and murder of aviator Charles Lindbergh's son in 1932, they had never stayed in any of them for more than ninety days at a time, careful to remain out of the public eye to protect their six children, who ranged in age from nine to twenty-three.[6]

Two weeks after the arrival of Violet and her daughters, the West-inghouses' dashingly handsome eldest child, Tom, arrived in dramatic fashion, flying from Seattle in his open-cockpit biplane, wearing a leather pilot jacket, helmet, and goggles.[7] Tom was a sportsman, and he hoped to hunt bighorn sheep and mountain goats during his visit.

Julia entertained the family with excursions to sites including Custer National Battlefield and Yellowstone National Park, where they planned to take home movies of wild game. While Julia drove the Westinghouse women to Yellowstone, Tom flew Marge there in his Gypsy Moth.[8]

Although they hailed from a completely different world, the Westinghouses were Julia's kind of folk—down-to-earth, friendly, and unpretentious. Mrs. Westinghouse, born Evelyn Violet Brockle-bank, was an Englishwoman known to her friends simply as Vi. Like Julia, she was a horsewoman. She had grown up riding on her family's summer estate in the Lake District of England, and she and her twin sister, Daisy (also an accomplished horsewoman), had learned to drive four-in-hand in Paris in 1899.[9]

Violet—whom Julia always called Mrs. Westinghouse—was just two years older than Julia. The Westinghouses "were wonderful people and we had a fine time," Julia wrote. During their stay, Julia asked Violet if she knew of a ranch in Tucson she could rent for the winter.

"Why don't you take our home?" Violet suggested. "It could be made into a fine dude ranch." She apparently was not as fond of the place as her husband was. When Daisy visited a year earlier, George had asked his wife's sister what she thought of it. "Oh, I think it might sell well," she had replied.[10]

Violet added a caveat: Julia would have to visit her husband and discuss a potential lease with him. At the time, George was at their Canadian home, Springwood, on Vancouver Island in British Columbia.

Violet and her daughters left the Diamond J in late October, while Tom stayed on to hunt with Julia. She likely was out on a hunt on October 24 when Anson Bennett died at the age of fifty-two in a Butte hospital, "following an illness of several weeks," a newspaper reported.[11] On his death certificate, the doctor listed her ex-husband's cause of death as heart disease, adding that the secondary cause was

21. Marjorie Bennett, Violet Westinghouse, and Julia Bennett at Julia's camp in the snowy Spanish Peaks, circa 1935. Julia Bennett scrapbook, Sherry Merica Pepper private collection.

"luers"—a disease better known today as syphilis. Julia never mentioned his death in her memoir.

At the end of the hunting season, Julia decided to pay a visit to George Westinghouse III. She proposed that she and Marge drive Tom home by way of Seattle, where Don and his wife lived in an apartment near the University of Washington.

In Seattle Tom tried to discourage Julia from making the four-hour ferry trip to his parents' home, telling her he was sure his father would not even talk to her, let alone lease her the ranch. Julia refused to be deterred.

One morning soon after, Julia, Marge, and Tom drove onto the ferry for the departure to the city of Victoria on Vancouver Island. Once on land, they headed north and then turned west onto the pastoral Mount Newton Cross Road to reach Springwood, the Westinghouses' large, shingled arts-and-crafts-style house. Marge and Julia took in the stunning view from the hilltop, which overlooked grass-covered pastures, the waters of Squally Reach, and the distant mountain known as the Malahat. Then they walked up the front steps to the porch of the gabled home, where the Westinghouses had invited them to dinner. Following the meal, Tom, his sisters, and Marge left to go to a party.

"To my surprise, Mr. W. invited me to have a cup of tea with him," said Julia. "So we sat in front of the fireplace."

Westinghouse was an intelligent man, hard-nosed yet generous.[12] "So you want to lease my place for a dude ranch?" he asked her. "I don't think much of dude ranches, but I want to sell, and have decided to lease you the place. Perhaps you will buy it or sell it for me. Mrs. Westinghouse says you will take good care of it."

He told Julia she could rent the Diamond W for $750 a month. Julia told him she couldn't afford it. He thought for a while and then asked, "Could you pay $400?"

"I said yes," Julia remembered, "although I did not have a cent to my name."

Perhaps sensing that finances might be a problem, Westinghouse said, "I want the money in advance, and will wire my lawyer to give you possession."

Julia agreed to the deal without a clue as to how she would cover the rent. Marge and Don were "very worried" and tried to dissuade her. But "Mrs. W. and girls were delighted," Julia added. So was she.

Chapter 48

Every star I know in Hollywood acknowledges
the same fact. With luck you can climb.
Without it, your brakes don't work even when you coast.

—Myrna Loy, 1938

It was late December 1935, and Julia was driving. She and Marge were on the road from Seattle to Tucson, a 1,500-mile trip. They were planning to make a stop in Hollywood, California, where Julia's childhood friend Della Williams—the mother of movie star Myrna Loy—had invited them to spend the New Year's holiday at her home in Beverly Hills.

Marge was thrilled about the opportunity to cross paths with a movie star who soon would be named Queen of the Movies in a national poll—but she also was terrified.[1] Her mother had never driven in a big city before, and Marge was afraid to be a passenger in her car.

Julia insisted that they take this detour to Los Angeles. While she didn't have enough money to lease the ranch, she did have enough to embark on this road trip, and she wanted to spend time with Della at her Spanish-style house on Crescent Hills Drive in Beverly Hills.[2] They arrived in Los Angeles on New Year's Eve; Julia thought the traffic abominable. There were no lane markings in the streets, with cars driving two or three abreast. She wound through the busy streets for two hours trying to find the house but couldn't.

"Marge was praying; she thought we would be killed," Julia wrote.

Julia saw a road sign for Long Beach. She exited, exhausted. They stopped at a large hotel "filled with old people playing bridge," where she decided they would spend the night. Marge was heartbroken that she would not get to meet the famous film star. Her New Year's Eve consisted of having a "big cry," Julia wrote. "She was so disappointed."

It was one of the few times in her life that Julia had given up on a plan. And it was the traffic that finally had defeated her. Early the next morning, the two got in their automobile and headed back toward Tucson. They didn't get far. The car stopped soon after they started; Julia couldn't get the engine to turn over again. As she put it, a "big Irish cop" came to the rescue. After he fiddled with the motor for a few minutes, it sputtered back to life, and he sent them off with a "Happy New Year."

Julia drove for sixteen hours straight, arriving in Tucson at two in the morning. She was so exhausted she had nearly lost her voice. They checked in to the luxurious six-story Santa Rita Hotel in downtown Tucson, which billed itself as "the finest hotel under the happy Arizona sun."[3] She informed the manager that she had leased the Westinghouse home to start a dude ranch. That morning, she and Marge ate breakfast in the hotel dining room, where she charged the meal to her room because she had only $2.50 left in her purse.

✤

Julia and Marge drove northeast through the Sonoran Desert toward the dark foothills of the Santa Catalina Mountains. Giant saguaro cactuses, stubby mesquite trees, and an occasional cottonwood dotted the vast valley. Along the fifteen-mile drive, they saw only two or three houses—Julia noted that one was the home of novelist Harold Bell Wright, the nation's top-selling author at the time.

Pulling up to the walled Westinghouse ranch, Julia and Marge introduced themselves to the caretaker of the three-hundred-acre property. "The location was beautiful. . . . The place cost $200,000," Julia noted (about $3.6 million today).

Although the Westinghouse family had money, their tastes were not fancy. Instead of taking the train to Tucson, they hauled their six children (along with five dogs, a parrot, and their retired butler and his wife) "in a fleet of old cars, right out of Steinbeck," their grandson recalled.[4] When Violet Westinghouse first entered the Co-ed Shop, an exclusive Tucson women's clothing store, wearing a "$1.95 house dress" and stockings riddled with runs, the owner thought she had intended to enter the Montgomery Ward next door. A local florist mistook George Westinghouse, who was wearing a shabby black suit, for a panhandler.[5] But after building their stately Tucson home in 1931, the Westinghouses became recognized members of the community. They showed their generosity by opening their estate for an "English Lawn Fete and barbecue" to benefit Tucson's Temple of Music and Art. A local newspaper noted that "the Westinghouse Manor . . . with its velvety smooth lawns and dense cottonwood grove will form the perfect English setting for such an affair."[6]

The Westinghouses' home was actually Spanish in design, simple yet elegant. Designed by noted Tucson architects Roy and Lew Place, the main house had stucco walls and a red-tiled roof. The third floor featured an open sun porch with a splendid view of the Santa Catalinas. Filled with Spanish furniture and ornate wrought iron fixtures, the house included a large living room, four bedrooms, and two baths. Julia especially loved the "library filled with books" and "two beautiful fireplaces" bordered with hand-painted Mexican tiles. Attached to the main house was a large dining room, along with a "kitchen help's dining room" and four bedrooms for servants.

As Julia and Marge walked through the property accented with flower gardens, they spied a swimming pool, corrals, garages, picnic groves with tables, a barbecue pit, a small schoolhouse built for the Westinghouses' youngest daughter, Margaret, and even an ancient Indian doghouse.

Poultry and birds wandered the grounds: "three peacocks, a cock, two hens . . . twelve guinea hens, chickens and lots of pigeons," wrote Julia. "The cock was beautiful."

And then there were the furnished brick cottages, which would be perfect for "dudes"—two with covered porches near the main house, each with four bedrooms and two baths—as well as three more cottages for the help.

Although a caretaker was living on the property, Julia thought "the place was neglected." The Westinghouse family hadn't been there

22. Julia Bennett's Diamond W Ranch in Tucson, undated. Courtesy of George Westinghouse IV.

recently, and there were "weeds all over and many flowers dead," with Julia concluding that the grounds "needed lots of work to get in order."

The run-down condition of the property would be Julia's saving grace. When she returned to the hotel, she sent George Westinghouse a telegram asking if he would give her a month to clean up the place before she sent him the rent money. He wired back, giving her permission to take possession and agreeing to delay payment.

Julia and Marge set to work. "The caretaker was a fine young man," Julia said. "He got me four Mexicans to clean up weeds and grounds."

In another stroke of good fortune, Julia's Montana neighbor Wetmore Hodges, the wealthy businessman who owned the immense Jumping Horse Ranch, was wintering a few miles away at the Tanque Verde guest ranch with his wife and three sons. The forty-six-year-old Hodges was one of the original investors in General Seafood Corporation in Gloucester, Massachusetts, founded by Clarence Birdseye, the creator of flash-frozen foods.[7] He recently had been mentioned as a possible contender for the position of assistant U.S. secretary of commerce.[8]

Hodges was fond of Julia and stopped by, she recalled, "to see how I was getting along." He asked if she had enough money to open the ranch.

"No," she replied.

"Would $250 help you any?" he asked, loaning her the money after she replied that it would.

That $250 solved the sticky problem of Julia's hotel charges. She drove back to town and paid her bill at the Santa Rita, and she and Marge moved into their new ranch.

On January 10, 1936, Violet Westinghouse and her three daughters became their first guests, arriving for a two-week stay on their way to the family's home in Nassau, Bahamas.[9] Violet took Julia into town, where she introduced her to the local merchants—an endorsement that enabled Julia to establish credit accounts. She also brought "a barrel of beautiful china" from the family's warehouse for Julia to use at the ranch.

Three days later, Violet was even more generous—she threw a large party to celebrate Marge's twenty-second birthday. She invited sixty guests—"all her best friends," Julia wrote—to a picnic in the ranch's shaded cottonwood grove.

When it was time for Violet to leave for the Bahamas, she asked if Julia had the $400 in rent to send to her husband. Julia told her she did not. With that, Violet handed Julia $400 in cash, saying, "My son's wife will come and stay awhile, and that will take care of it."

And then Julia sent Violet Westinghouse's money to George Westinghouse. "So that was how I paid first month's rent," she wrote.

Chapter 49

The vogue for following the sun in its orbit grows and grows. . . .
Easterners have discovered the Sun Country of the Southwest
and are flying there each winter in larger numbers.

—*Brooklyn Daily Eagle*, December 20, 1936

The land surrounding the Diamond W had been known for centuries as Tanque Verde, Spanish for "green pool." In earlier days, there indeed had been lovely green pools nestled in Tanque Verde Creek, but they had dried up decades earlier. The area around Tucson had been home to several Native American tribes: the Apaches, the Pimas, the Papagoes, and the Sobiapuris. After the establishment of Fort Lowell in 1873, ranchers from both Mexico and the United States brought their cattle to roam the mountain-ringed valley, surrounded by the Santa Catalinas to the north, the Rincons to the east, and the Tucsons to the west. As Julia's brochure noted, it was a place where "the sun sinks in all its glory behind the Tucson Mountains."

Julia fell in love with the open landscape, which she declared was "beautiful riding country" with "no fences [and] miles of beautiful blooming cactus."

Tucson was the ideal spot for a winter guest ranch. It was on the main line of the Southern Pacific Railroad, which advertised that southern Arizona guest ranches offered "all the comforts of modern living, plus the fun of horseback riding on real cattle ranches."[1] As the chamber of commerce boasted in the 1936 *Tucson City Directory*, the town was intersected by U.S. Highway 80, "'the Broadway of America'—all year, high gear, coast to coast highway, 100% paved," and served daily by American Airways, known as the "Sunshine Airway." The chamber called Tucson's climate the "'finest in America' for health, rest or recreation." It may have exaggerated a bit. Julia herself wrote that "Tucson was only a village filled with Indians, Mexicans and cowboys and cattlemen." But she also knew that an attraction near the Westinghouse ranch was Saguaro National Monument, the desert home to the largest cactus species in the United States. The area had been preserved just a few years earlier, in 1933, by proclamation of President Herbert Hoover.

Now that the ranch was hers, Julia had a dozen beds to fill—pronto. She contacted George Westinghouse, asking for permission to install electricity and a telephone, which, she told him, "we just had to have" (although her Montana ranch didn't yet have either of those conveniences). He agreed.

Wetmore Hodges continued to stop by to see how Julia and Marge were faring but wasn't optimistic about their future. "You can't make this a guest ranch, for you haven't any money," he told Julia. He offered to take over the lease and employ her as the housekeeper.

She politely thanked him and then firmly turned him down. "I told him I had come there to establish a guest ranch and was going to do it."

In an effort to help fill those twelve beds, he offered to move his family from the nearby Tanque Verde ranch as soon as the telephone was installed. She took him to see the cottage the Westinghouse family had named the Prussian, which was ready for occupancy.

Soon the Hodges family would be the first guests at Julia's newly named Diamond W, branded with a W—most likely in honor of the Westinghouse family.[2]

Julia hired a cook and two maids, and a few more paying guests arrived. Gus and Dorothy Cobb, guests at the Diamond J in 1933 who had become friends with Julia during their stay, arrived from New York and rented the second large cottage, named Catalina. The couple took up residence for the entire winter, "and I did not have to ask their help," Julia proudly noted.

She couldn't afford to buy horses that first season but had a long list of activities to keep her guests entertained. She led them on trips to Sabino and Tanque Verde Canyons, Saguaro National Monument,

Native American ruins, and the seventeenth-century San José de Tumacácori and San Xavier Missions.[3]

Although Julia thought her guests would enjoy the assorted birds the Westinghouses had left behind on the ranch, they most decidedly did not. They complained about the crowing and squawking of a cock and guinea hens, and Julia felt compelled to give them away. "Someone stole the peacock, and we had to shoot the many pigeons," she said.

Julia also had a new pet, a one-year-old wild boar that a rancher friend named Jack Kenny had brought her from Mexico. The pig followed her everywhere, curling up on the floor by her side whenever she sat down. Unfortunately, the boar had scent glands that emitted a noxious odor when he became excited or angry. One day, the pig walked into the main house, and Julia reported that a few of the guests "threw things at him and drove him out." She took him to the vet, who said he could remove the glands, "but the operation killed him."

A New York physician who was a friend of Wetmore Hodges referred a guest named Bill Smith, who recently had suffered a nervous breakdown. Julia picked him up at Tucson's medical center. During the drive to the ranch, he told her "all the things he needed"—including twin beds, because "he could not sleep with his wife."

Julia replied that she could provide him and his wife with a large room with a double bed in the main house, but she did not have twin beds. He accepted her offer in spite of that, and Julia noted that he "slept with his wife and improved every day."

She drove Bill Smith to Mexico—about sixty miles south—and arranged for him to have a short stay at a large cattle ranch owned by the same friend who had presented her with the pet boar. The Smiths spent five months at the Diamond W, and by the time they returned to New York in the spring of 1937, Julia reported that Bill was "a new man."

She also reported that she had grossed $5,000 in only three months' time.

23. Julia Bennett leading dudes on a ride near the Diamond W Ranch in Tucson, undated. Photograph by Chuck Abbott. Julia Bennett scrapbook, Sherry Merica Pepper private collection.

Chapter 50

Only real people visit dude ranches.

—Julia Bennett, memoir

In the spring of 1937 Julia made another booking trip to New York City, and this time her son, Don, joined her. Since meeting W. H. Jackson four years earlier, she and the renowned photographer had become good friends, and he sent her an invitation to an April 4 reception hosted by the Explorers Club in honor of his ninety-fourth birthday. She couldn't attend, so Jackson invited Don and her to dinner the following week at the Town Hall Club on West Forty-Third Street, a coed organization for "people of cultural interests" built by women suffragists in 1921.[1] "I like the Town Hall Club because it is for interesting men and women who have interesting things to keep them busy," wrote a member in the club newsletter.[2] Guthrie Barber also had been invited but was ensconced at his camp in the Adirondacks. When the Bennetts arrived at the Town Hall Club, it was "cocktails all around," wrote Jackson in his diary, noting that then a "game of 'You Ask Me' got underway and the Bennetts and I went to the Demings for the rest of evening."

Julia and Don also dined with Herbert and Pete Stursberg. Pete had just returned from a spring break trip to the Diamond W before heading back to Yale for the end of his senior year. This was the final time Julia would travel to New York for a booking trip. Thanks to the Diamond W, "one ranch booked the other, and I have had a very fine group of people," she said. Like Jackson, many became her friends for life.

❖

Marge and Pete also had fallen in love with Tucson, and they soon would return—as a married couple. On June 30, 1937, just nine days

24. Marjorie and Julia Bennett with their horses in 1937,
the year Marjorie married Pete Stursberg. Stursberg 1937
scrapbook, Sherry Merica Pepper private collection.

after Pete's college graduation, they tied the knot in the chapel of
St. Bernard's Episcopal Church, a turn-of-the-century Gothic stone
edifice nestled in the woods of Bernardsville, New Jersey, not far from
the Stursberg family's imposing summer estate. The nuptials received
a brief mention in the Butte, Montana, newspaper, which noted
that the wedding was the culmination of "a dude-ranch romance."[3]
Although Pete's aunt, sister Babs, and Yale friend Charles Miller
and his wife attended, Julia did not—she was tending to her guests
at the Diamond J.[4]

Chapter 51

Did I say . . . that her energy was of the quiet kind. Well . . . that still goes double . . . but it's also an endless, ceaseless, limitless energy.

—Betty Cass, Diamond J guest, writing about Julia Bennett
in the *Wisconsin State Journal*, August 17, 1939

They called Julia Bennett "Boss." Not just her employees—her guests too. And they also called her "GoGo," because she was always on the go, forever encouraging everyone to join in the fun. Julia rose at five every morning to start the daily chores, along with the rest of her crew. She'd go to bed after everyone else. She could outwork anyone. And she never complained.

Betty Cass, a journalist from Wisconsin who stayed at the Diamond J over several summers, had this to say about Julia's stamina:

Yesterday, after overseeing her ranch, with 35 horses, five cowboys, 20 dudes, a herd of cows, she rode the 15 miles into the mountains and back with us . . . and then danced until 3 o'clock in the morning. And she was the most popular girl at the dance. While some of the prettiest young girls in the place sat out dances against the wall, there were always two or three males . . . all the way from 19-year-old cowboys to grey-haired ranchers, waiting to dance with Mrs. Bennett . . . and she was the least-tired one in the crowd when we arrived back at the ranch at daybreak.[1]

"Everyone was a little in love with her," said Julia's granddaughter. "She loved them, and they knew they were loved."[2] She was discreet, and she never complained.

"There's just one rule on this ranch," Julia told her new dudes when they arrived. "Do as you please . . . and we'll help you do it."[3]

Julia's guests said she made them feel at home—no matter who they were. The famed *Chicago Tribune* cartoonist Carey Orr, a regular at both the Diamond J and Diamond W, drew a cartoon that playfully expressed Julia's personality. He's stretched out on a chaise longue while six versions of Julia encircle him, pulling on his arms and legs and saying, "Let's GO to Nogales! Let's GO see the Indian writings! Let's GO to Guaymas! Let's GO to Phoenix! Let's GO to the rodeo! Let's GO to Mt. Lemmon!"[4]

Orr inscribed the piece, "To 'GO! GO!' from 'NO! NO!' in appreciation of another wonderful vacation."

Many guests relished the fact that if they chose, they could do nothing but bask in the beautiful surroundings. Betty Cass wrote of the Diamond J,

> Once more I'm in one of those choice places in this old world which is all silence and serenity except for wind-in-the-pines and the song of a mountain stream. Now and then I hear a cricket singing outside my cabin, as I write I can hear the far-off tinkle of cow bells as Buck, one of the cowboys, drives the milk cows home from the hills. That is all. The ranch house and the other cabins are too far away to hear their quiet, leisurely sounds. . . .
>
> Beginning at our back doors, too, are the tall lodge pole pines and the Douglas firs which cover the mountains. . . . and in which the wind sighs softly day and night. Down from the mountains and across one end of the meadow runs Jack creek, the singer.[5]

Julia's main goal was to make sure all her guests had fun. They could ride horses up into the mountains, bringing along sandwiches and napping at midday on a bed of pine needles along Jack Creek. At night they could join Julia as she led guests in sing-alongs around the campfire. She even published a songbook with the lyrics to more than one hundred tunes, including "Home on the Range" and "Oh! Susanna." One of her 1937 guests, a musician named Gene Quaw, who had written "Yellowstone," the park's theme song, rewrote its lyrics in tribute to Julia. He penned these altered lyrics, along with the notes of the tune, in her guest book:[6]

"Diamond J," "Diamond J,"
That's the ranch where ev'ry-body likes to stay;
Skies of blue, friends so true;
In the west you find the best at "Diamond J."

He added this note: "A mountain symphony of beautiful scenery, sunlit days and starlit nights, good food, and good cheer, and warmth of hospitality that is as fine as it is sincere. . . . You have given me the happiest vacation of my life. I shall never forget it."

When Julia led guests to her camp high in the Spanish Peaks, she loved to sit by the campfire and tell stories from her early years. The trip took about seven hours along a steep and rugged trail, and once guests reached the destination, they would stay for two or three days. A professional photographer sometimes tagged along to document the journey. Wrangler Art Smith, a retired forest ranger, stayed there for six weeks each summer to keep it in shape. She always kept some supplies on hand, storing pots and pans under rocks, and supervised the packing of the food. She knew exactly how she wanted it packed, in boxes that were carried up by the horses. "Packing those boxes was an art," said her granddaughter. "Then, you had to take bed rolls."[7] All were balanced on the horses and secured with a diamond hitch.

Julia was insistent that the camp be comfortable for the dudes, who were used to expecting the best. One was Eddie Hastings, general manager of the luxurious Waldorf Astoria hotel in New York City; he presented her with a Waldorf Astoria chef's toque, which she loved to wear while she cooked. Julia cooked all the meals, which included cakes she baked over the fire in a dutch oven. After a long day at the camp, she would put on her flannel nightgown, slather her face with cold cream, and turn in on a custom-made feather mattress that had been lugged up the mountain by a packhorse.

Julia was renowned for her themed barn dances at the end of every summer, which she had hosted every year since 1932. She invited hundreds of people—ranch guests, neighbors, friends, even celebrities. In 1936 her friend Della Williams—Myrna Loy's mother—

25. Julia Bennett serving supper to Diamond J guests, undated.
She sports the chef's hat given to her by Eddie Hastings, manager
of New York's Waldorf Astoria hotel. Photograph by Chris
Schlechten. Sherry Merica Pepper private collection.

"made a special trip from Hollywood," according to one newspaper, to attend the Diamond J's Spanish-fiesta-themed dance "held during the full moon of August."[8] The Butte newspaper covered a 1939 event, reporting that several hundred guests gathered in the barn's hayloft, "where a canopy of balloons gave a colorful glow and stately pine trees formed a background." The guests danced from 9:00 p.m. to 3:00 a.m. to music by a Bozeman orchestra and sustained themselves with sandwiches, pickles, cake, and coffee served at midnight. Some of the guests "dressed in clever movie star costumes, as was the hostess who represented Aunt March of 'Little Women' fame."[9] At the Diamond W in 1937, Julia hosted an afternoon barbecue for more than two hundred people that included both a cowboy orchestra and a Mexican orchestra.[10]

Although Julia told her help that "the guest is always right," she also held her guests to high standards.[11] Like her father, she followed the Golden Rule. She didn't tolerate rudeness, meanness, or disrespect. At the Diamond J, when a neighbor girl reported that an adolescent guest had said something lewd, Julia insisted that the young man apologize. One couple brought their mentally disabled adult daughter with them to the Diamond W, and a few guests complained. "Well, pack your bags, then," she told the complainers. A wealthy woman from Butte demanded that she be served breakfast in bed. Julia told her she would take her meals in the lodge, along with all of the other guests.[12] And when a man described by a fellow guest as a "good-looking ne'er-do-well" offered to pay Julia $1,000 to sleep with nineteen-year-old Marge, she blew her top.[13]

There were contradictions, however. The Diamond J's brochure included the words "clientele restricted." The Diamond W's was even more specific: "The Diamond W Ranch accepts Gentiles only and does not accept any guests with communicable diseases." Before World War II—and often after—many U.S. country clubs, social organizations, and dude ranches did not welcome Jews. However, Julia didn't enforce the restrictions printed in her brochures. A Jewish

26. Charlie Anceney, owner of the Flying D Ranch, and Julia Bennett, circa early 1930s. Julia Bennett scrapbook, Sherry Merica Pepper private collection.

couple from New York and their young son were three of the earliest guests at the Diamond J, returning year after year. Julia later hired their son as a wrangler. And when some guests at the Diamond W asked her to tell some Jewish guests to leave, she told them she would not. "She was nonjudgmental, which people sensed," her granddaughter remembered.[14]

Julia treated everyone, including her employees, with respect, although she did set high standards for those who worked for her. "I never saw her jump on somebody and yell at them or flail at them in any way. . . . When she told you to do something, you did it," remembered Frank Seitz, who spent time at the Diamond J as a young boy.[15] One of Julia's chore boys, Jack Mayo, told her granddaughter, "We all loved that woman—she was like everybody's mom."[16]

Discretion was key—and not only in Julia's professional life. Her love life was a well-kept secret. She had a few love affairs after her divorce. One was with M. S. Cunningham, a partner with the Butler brothers in the Rising Sun Ranch. But the most important seemed to be with her friend Charlie Anceney after the death of his wife in

1931.[17] A photo of Charlie and Julia lying in the grass at the Diamond J, both of their eyes glistening with happiness, clearly illustrates the depth of their relationship.

Sadly, their romance would be short-lived. In January 1936 Anceney, still actively managing his ranch at age seventy-two, was injured in a near-head-on auto accident south of Bozeman.[18] A doctor told a newspaper that "he is given a good chance to recover because of his rugged constitution and good health," but he died one month later.[19] Julia, tending to her guests in Arizona, was unable to attend his funeral.

When friends asked her why she didn't get remarried, she told them, "I've been looked at, thought about, and passed over."[20] Her granddaughter believed, however, that she was "very independent and not inclined to be married."[21]

Chapter 52

The typical western ranch takes the tired children of the world
to its arms and rocks them to deep and refreshing sleep. By
sunlit trails it takes them to beauty spots reflecting nature's
majesties, whether they are dudes or ultra sophisticates.

—*Great Falls Tribune*, November 24, 1929

In October 1937 Julia loaded up a truck full of blankets, tack, bed
linens, and rugs and—along with two wranglers from the Diamond
J whom she had hired for the winter season—embarked on the four-
day drive to Tucson. The wranglers, Buck Cheney and Arthur
Dusenberry—"wonderful boys," she called them—helped her turn
the Diamond W's four-thousand-year-old Native American doghouse
into a two-bedroom guest cottage. She also hired the late Charlie
Anceney's son, Charlie Jr., as a "guest wrangler."

The team built two cottages for the staff, each with three bedrooms
and a bath. Young Margaret Westinghouse's schoolhouse became an
apartment that Julia named Sunset. Two buildings far from the main
house also became cottages; she dubbed them Faraway and Demijohn.
Now she had six guest cottages—along with the rooms in the main
house—that could accommodate forty guests altogether.

She placed an ad for the Diamond W, which she billed as "the
former Westinghouse ranch," in a local newspaper: "This guest ranch
offers all the comforts and conveniences of a fine house. . . . All buildings have heat and electricity . . . excellent beds . . . beautifully furnished . . . and food of the best quality. . . . Rates are $50.00 to $70.00
weekly but include all ranch activities, food, lodging, horses, etc. An
ideal place for rest, recreation and health."[1]

The season started on November 1. By mid-December, all the
rooms were occupied.

A promoter for the Santa Fe Railroad told New York radio listeners about the possibilities for fun on an Arizona dude ranch. "If not too far from the pueblo country, everybody piles into the ranch cars and goes off to the terraced towns for native fiestas and dance days," she reported. Horseback riding also was an option, along with hunting. "At night the headlights of your car pick up the glaring eyeballs of coyote or bobcat. Even if you want a mountain lion, a strange taste occasionally manifested by visitors, there are lion guides and trained lion dogs that go after their quarry with the same certainty as the Mounted Police. Also, even bear hunting, if you want it."[2]

Julia offered all those options. Her promotional brochure outlined the possibilities: "A fine string of horses and experienced cowboys wait to accompany you on beautiful rides through miles of open country on mesa, through desert, mountain trails and canyons. Pack trips and hunting parties may be arranged if desired. . . . Wonderful motor trips include Grand Canyon, Old Mexico, Prehistoric Indian Ruins, and famous old Spanish Missions. Guests also enjoy tennis, ping-pong, target range, croquet, moonlight picnics, and barbecues or resting and relaxing on the spacious sun-decks, in the land where it is 'June in January.'"

A brochure photo featured three women in bathing suits lounging on cots on a sundeck—one with a leg coyly kicked in the air—while a man wearing a three-piece suit sits between them in a chair, reading a book.

If they desired more than sunbathing, Julia jumped at the opportunity to take guests hunting for quail and wild turkey, antelope jackrabbit, coyote, deer, bear, and even mountain lion. She also would lead groups—sometimes up to twenty-five at a time—on bobcat hunts. Dell Mercer, a friend who owned hounds, would catch wildcats and truck them into the desert, where he would release them and—after giving them a head start—let loose the hounds. "We would have a wild ride," Julia said, but "we never killed the cats."

27. Diamond W Ranch brochure cover, undated. Julia Bennett
scrapbook, Sherry Merica Pepper private collection.

She also relished creating games in the desert, where guests pre-
tending to be Pony Express riders would try to pass a sack containing
$50 without having it stolen by a "bandit." If the bandit nabbed the
bag, he or she would try to escape the "sheriff." One such game ended
in a dispute over whether the bandit had succeeded. To determine
the winner, Julia decided to lead thirty-five guests to supper on a
mountain, where two guests—both New York lawyers—argued the
case. The bandit was declared the winner.

One winter, she drove some guests to the Mogollon Rim, north of
Phoenix, to hunt mountain lions with the same dogs. "We chased the
lions over forty miles and camped in a cow camp with the cowboy. I

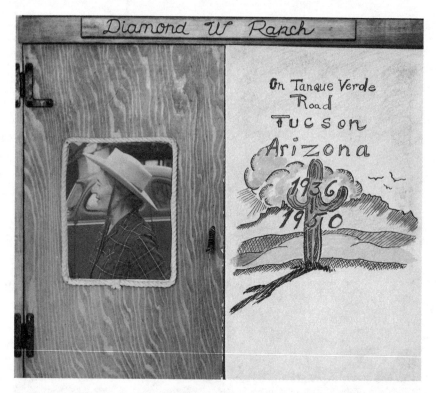

28. The cover of one of Julia Bennett's Diamond W scrapbooks, decorated by her son-in-law Pete Stursberg. Sherry Merica Pepper private collection.

cooked," Julia remembered. She loved nothing better. If guests liked to fish, Julia would offer to take them south of the border, to Guaymas, Mexico, to angle for marlin in the Gulf of California.

About once a month, when the moon was full, she led her guests on an evening picnic to nearby Saguaro National Monument. Some people rode single file along the equestrian trails; others who weren't up to the ride came in a station wagon.

No matter the transportation, the guests were enthralled: "Pack up your duds and don't waste another minute! At last I've found out what people mean when they say, 'This is the life!'" one unnamed Diamond W guest gushed in an article that the local paper published every year in its annual rodeo edition. "Round up your children and your dogs and join us post-haste at the Diamond W," she wrote. "Brain-trusters, bricklayers, social butterflies or highbrows all owe themselves a periodic dose of relaxation. The Diamond W is the best place to get it because here fun and health march hand in hand."[3]

The fun included a five o'clock cocktail hour served in the ranch house's living room or on the sundeck—to which the guests brought along their favorite liquor. Julia joined them but never drank to excess (she smoked, too, but didn't inhale).[4]

Planning parties was one of Julia's specialties—she hosted an "outdoor roundup" Easter breakfast; dances featuring local bands (including one called the Rhythm Rangers); and a Gay Nineties New Year's Eve party, with ranch staff dressed as "gamblers, prospectors, bartenders, barmaids, and dance-hall girls," where Julia served her guests smoked venison shipped from the Diamond J.[5]

❋

Julia's year-round business now had established a successful routine, with her sister, Diddy, along with Lee Smith and a few other long-time ranch hands, maintaining the Diamond J in the winter while Julia was running her Arizona operation. And when it was time for her to return to Montana at the beginning of June to prepare for her summer guests, Marge and Pete stayed behind as caretakers at the Diamond W. On June 22, 1938, Marge gave birth to her first child there—a son, Peter. Julia left the Diamond J in the hands of staff and headed to Arizona to meet her first grandchild. She also would be on hand that December, when Don's wife, Vi, also delivered a son, named Marshall, in Tucson.

Chapter 53

Mrs. Bennett is small and plump, with grown children and greying
hair, but her face is as smooth and unlined as a girl's, her laugh is
as merry, though quiet, and her spirit is as shining as her eyes.

—Betty Cass, Diamond J guest, *Wisconsin State Journal*, August 17, 1939

Never one to sit still, Julia hatched a new business in the fall of 1939—a
store on South Sixth Avenue in downtown Tucson called the Stable.
The shop, which she designed herself, carried a clothing line of her
creation, called Diamond Hitch Ranch Clothes.

Her timing was right. Western outfits were all the rage; even New
York's chic Bonwit Teller was promoting a dude ranch clothing line.
A fashion columnist told female readers they'd be "tops" on a dude
ranch vacation if they wore an "ensemble" of wide-legged trousers
and a fringed suede jacket. "A bold plaid flannel shirt will brighten it
up, and to keep the sun out of your eyes you will wear a felt sombrero
with punch holes for air."[1]

The newspaper ad for the Diamond Hitch brand assured the western authenticity of Julia's clothing: "Made by ranchers—for ranchers
and their guests. Ready made or made to your measure." A Tucson
newspaper found the Stable to be "a delightful experience, with its
rough board stalls and feed bins (in which are found rolls of beautiful color denims), its row of saddles, and, perching on high, a wise
old owl."[2]

Julia hired a few local women to sew the designs, which included
"tailored denim suits, nifty little zipper fastening vests ideal for wear
with frontier pants, smart sport dresses and slacks." She gave each
piece a name, as well (Lady Denim and Durability were two).[3]

Julia thought the shop might provide a productive outlet for Marge.

But at about the same time it opened, Marge gave birth to her second child, a daughter named Sherry. With two young ones under the age of two, Marge had neither the time nor the inclination to oversee the shop, and Julia's new venture lasted less than a year.[4]

❧

Meanwhile, much like Julia's former husband, her son-in-law, Pete Stursberg, could not seem to find what he wanted—although, unlike Anson, he had a substantial trust fund to keep him afloat. In January 1939, after the birth of his son, he started, at the age of twenty-six, what he called "my first enterprise in the field of business." The venture was a community auction center he opened with a friend in Tucson.[5] The first day did not go well. The pair had hoped to attract potential cattle buyers, but only three horses were put up for sale, along with "a good deal of odds and ends." Those "odds and ends" included some of Julia's guns, along with other items from the Diamond W belonging to the Westinghouse family, that Pete had taken without her knowledge.[6] The auction lasted just thirty minutes. Pete and his partner continued promoting the weekly sales, noting in their newspaper ads that they'd accept anything "from a pin to a battleship."[7] Dropping the unsuccessful plan for the auction center after several months, Pete then decided to enter the real estate business. In June, whether from his inheritance or from his work earnings, he paid off an $800 loan from Unk. In July Pete started a mail-order cartooning class, hoping to parlay his artistic talents into a career. That fall, he began working at the Diamond W but was none too successful. Once, he picked up a guest at the train station, brought her to the ranch, and then drove to Mexico on a drunken bender, taking her luggage with him.[8]

He invested $600 in an Arizona tungsten mine and gave Julia $500 to help fund Diamond Hitch Ranch Clothes. And in December he gave Julia's longtime ranch hand "Irish" Frank McRedmond $100 to head to the Diamond J to build a summer cabin for his growing family. They wouldn't end up living in it for long.

Chapter 54

Strange as it may seem, of 35 names drawn
from the jury-box, nine were women.

—*Townsend Star*, January 18, 1940

Just ten days before Marge delivered her daughter in Tucson, the first murder in Broadwater County, Montana, in twenty-two years came to pass. In the early morning hours of Sunday, October 1, 1939, thirty-eight-year-old James T. Olary, a 240-pound Nevada tractor driver working on an irrigation dam project in Toston, was shot in the chest near the Brown Brothers lumberyard.[1]

A few hours later Deputy Sheriff Boyce Robbins showed up at the house of Julia's brother Jim and arrested him for murder. Robbins led him off to jail at once, telling a reporter that, according to eyewitnesses, the shooting was "the climax of an argument."[2] Three days later, Jim officially was charged with first-degree murder.[3]

The *Townsend Star* reported that the incident occurred after a night of "making the 'joints' and mingling in the festivities of a Saturday night out." Jim, now the owner of a Toston butcher shop, had been seen at several local beer halls with twenty-one-year-old Dick O'Hearn Jr., the son of a friend.

"The story as we get it runs something like this," the *Star* reported. "It seems that words passed between O'Hearn, Bembrick and Olary and a slight fistic encounter ensued."

Olary reportedly followed Jim and Dick as they moved to another saloon, saying, "I want to talk to you fellows," and then trailed them to the lumberyard. "Bembrick, who was standing with both hands behind his back, suddenly fired, hitting Olary, and as Olary fell, he said, 'you didn't need to do that, I only wanted to talk to you.'" Three witnesses claimed that Bembrick fired the shot.[4]

Jim was charged with first-degree murder and held in the Townsend jail without bond. Two weeks later he pleaded not guilty. His trial would be the first murder case tried in the county since 1911.[5] The county attorney announced that he would seek the death penalty.[6]

Jim hired Montana's former attorney general and U.S. attorney Wellington D. Rankin to represent him. A prominent Republican, Rankin had managed the congressional campaign of his sister Jeannette, the first woman ever to be elected to the U.S. Congress.[7] As a young lawyer, Rankin also had served as the defense attorney in Broadwater County's 1911 murder trial, winning his client's acquittal.[8] Pete Stursberg sent Jim a $100 check—probably to help cover what must have been Rankin's hefty legal fees.[9]

On Monday, January 15, 1940, jury selection began in district court. Sixty-two people—including the first twenty women ever to be called as potential jurors in a Montana murder trial—were interviewed. None of the women were seated. "The jury now sitting includes men who are young and some who have white heads," reported the *Star*. "For the most part they are middle aged."[10]

Rancher Dan Sullivan of Townsend was one of those who received a summons for jury duty. Many years later he recalled, "I didn't want to sit on the jury because the guy [Bembrick] was as guilty as could be, you know, and when the judge said 'You're excused,' that's just what I wanted. . . . The guy was so goddam cold-blooded . . . murderer, you know." He added, "Everybody who was in a tight place got Rankin. He could sure influence a jury."[11]

On January 16 the trial got underway during a winter snowstorm with subzero temperatures.[12] Jim walked into the courtroom followed by his wife, Sayde; his brother, Ben; Diddy; and Julia, "who had come from her Dude ranch [in] Arizona," reported the *Townsend Star*. "Large crowds have been packing the spacious court room of the courthouse interested in the first criminal case in six years and the first murder trial in almost 20 years," the newspaper noted.[13] In fact, the weeklong trial made the front page of newspapers throughout central Montana.

Broadwater County Attorney Frank Hooks presented the state's evidence, "declaring that eye witnesses to the killing would testify that Bembrick shot down Olary without warning."[14]

A married woman who was witness to the murder and who reportedly had been on the dance floor with Olary "drunk and kissing and embracing" was called to the stand, where Rankin "cross-examined her intensely." Rankin argued that Bembrick killed Olary in self-defense and "to protect a life-long friend" and that Olary had punched both men.[15] Rankin also called Jim's brother, Ben, to the stand to testify that he saw Olary hit them.[16] Undersheriff George Kieckbusch, meanwhile, testified that officers had sent Olary's fingerprints to the FBI, which discovered that Olary (using a pseudonym) had served six months in a Bakersfield, California, prison for writing fake checks. In 1938, using yet another pseudonym, Las Vegas police had arrested him for drunkenness.[17]

Dick O'Hearn, who also "admitted having imbibed heavily of intoxicating liquor, and remembered part of what happened," testified that as he and Jim walked into the saloon, they "accidentally collided" with Olary. O'Hearn claimed that Olary then struck him "on the side of the head while I was turned away from him."[18] He added that he and Bembrick left the bar and that during the rest of the evening, "whenever Olary came into sight," O'Hearn ran away and "tried every way possible to avoid any trouble."[19]

When Douglas Pease, the fourteenth defense witness, took the stand, the county attorney asked him to describe how Olary approached Bembrick. Pease "appeared at a loss for words," so Hooks asked him to demonstrate. He did, punching the county attorney in the face—twice.[20] District Judge George W. Padbury Jr. promptly fined Pease $10 for contempt and called for a recess.[21]

"Bembrick, a small man, 54 years old, has not yet taken the stand," reported the newspaper. "He sits quietly watching the proceedings and listening. Sometimes he appears a little nervous."[22]

When Jim finally did testify, he spoke "in a low but clear voice." He told the jury that he and Sayde had gone to bed early that Saturday.

They were awakened in the middle of the night by a local beer parlor owner who told him that a man who had ordered meat from Jim was leaving town. If the man owed him money, he said, Jim should come into town to collect it. Jim testified he had done just that and then ran into O'Hearn, and Olary later assaulted them. He also testified that twice he had told Olary to "stand back," before shooting, adding that he had been on his way to tell the sheriff about the shooting when he heard another shot and decided to go home instead.[23]

Early in the evening of January 18, the case went to the jury, following Wellington Rankin's three-and-a-half-hour final argument. The judge's instructions included a reminder of Montana's liberal law concerning self-defense, which stated that if the jury had "reasonable grounds for believing [Bembrick] was in danger of receiving great bodily harm at the hand of Olary, then Jim Bembrick was justified in shooting to protect himself," and they then "must acquit him."[24]

The jury deliberated for seventeen hours before reaching its verdict: not guilty. "The two words that gave Mr. Bembrick his freedom were read at 9:27 and a few minutes later the news was flashed by radio across the nation," noted the *Star*.[25]

"During all those grilling days Mr. Bembrick and his wife and close relatives sat calmly under the strain," the article continued. "When the verdict was read the defendant's face lighted up and every muscle in his face reflected his feeling of gratitude. . . . Mrs. Bembrick received the news at her hotel where she was waiting with other relatives."

When Jim died in October 1965, his obituary noted, "He gained a reputation as an excellent shot."[26] But it made no mention of the murder trial.

Chapter 55

The devotion of thought to an honest achievement makes
the achievement possible. Exceptions only confirm this rule,
proving that failure is occasioned by a too feeble faith.

—Mary Baker Eddy, *Science and Health with Key to the Scriptures*

In 1940 the nation's economy was slowly creeping out of the decade-
long Great Depression. But the unemployment rate, while dropping,
still stood at nearly 15 percent. And the United States watched anx-
iously as Adolf Hitler was continuing his blitzkrieg across western
Europe.

Closer to home, although "the dude season and income was good,"
Julia Bennett was in debt to the tune of more than $20,000. She had
spent more than $8,000 to expand the capacity of the Diamond W
to thirty-five guests, which had increased income but drained her
bank accounts.[1]

At the end of June 1940, Herbert Stursberg—this time joined by his
nephew and Julia's son-in-law, Pete—offered relief. They purchased
the Diamond W from George and Violet Westinghouse for $45,000
and a few weeks later established the Diamond Ranches Corporation,
which also included the Diamond J.[2] The articles of incorporation
stated that its purposes were to "acquire, own, hold, operate and
dispose of ranches and ranching property," as well as a laundry list
of other activities, including farming, stock raising, and lumbering;
buying, selling, and owning houses, inns, restaurants, and mines; and
buying and selling stocks and bonds. Julia was listed as president of
the corporation, while Pete held the titles of both vice president and
treasurer.[3] Both would receive a salary of $150 per month, but Pete
and Herbert would be the majority stockholders. As part of the deal,
Julia signed over to the corporation her two bank accounts in Bozeman

and Tucson; her Ford station wagon, pickup truck, and sedan; and all her horses, furniture, and ranch equipment. However, she made it a point to keep for herself her saddle and riding equipment.[4]

There was another component of the deal: Herbert Stursberg would have to approve any proposal to borrow money or to make any capital expenses of more than $1,000.[5] With the agreement of the Westinghouses, who held the mortgage, they sold one hundred acres of Diamond W land to Albert Morrill, president of the Kroger Grocery and Baking Company in Cincinnati, for $7,500. He had been a guest there earlier that year.[6]

Now things were starting to look up. Recommendations from satisfied guests, along with positive publicity, had made both ranches vacation destinations not only for the wealthy but also for celebrities. That summer, the famed ventriloquist Edgar Bergen, whose *Chase and Sanborn Program* was then the top-rated radio show in the nation, stopped at the Diamond J as he made a cross-country trip to pick up his new Stinson airplane.[7] He drew a cartoon of his monocle-wearing dummy, Charlie McCarthy, in the ranch guest book and, upon his return home, shipped Pete a Confederate army uniform to wear at the annual barn dance, which that year had an Old South theme.

Norwegian Else Hall, the nineteen-year-old daughter of world-famous Metropolitan Opera singer Kirsten Flagstad, had come for a stay at the Diamond W in the winter of 1939. Else was described in a newspaper article "as sophisticated and smart as a page from Vogue . . . the idol of all the cowboys in the county."[8] One cowboy, Julia's former wrangler (and now the ranch accountant) Arthur Dusenberry, caught Else's eye as well. The following summer, she married him in Bozeman.[9] Another ranch marriage would take place later that year. In October Diddy, now sixty-three, married Julia's longtime ranch hand and hunting partner Lee Smith, who was eleven years her junior.

❖

Right when many guests were becoming regulars at Julia's two ranches and finances were starting to get back on track, the outside world

29. Popular entertainer and ventriloquist Edgar Bergen, a guest
at the Diamond J in 1940, riding with Julia Bennett. Stursberg
1940 scrapbook, Sherry Merica Pepper private collection.

intruded. On December 7, 1941, the Japanese attacked Pearl Harbor, and suddenly, America was at war.

A few days earlier, Tucson's municipal airport had been renamed Davis-Monthan Army Air Field and became the site of training for U.S. Army Air Corps bomber crews. Sugar rationing went into effect throughout the nation in May 1942, with each person limited to one pound every two weeks.[10] Automobiles and tires also were tightly rationed. The women's section of the *Arizona Republic* tried to put a positive spin on the state of affairs. An article titled "War Simplifies Women's Lives" pointed out, "One thing we women have learned from the national defense program is how easy it is to get along without some of the things we used to figure were absolute essentials."[11]

Members of the Southern Arizona Dude Ranchers Association, concerned whether guests would visit during the winter of 1942–43, discussed converting their ranches to housing for the families of army officers stationed at nearby air bases.[12] They didn't need to worry. In December 1942 the association reported that despite gas rationing, the occupancy rate of dude ranches in the area stood at 60 percent— even higher than the previous year. But rumors were rampant. One rumor alleged that "the government had taken over all guest ranches in the area." The head of the association denied that claim, saying, "Not a single dude ranch has been taken over by the government."[13]

Times were tough, however. Julia sold chickens to help make ends meet.[14] A laundry sued her for not paying a bill. Rationing put a crimp in meal planning, but she tried to keep her guests' minds off the war. She took them on horseback rides to Sabino Canyon. She planned countless parties, including one called Upside Down Day, in which the guests took on the roles of staff. The female guests cooked, washed dishes, waited tables, made beds, emptied wastebaskets, dusted, shopped for supplies, and did the books, while the men fed the livestock, collected the mail and garbage, and took their "guests" on a desert horseback ride. "The very eventful day came to a close with a good poker game, and guests and staff decided that the day should become an annual event," reported a Tucson newspaper.[15]

Julia proved she even knew how to make work fun (and perhaps give herself a break at the same time).

She loved taking the reins in annual rodeo parades in both Arizona and Montana. Four burros pulled her covered wagon, which carried the names of the Diamond W and the Diamond J.[16] In Tucson the Diamond W dudes dressed up as cowboys and Indians and rode in a horse-drawn wagon draped with an American flag. Julia's Old West float won first prize in 1941.

Tucson was a popular Hollywood filmmaking location. Some ranch guests were hired as extras in the Paramount musical *Riding High*, the story of a burlesque queen who takes a job as an entertainer at "an exclusive guest ranch."[17] Marge was hired to ride a horse in Paramount's *Incendiary Blonde*, starring Betty Hutton.[18] And true to her style, Julia won the award for Best Cowgirl Costume at MGM's world premiere of the movie *Let Freedom Ring* at Tucson's Fox Theater in February 1939, portions of which had been filmed in the city.[19]

Now nearing sixty, Julia continued her constant whirlwind of activity. In 1942 she was the only woman to serve as an executive director of the Southern Arizona Dude Ranchers Association. That same year, she also chaired its committee for the town's annual La Fiesta de los Vaqueros Rodeo Parade and took her guests to fashion shows and a Tucson charity ball—all while running both ranches.

Chapter 56

A fire on a ranch, far from firefighting equipment, is a terrible thing.
—Undersheriff John Higgins, *Tucson Daily Citizen*, February 24, 1943

The weather was clear and balmy in Tucson on the evening of February 23, 1943. A few hours before midnight, guests at the Desert Willow Ranch, about a half mile north of the Diamond W, spotted flames shooting into the sky. They called the sheriff's office in Tucson to report that the Diamond W was ablaze. The sheriff told them he could do nothing since the ranch was located outside the area of his authority.

At the ranch, Pete was scrambling. He had discovered the fire, which was spreading rapidly through the annex that housed the dining room, kitchen, and pantry. The blaze was approaching the thin walls that separated those rooms from the main house.

Pete began throwing buckets of sand on the flames and slamming doors and windows. He telephoned the Tucson Fire Department, which also told him there was nothing it could do because the Diamond W was outside its service area. Then, according to newspaper accounts, both he and the sheriff's office telephoned the Davis-Monthan Air Base, about ten miles south of the Diamond W, hoping that military firefighters could come to the rescue. Its fire crew arrived about fifteen minutes later, "plough[ing] through fence and cacti to string 1,150 feet of hose from [a] well to extinguish [the] blaze."[1] Pete told a reporter that it took them nearly six hours to finish the job, hindered by a lack of water pressure in the remote desert location.

The annex was destroyed. Along with its furnishings, Pete reported that the losses included a new icebox and the contents of the pantry, including a month's ration of coffee and sugar they had picked up from the ration board the day before. Pete also told the *Tucson Daily Citizen* that the damage stood between $7,000 and $10,000, an amount he later crossed out on the newspaper clipping he had pasted in his scrapbook and changed to between $10,000 and $15,000. But the good news was that the Diamond W was insured.

The day after the fire, Pete told a newspaper reporter that he had discovered the blaze. He said he thought it had started in the cellar after oil had leaked from a "faulty tank on the heater," spread to boxes on the floor, and "was ignited by soot dropping from the chimney."[2]

Reporters from two newspapers interviewed Pete and Undersheriff John Higgins. Their accounts differed. Pete's story was much more dramatic. He said he had first seen flames at about 8:30 p.m.; the undersheriff reported that he received the call from the Desert Willow nearly an hour and a half later. Higgins also said, "In about 30 minutes from the time the first call was received here at 10 p.m., the fire was under control."

Pete attached a photo in his scrapbook that showed Julia surveying the remains. Only one wall, a fireplace, and two chimneys were intact. "If the equipment from the field had not responded it is likely the whole place would have burned to the ground," Higgins told reporters.[3]

Pete concurred. "If it hadn't been for the Davis-Monthan firemen the ranch house would have been a complete loss," he said, adding that during the rebuilding, Diamond W guests would take their meals at a neighboring ranch, which he told the reporter was "a real neighborly act."

❖

Unbeknownst to Julia, this was not the first time Pete Stursberg had been near the scene of a mysterious blaze. Over the years, he had pasted into his scrapbook several newspaper clippings about fires of undetermined origin, all at locations near the Stursbergs' New Jersey summer estate. Ten years earlier, on April 30, 1933, a fire believed to have been started "by someone throwing a match down into the elevator shaft" had destroyed a landmark replica of a Japanese pagoda at a nearby estate. In late March 1935 the Bernardsville Fire Department had responded to eleven fire alarms in twelve days, including "a blaze of unknown origin at 1:30 a.m. Sunday morning [March 24] that destroyed an unoccupied cottage on the A. H. Stursberg estate."[4]

Did Pete's scrapbook clippings simply reflect a consuming interest in local fires, or was something more sinister involved? Arthur Dusenberry, one of Julia's longtime wranglers, had his own suspicions. "Your father burned down the Diamond W dining room," he told Pete's daughter many years later. "He was a pyromaniac."[5]

Interestingly, nearly thirty years earlier, Pete's older brother Laird had had his own experience with fire. In 1917, at the age of seven, Laird had used a cap gun to shoot at a window shade in the family's New York City mansion, setting the shade ablaze. The family servants extinguished the blaze but not before a fire brigade arrived and a reporter from the *Sun* and several hundred spectators gathered outside to watch. The newspaper crowed, "Fire Thrills Fifth Avenue."[6] Had young Pete also found the fire and resulting commotion thrilling?

Although Dusenberry fingered Pete, others—including Julia—clearly did not connect him with the blaze. Quite the contrary, he was heralded as a hero. Pete included a handwritten note by an unidentified woman in his scrapbook, hailing his actions at what she called the "ghastly" event: "Dear Pete, I do want to tell you again how *wonderful* you were the night of the fire. If it had not been for the marvelous work you did the whole house would have gone."

The story even managed to reach Chicago, where the *Tribune*'s society page reported, "Ranch life out at the Diamond W. is back to normal following a fire which damaged the ranch commissary. Resourceful Pete Stursberg, co-manager of the ranch, arranged improvised eating quarters for the guests for a time and now all is in order again." The article went on to list the names of prominent Chicagoans who spent their vacation at the Diamond W, including the British vice consul in Chicago.[7] Pete's classmates learned in the Yale newsletter that he had "been engaged in ranching since graduation," as vice president of the Diamond Ranches Corporation.[8]

There was no mention of Julia in any of these articles.

❊

Less than two months after the Diamond W fire, Pete's sister called him on April 10, 1943, to tell him that their brother Laird, who, at the age of thirty-four, was managing the family's Livingston Worsted Mill, had taken his life "while in a state of depression because of ill health," according to a local newspaper. He had shot himself in the right temple with a .22-caliber pistol in the closet of an upstairs room of his house, the grisly details described in the news account Pete preserved in his scrapbook.[9] Pete left immediately to travel to Massachusetts, where Laird had left behind a wife and three daughters.

Back in Arizona the following month, he successfully applied for a commission as a lieutenant JG in the U.S. Navy. A vice president at American Airlines in New York wrote his recommendation letter: "He is well educated and intelligent and of high moral character. Mr. Stursberg is exceedingly personable and he has been successful in relations with all kinds of people."[10]

Around that time, Pete also began having successful relations with a young widow named Florence Hartzell. He had met the twenty-three-year-old, blue-eyed blonde from Cincinnati in New York.[11] Her husband, Lawrence, a civilian flight student, had been killed in a midair collision of two planes over Miami in April of the previous year. At the time of his death, Florence and their two young children had been living in the wealthy enclave of Bryn Mawr, Pennsylvania, with Lawrence's mother, whom a Cincinnati newspaper described as "prominent socially."[12]

A connected friend supplied Pete with a 1940 Plymouth convertible, and in August 1943 he managed to wrangle a supplemental mileage ration so that he could drive back east. He stopped in Cincinnati (home of Florence Hartzell), where he stayed at the luxury Netherland Plaza Hotel (with Florence?), in Bryn Mawr (home of

Florence's mother), and in New York City, where he spent the night at the Waldorf Astoria.[13] Marge remained at the Diamond W with their children—Peter, now five, and Sherry, nearly four.

Upon Pete's return to the Diamond W, he walked into their bedroom, where Marge was sitting on the bed with their children and nanny, and announced that he wanted a divorce.[14] Marge was stunned. She divorced him in Montana the following month, citing "extreme cruelty."[15]

On November 12, 1943, Pete became one of four hundred or so student officers to graduate from the Naval Reserve Officers' Indoctrination School at the University of Arizona and was shipped off to service.[16] He married Florence a few months later in California. She divorced him in September 1946, also claiming "cruel treatment,"[17] stating in her divorce filing that he had hit her when he was intoxicated and hadn't stopped seeing Marge. Pete had, in fact, attempted to reconcile with Marge, but she refused.[18] In November 1946 Florence and Pete remarried.

❖

Despite his many transgressions (which included an alcohol problem so severe that he once got drunk on a bottle of vanilla from the Diamond J kitchen and passed out in the woodbin), Julia continued to have a soft spot for her former son-in-law. He visited his children frequently and bought his daughter horses and ponies.[19] "Every time we were around him, he was Santa Claus," said Sherry. "I adored him. He was always fun."[20] And perhaps Pete reminded Julia of her brothers, whom she loved deeply, flaws and all.

Chapter 57

To Julia—A real woman of the Golden West—
the truest and the finest I've ever known.

—Carey Orr, *Chicago Tribune* cartoonist, Diamond W
guest book, February 21, 1946

Hunting continued to be the thing that Julia looked most forward to in the world. Whether she was sleeping in a tent at her camp in the Spanish Peaks or on a bed of leaves in the Sierra Madre, being in the wilderness brought her joy.[1]

Although Julia loved to hunt big game, she also loved animals and played by the rules of hunting, unlike others. The Dude Ranchers Association quoted a letter it received from the Diamond J one November, probably written by Julia: "So glad hunting season is over. Doe season . . . was dreadful, killed does and little fawns—killed my burros right on the ranch."[2]

She took good care of her own animals, even buying cases of Sego condensed milk to feed the dozens of stray cats that roamed the Diamond J in the winter.

In her sixties, still running both ranches, Julia continued to plan rugged adventures. She told guests that if she could convince five people to join her, she would ride on horseback from the Diamond J to the Diamond W in the fall. It was not a trip for the faint of heart. The ten-week, 1,200-mile trip would include riding through the Grand Canyon. She apparently couldn't talk anyone into coming along, because she never went.[3]

She did, however, go on a jaguar hunt in Sonora, Mexico. (Julia called them tigers, appropriating the Spanish word for jaguar, *tigre*.) She was the only woman in the group of eight, joined by her hound-supplying friend Dell Mercer, young wrangler Charlie Anceney Jr., two Diamond W dudes, and two other men. The group rented a pack of burros from a local rancher who couldn't speak English but who knew how to make jaguar calls. He joined them on the hunt.

It was late April and very hot. "We trailed through beautiful country," Julia recalled. They camped in groves of wild palm, ate wild bananas, and encountered parrots large and small, along with "many snakes." Then they began to ride high into the Sierra Madres. On their first night in the wilderness after a long day of riding, they were "delighted" to come upon a large stream. They drank the water, went swimming, and set up camp. The next morning, they headed even higher into the rugged mountains. "We had only gone a little ways when we came on to an Indian village," wrote Julia. "They were washing clothes in the stream and swimming," and suddenly, her group "did not feel so good about the water" they'd quaffed the night before.

Although the encounter made them uneasy, they rode on and found a new campsite later that day. At night the moon was full, and the rancher walked out onto a high point with his horn to make jaguar mating calls. They heard the big cats respond with their own screeching calls and move closer to the camp. The next morning, the group directed their hounds to follow the cat tracks, which unexpectedly led them toward a camp of what Julia said were bandits. Quickly they turned and headed in the opposite direction, where they stumbled onto yet another camp deep in the wilderness. Julia described this one as populated by "very dangerous . . . wild Apachies" and "did not dare to ride near them." She may have been correct in identifying them as Apaches. There were, in fact, Chiricahua Apaches who had headed south decades earlier while escaping the U.S. Cavalry. They lived hidden in the Sierra Madres at least into the 1930s and perhaps later.[4]

Surrounded by what they believed to be danger, the hunters had nowhere to go but up—or else abandon their trip. They decided to head higher into the mountains and change their prey to wild pigs and turkeys. They could find no clear spot to set up camp, so they dined on crackers, cheese, and juice. The rancher made Julia and one of the men a bed by spreading a pair of chaps on the ground, which he covered with two feet of dry leaves. If past experience held true, Julia slept like a log.

❧

Throughout her life, Julia collected an assortment of rugged male friends. Another one of her pals, George Parker, frequently traveled to Africa to hunt big game. Like her father and her longtime friends Lee Smith and Tom Lincoln, she shared with them a love of hunting and the great outdoors.

An Arizona friend named Jim Converse was in many ways like Julia's brother Jim. Converse, a native Texan, had bought the nearby Tanque Verde Ranch in 1928, intending to herd the wild cattle that roamed the nearby mountains.[5] Converse's ranch hosted guests, too, but he frequently was away either on a hunt or, when he had too much to drink, raising hell. His wife tended to the dudes.[6] A friend described Jim as "generous, impulsive, playful, and possessed of a wild streak which made him at once attractive and a little danger-ous. He was his own man, caring little for society's impediments. . . . This included such activities as shooting targets from a moving car, shooting the numbers from a cash register in a hotel bar, and in one tragic incident, shooting too close to a friend's head."[7]

That description fails to reflect the severity of the "tragic incident." On the evening of September 29, 1945, Converse, fueled by wine and whiskey, stopped by what a newspaper called the "three-room, mud and cactus shack" of the family's laundress to pick up clothes. While there, he shot a twenty-seven-year-old ranch hand and father of seven in the forehead with a .22 automatic pistol, shattering his skull and killing him.[8]

Hearing about the shooting must have taken Julia back to about the same date six years earlier when her brother had been charged with murder. Like Jim Bembrick, Converse claimed the shooting was an accident. He testified that the victim, Francisco Romero, had walked into the house and loudly interrupted a conversation. Jim told the court that he only had intended to fire above Romero's head to quiet him down but that his gun had misfired. Unlike Jim, however, Converse had called the sheriff to report the shooting and waited outside to direct him to the house. He was charged with first-degree murder, and fellow local ranchers paid his $40,000 bail. In the time between the shooting and his trial, Jim was reelected to Tanque Verde's district school board and attended a meeting of the Southern Arizona Dude Ranchers' Association, of which he and Julia were both directors.[9]

After a first trial, in which the jury could not reach a verdict (and which included an attempt by his attorney to challenge "the legality of the whole jury panel . . . on the grounds that the Arizona constitution and common law are both violated by the presence of women on the panel"), Converse was convicted of manslaughter and sentenced to two to four years in prison.[10] After Converse had served only ten months and paid Romero's widow $7,000 to settle a wrongful death suit, the governor of Arizona commuted his sentence to time served, and he was released on Christmas Day 1946.

Converse and his wife, Katherine, divorced soon after. She was found dead in her apartment kitchen six months later of a gunshot wound, a revolver at her side. The coroner ruled her death a suicide.[11]

Chapter 58

The west's greatest charm lies in being just itself.

—*Great Falls Tribune*, November 24, 1929

At the age of sixty-seven, Julia, aka the Boss, was still full of energy. A visitor to the Diamond W wrote the following poem in her guest book in March 1947:

> Here's to the Boss—the best dancer in town
>   Oh Boy, what a thrill
> When she whirls around
>   Till some dam goon says
> Oh Jesus! *Let's sit down.*

Another frequent Diamond W guest, John Frey—a portly, cigar-smoking bachelor and American Federation of Labor executive from Washington DC—seemed to have been smitten with Julia. He penned long tributes in her guest book every time he visited. "You give your guests the gracious presence of a true pioneer woman of the Southwest and of Montana," he wrote in April 1947, "the courageous, self reliant hospitable woman who faced the problems of life without flinching, and because they enjoyed doing things for others, for their comfort and enjoyment, reaped a rich reward in the friends they made and kept. Without you the Diamond W would be only a name, with you it is a place where people enjoy to a greater extent than elsewhere the generous hospitality of the South west."[1]

More than one man even gave Julia and the Diamond W credit for restoring his health. A Portland visitor wrote in the 1948 guest book, "January 21st Arrived a Creeping Invalid / May 3rd Departed a Roaring Tiger." A couple who wrote a feature article for the *Phil-*

adelphia Inquirer about their stay at the Diamond J called Julia "a courageous, composed grandmother."[2]

The grandmother's grandchildren, who all called her Dudu, now were integral members of the ranch staff as well. Julia still led the charge, while Marge kept the books and helped with the guests. Don, an insurance agent, and his wife had returned to Bozeman with their son, Marshall, in the early 1940s. Marshall, along with Julia's other two grandchildren, Peter and Sherry, helped saddle up horses for the dudes and handled chores like mowing the lawn. Julia recruited them to scrub the log walls of every cabin before the ranch opened for the season.

Sherry also helped in the kitchen, waited tables, and washed dishes. One day, a wealthy woman from Butte showed up in the dining room, late for lunch. "Lunch is over," Sherry bluntly told her. Julia was not pleased with her granddaughter's response. She ordered Sherry to apologize. "Remember one thing," she said. "The dude is always right. Don't ever forget it.'"[3]

But Julia didn't always follow her own advice, depending on the guest. One difficult woman asked Sherry to bring breakfast to her cabin. Julia intercepted the tray of food, took it to the cabin, and told the dude, "Next time, if you want breakfast, you'll get it yourself."

＊

The financial burden of successfully running two ranches didn't diminish, and the Stursbergs were no longer her in-laws. So in October 1948, when Julia was sixty-eight, the Diamond Ranches Corporation sold the Diamond W for $200,000 to one of her former guests, J. D. Gardner, a Salt Lake City realtor, hotel owner, and former Wyoming sheep rancher.[4] Julia would continue to serve as its manager until the end of the 1950 season, after which Gardner sold it to the widow of famed race car driver Barney Oldfield, who planned to turn the ranch bungalows into "small kitchenette apartments for families."[5]

Six months after the sale of the Diamond W, the corporation turned the Diamond J back over to Julia. Finally, she once again owned the land she so loved, as well as everything that sat on it.[6]

Meanwhile, Julia's daughter's life was also in transition. In the fall of 1949 Marge walked into the ranch house at the Diamond W and informed her children that she had just married Jim Van Auken, one of Julia's wranglers. Peter and Sherry, not yet teenagers, were shocked by the news, as were Jim's family, devout Catholics who frowned on the marriage. Van Auken was seven years younger than Marge. He was remarkably similar, in many ways, to Pete Stursberg: handsome, five foot six, with dark hair and a broad smile. Like Pete, he, too, had served as a navy officer during World War II. Unlike Pete, he was a native westerner. His father had run a horse-breeding operation in Wyoming, and Jim, who attended the University of Notre Dame, had taken it over following his father's death in the 1930s. His sister worked at the Diamond W, and when Julia hired Jim, one of his jobs was to saddle horses for dudes every day but Sunday. He'd been working at the ranch for two years when he and Marge married.

Julia returned to the Diamond J to prepare for the season, and Sherry and Peter moved with their mother and new stepfather to a rented house across the road from the Diamond W. The marriage was rocky from the start. Jim and Marge were drinking heavily and fighting loudly. When she was in the seventh grade, Sherry called Julia in Montana. In addition to the constant conflict, Marge had made Sherry give away her beloved American paint horse.[7] "I can't stand it," Sherry told Julia, begging to come live with her at the Diamond J. Julia drove to Arizona to pick her up. Peter decided to stay in Scottsdale with his parents. But a year later, he changed his mind, and in addition to running the ranch, Julia now was the surrogate mother of two of her grandchildren. Sherry was thrilled. "Peter and I thought we'd died and gone to heaven."[8]

In the middle of winter at the Diamond J, Sherry and Peter rode to school the same way their grandmother had—pulled on a sled by horses—but this time, the sled ride ended when they reached the bus stop.

Chapter 59

Good thoughts are an impervious armor; clad therewith
you are completely shielded from the attacks of error
of every sort. And not only yourselves are safe, but all
whom your thoughts rest upon are thereby benefited.

—Mary Baker Eddy, *First Church of Christ, Scientist, and Miscellany*

Now that she no longer operated the Diamond W, Julia had more time to devote to her passion for hunting. Although she was in her seventies, her energy and stamina hadn't diminished. Her grandson Marshall, now out of high school, frequently joined her on hunting trips. A neighboring ranch owner called her "the best woman shot I ever saw in my life."[1]

One morning in the middle of winter, Julia and Marshall, along with Lee Smith, left the Diamond J around 6:00 a.m. The temperature stood at twenty-five below zero. The trio rode all morning and then stopped to build a fire and eat lunch. Later, as they tried to make their way through a thicket of downed timber, their horses became trapped. After hours of trying to work their way out, they managed to find a game trail well after dark. They didn't arrive back at the ranch until nine that night—fifteen hours after they had left. Marshall remembered being so exhausted that he couldn't hold his head up. Julia, on the other hand, built a fire in the ranch stove and cooked the three of them dinner.[2]

The Norwegian family of skier Sverre Engen lived on a small ranch across the road from the Diamond J—in fact, they had purchased a small parcel of land from her. Julia invited Engen to join one of her pack trips in the Spanish Peaks. "It was a sight to remember when the party returned after roughing it in the wilderness for a week or ten days," he wrote. "Julia's horse would be in the lead, with Julia sitting tall in the saddle, head up, back straight, never looking the least bit tired nor anywhere near her seventy-odd years."[3]

Her physical stamina also saved her from what could have been a debilitating accident. Once, when she got out of her pickup truck to open the gate at the Diamond J, she failed to set the brake. As it began to roll down an incline, one of its wheels ran over her leg, but she escaped unscathed.

Julia's hearing, however, was terrible. The first time Marshall rode with her on a trip to the Spanish Peaks, he shared her tent. He awoke in the middle of the night to the sounds of a bear raiding the garbage. He was terrified but couldn't manage to rouse her. "She slept like a log," he said. "She had a hearing aid, but she and the hearing aid didn't get along."[4]

Growing old didn't seem to bother Julia. "I don't think I ever heard her complain—she never talked about aging," said Sherry.[5] But inevitably, the ravages of age were catching up with the Bembrick siblings. On July 17, 1953, Julia's beloved sister, Diddy, died of ovarian cancer at her home in Bozeman at the age of seventy-seven. Her youngest brother, Ben, had also died of cancer in September 1947, at sixty-three.

❖

On October 6, three months after Diddy's death, the shrill strains of a fire siren blew through the town of Ennis. It was ten years after fire had threatened the Diamond W. Sherry was headed home on the school bus when she heard someone shout, "There's been a big fire at the Diamond J." As the bus approached the ranch, she couldn't see a thing—thick, black smoke obscured the canyon. Then she spotted the wooden farmhouse that Julia had first laid eyes on in 1929—the house that was now their home. All that remained was a scorched foundation.

The blaze apparently had started when Lee Smith, who continued working at the ranch after Diddy's death, lit the oilstove in the living room. Then he joined Julia and a few other ranch hands for lunch in the lodge. The heat of the stove ignited old newspapers and sawdust that had been stuffed behind the wall decades earlier as insulation. The fire smoldered unnoticed until it burst through the outside walls. When flames were finally spotted, the ranch hands and neighbors tried to extinguish it, but to no avail.

Everything was lost: all of Julia's and Sherry's clothes, attic trunks filled with family memorabilia, and Julia's Savage hunting rifle. The Virginia City newspaper noted, "Nothing was saved from the building but automobiles and other things which stood nearby."[6]

Left lying in the rubble were a delicate, white china mare and foal—a gift to Julia from two of her longtime employees—and a few silver dollars.

A longtime friend of Julia's said, "That's the only time I ever saw her depressed."[7]

Julia and Sherry moved into the tiny cabin Julia had named Mickey Mouse, and by June the hostess was once again ready to welcome summer guests to the Diamond J.

Chapter 60

The west, traditionally cheerful and carefree,
dodges self-analysis like a plague.

—Joseph Kinsey Howard, *Montana: High, Wide, and Handsome*

In 1957 Julia, now seventy-seven, and Sherry, sixteen, were back in Arizona, living in a rented house on Elm Street in Scottsdale. Peter was a freshman at his father's alma mater, Yale. Marge and Jim Van Auken's tumultuous eight-year marriage was falling apart, and Marge moved in with Julia and Sherry. On April Fool's Day, she filed for divorce. Two days later, Marge was quiet and despondent. Sherry saw her go into the bedroom and take a handful of sleeping pills. She ran to tell Julia, who found it difficult to believe. Sherry ran to the neighbor's house and asked them what to do. "Give her mustard and water," they replied, and then they called an ambulance.[1] When it arrived, Sherry rode with her mother to Good Samaritan Hospital, where Marge was pronounced dead on arrival at 7:30 p.m. She was forty-three years old.

Phoenix's daily newspaper, the *Arizona Republic*, provided its readers with all-too-graphic details: "Sheriff's Sergeant Lester Jones said his investigation revealed Mrs. Van Auken became despondent after a three-day divorce proceeding against her husband. . . . Jones said a nearly empty bottle of pills was found in the bedroom where Mrs. Van Auken was discovered."[2]

Marge had not inherited Julia's natural resilience. Sherry described her mother as "a different breed of cat. She was shy and quiet, and she was too damn pretty."[3] Marge's beauty had worked against her most of her life, bringing with it a special kind of insecurity.

Julia dealt with Marge's death the same way she had coped with previous tragedies. She soldiered on, buoyed and strengthened by her faith in and practice of Christian Science and, perhaps, by the words of its founder, Mary Baker Eddy: "Hold thought steadfastly to the enduring, the good, and the true, and you will bring these into your experience proportionately to their occupancy of your thoughts."[4]

Julia believed that the spirit is eternal and, no doubt, was comforted by that conviction as she came to terms with her daughter's death. She may have turned to Eddy's *Science and Health with Key to the Scriptures*, which posited, "There is no life, truth, intelligence, nor substance in matter. All is infinite Mind and its infinite manifestation, for God is All-in-all. Spirit is immortal Truth; matter is mortal error. Spirit is the real and eternal; matter is the unreal and temporal. Spirit is God, and man is His image and likeness. Therefore man is not material; he is spiritual."[5]

Julia wanted Marge to be buried in Bozeman, so she arranged for the casket to be shipped there by train. She and Sherry accompanied it, and when the train stopped at Union Station in Los Angeles, Julia treated her only granddaughter to lunch in the station's elegant two-story dining room.

Later that year, Julia turned over the day-to-day management of the Diamond J to a man named Elliott Redmond, who managed a ranch in Spokane, Washington.[6]

❖

The following years brought more grief. In August 1959 an earthquake measuring 7.1 on the Richter scale caused a mountain landslide near Ennis that killed twenty-nine people, most of whom were asleep at a campground. Two months later the Diamond J Ranch, which Julia had turned over to her son, Don, was sold to Virginia and Peter Combs, whose family continues to own it in 2021. In November 1959 Pete's Unk, Herbert Stursberg, died in Norwalk, Connecticut.

Julia's brother Jim died in October 1965. Her son, Don, was felled by a heart attack at the age of sixty-one on April 3, 1966—the exact date of her daughter's death nine years earlier. Seven months later Pete Stursberg died in Tucson on November 22, 1966, at the age of fifty-four. (His son, Peter, would die on the same day thirty-three years later, at age sixty-one.)

Julia now had outlived her parents, her brothers and sister, and her daughter and son. Still, she managed to maintain her optimistic outlook and made the best of things. Now in her eighties, she spent seasons that she would have resided at the Diamond J staying in a cabin near the ranch that she had given to Don and Vi. "She would hunt with Lee Smith. She just loved entertaining. On Halloween she would always have a costume party at the cabin. . . . Every holiday was a party," remembered Sherry.[7]

She spent the winters with Sherry, Sherry's husband, and their two young children at the Sun Ranch (formerly called the Rising Sun Ranch), which they tended—one of the ranches where Julia had cooked for Julius Butler's guests nearly fifty years earlier. Or she visited her grandson Peter, who was living in Puerto Rico.

Julia continued to ride. "I'm putting so much lead into the mountainsides that they'll be mining here soon if I don't quit hunting," Peter recalled her saying.[8] She shot her last elk on a trip with her hunting partner of more than four decades, Lee Smith, at the age of eighty-four.[9]

When she turned eighty-five, Julia's doctor told her that he had found a tumor and that she would have to have surgery. She called her Christian Science practitioner and asked her to pray for her. When Julia returned to the doctor, the growth had disappeared—a story remarkably similar to the one her mother had told her decades earlier about her father's tongue tumor.

Julia Bennett loved to reminisce about the good times: the thrill of the hunt, shaking the hand of a U.S. president, and the two ranches she built from scratch. She never talked about the bad times: losing two babies, divorcing her wayward husband, seeing her brother on trial for murder, and Marge's suicide. As her grandmother Lizzie Martin wrote in her own diary in 1867, "The human family have their troubles, and I am one who tastes it often." Yet these women did not let

30. Julia Bennett poses with her horse Apache at the entrance to the
Diamond J Ranch, circa 1936. Sherry Merica Pepper private collection.

impediments deter them. "You must move on" was Julia's mantra—a
spirit of resilience she inherited from her mother and grandmother.

A passage from Eddy's *The First Church of Christ, Scientist, and
Miscellany* was likely a continual comfort as Julia coped with these
tragedies: "Remember, thou canst be brought into no condition, be
it ever so severe, where Love has not been before thee and where its
tender lesson is not awaiting thee. Therefore despair not nor murmur,
for that which seeketh to save, to heal, and to deliver, will guide thee,
if thou seekest this guidance."[10]

"I never heard her say 'woe is me,'" her granddaughter, Sherry,
remembered. "Nothing stopped her. She cruised right through."[11]

Epilogue

By the time Julia reached the age of ninety-one, her heart was failing. She had outlived by more than forty years the prediction of a doctor who had told her she wouldn't live past the age of fifty because she had a bad heart. Sherry and her husband prepared to take Julia to the hospital a few weeks before she died. "Get my gun," she told her great-grandson, Tyler. "They're not taking me." She finally relented, and her grandson Marshall drove her to the hospital in Bozeman. At 2:30 in the afternoon on October 25, 1971, her heart finally stopped. "She was ready," said Sherry. "She never let us know what she had to put up with."

Julia Bennett was buried three days later, next to her daughter, in Bozeman's Sunset Hills Cemetery.

The prayer she taught her grandchildren had given her strength:

Now I lay me down to sleep,
I know that God my soul will keep.
I know that God my life is nigh.
I live in him and cannot die.
I can't be sick;
God is my strength,
Unfailing, quick.
God is my all;
I know no fear,
Since God, love, and truth are here.

Afterword

JAMES E. PEPPER

Through the foregoing pages, you have become acquainted with a number of extraordinary women. No doubt you were surprised when they seemed larger than life as they traveled the wild and uncharted territory of the American West, enduring unfathomable hardship, grieving untimely deaths, and encountering shiftless as well as charming and worthy menfolk.

We witness them carving out lives amid the brutality and sorrow of the Civil War, enduring the inhumanity of the frontier conquest and Indian wars, and confronting the misery and despair of the Great Depression, as well as the uncertainties of two world wars. In sharp contrast, we must also recognize the associated joy and laughter, challenges, creativity and accomplishment, and the satisfaction of their full and meaningful lives.

These were women in what was undeniably a man's world, particularly prevalent in the emerging American West, where women were few and far between. In overcoming centuries of male domination, these women had to be uncommonly vigilant and steadfast, as well as fiercely strong and self-reliant.

As a youngster in the early 1940s, I met Julia Bennett on several occasions when she would periodically visit her son and his family in Bozeman. Dudu, as she was widely and affectionately known, would dress her grandchildren Peter and Sherry in their "city" clothes and drive her woody station wagon from the Diamond J Ranch for a day of shopping, lunch at the Bacchus Pub in Hotel Baxter, visiting, and time for the children to play. It was my good fortune to live close to Don and Vi Bennett's home and to have their son, Marshall, as a neighborhood playmate. During one such visit, I vividly recall meeting Sherry—a real cutie dolled up in cowgirl attire, complete with boots and a calfskin vest. Little did I know that a half century later I would again meet up with her, this time at a Gallatin County High School reunion. On this retrospectively momentous occasion, she asked me to dance, and dance we did, cheek to cheek, just as Ginger Rogers and Fred Astaire had in the 1935 movie classic *Top Hat*. We married a year later!

In our subsequent twenty-six years together, the spirit of Julia Bennett has been our constant companion, as Dudu stories are a staple—indeed, the foundation—of my wife's repertoire of "the good old days." Before long, I knew more Dudu stories than I could count and increasingly felt like she had been an instrumental part of my own life story as well, although my own parents and immigrant grand-parents had compelling stories of their own.

In the process of this storytelling, I slowly came to the realization that I had, in fact, married into the hospitality industry; Sherry has never met a stranger, treating every new acquaintance as a long-lost friend, drawing out their life histories, and sharing hers. She also made certain they knew what to order off a menu at our favorite bistro; where to go for the best horseback trails, the most beautiful walks, and the best breed of dogs (Scottish terriers, of course); and how to properly break a horse. I thus have borne witness to the pro-found influence of Julia Bennett's character, capacities, values, and spiritual life on her granddaughter, as well via Sherry's spellbinding storytelling to an expansive and growing audience of friends, neigh-bors, and complete strangers.

It is not surprising, then, that Julia's grandson Peter published a book about her, *Your Dream Mentor: How Role Models Can Help*, describing how his grandmother had influenced him, propelled him to Yale University, and led to his success in business as well as life in general. Similarly, her grandson Marshall became a successful businessman who in his eightieth year still loves to tell stories about Julia's horses, associates, cooking, and bone-chilling winter hunting trips, clearly revealing the profound influence she had on him as well.

Fair-minded, gracious, fearless—Julia Bennett was clearly an out-sized personality, but one who consistently considered and treated all as her equal. She was known to be strong but not tough, steadfast and never rattled, feminine but not fussy, and straightforward but not pushy, with never a complaint or word of self-pity—all attributes of the iconic western woman. We should all be so fortunate as to live lives so worthy of being memorialized in print.

I am honored to be an extension of this continuing account of the trials and tribulations of these indomitable western women, particularly Julia Bennett; I trust that you are likewise. We have much to learn from making their acquaintance.

Acknowledgments

I first "met" the remarkable woman named Julia Bennett in 2011 during a phone conversation with my brother, Peter, who at the time lived in Bozeman, Montana.

"Sherry wants someone to write about her grandmother," Peter told me. I had met his friend Sherry Pepper on one of my trips out west—she's a ray of sunshine, an unbridled ball of energy. A talented horsewoman who has managed her own ranch as well as a ranch that raises polo horses, she's as comfortable on a saddle as she is walking down the street.

I was immediately intrigued. Unbeknownst to my brother, I was on the lookout for a new writing project.

"What did Sherry's grandmother do?"

"She was the first woman to own a dude ranch in Montana."

Being a midwestern city girl, I'm a romantic for the West. I never liked "Westerns" as a kid—those male-dominated stories marked by violence didn't appeal to me. But as a traveler at heart, I've always been captivated by the stories of pioneers who left their entire world behind, setting out blindly on a horse or in a covered wagon in search of a new way of life. And that is the story of the family who gave birth to Julia Bennett.

At the time I learned about Julia, I didn't know if there was enough information available to fill a book—but as it turned out, there was more than I could even imagine. In September 2011 my husband and I visited the Diamond J Ranch, which sits in an idyllic valley outside Ennis, Montana. It's now owned by members of the Combs family, who have operated it for more than fifty years. The cabins and lodge built by Julia and her crew in 1930 still stand, and much of the china and furniture she carefully selected nearly one hundred years ago is still in use today. Sherry also owns many family heirlooms, including the draft of a memoir dictated by Julia, photo albums, scrapbooks, and ranch guest books.

A grant from the Matthew Hansen Endowment of the University of Montana's Wilderness Foundation funded my initial research. Later, after many trips to Montana and Arizona and hundreds of hours spent searching online archives and visiting historical societies, courthouses, and museums, I realized that this was the story of not just one remarkable woman but three generations of them.

During my research I met many remarkably kind and helpful people who made it possible to tell this story. First and foremost, it could not have been written without family members Sherry Pepper, Molly Merica, and Marshall Bennett, who selflessly shared family stories, photo albums, scrapbooks, ranch guest books, and memorabilia. James Nave, the grandson of Errendle Nave, tracked me down after reading a magazine article I had written about Julia Bennett and became an invaluable resource, tour guide, and friend. Arian Nave, who has done extensive genealogical research on the Nave family, also generously shared his knowledge. Sherry's husband, Jim Pepper, a Montana native himself, offered to track down facts and research maps and provided useful insight on several topics. Ginger Combs, whose parents bought the Diamond J in the 1960s, led me on a tour of the ranch. Her brother, Bruce, a Bozeman attorney, helped interpret old legal documents. George Westinghouse IV, whose grandfather sold the Diamond W to Julia Bennett, was kind enough to respond to an email from me, a complete stranger, and shared family lore, photos, and diary entries, along with details from his father's flight log. Before he passed away, Alexander "Sandy" Bing offered memories of his time at the Diamond J as a child and later as a wrangler, and his daughter Virginia provided additional information. Relatives Bobbi Stutzman and Frank Seitz also shared stories from their youth.

I also owe a huge debt of gratitude to many cheerful and diligent archivists, public and university librarians, and courthouse clerks in Montana, Arizona, Colorado, Missouri, and Indianapolis. Special thanks to Elizabeth Barnett of the Madison County, Montana, Clerk's

Office, who went beyond the call of duty to search real estate records that revealed the details of Julia's Montana land holdings. Judy Donald at Choate Rosemary Hall provided photos of Pete Stursberg from the school's 1932 *Brief* yearbook. Rich Aarstad, Molly Kruckenberg, Zoe Ann Stoltz, and Natalie Waterman of the Montana Historical Society helped in the search for information about the Nave and Bembrick families and Lizzie Martin's diary. Linda Huth at the Broadwater County Museum, Carmen Clark at the Bozeman Public Library, Rachel Phillips at the Gallatin History Museum, Carolyn Marr at Seattle's Museum of History and Industry, Kim Allen Scott at the Montana State University Library, and Katie O'Connell from the Brooke Russell Astor Reading Room at the New York Public Library (which holds the diaries of William Henry Jackson) also were rich resources. The Arizona Historical Society provided details about the Westinghouse estate and the Diamond W, and the staff at the Circle Tree Ranch, which now owns the Diamond W property, kindly led me on a tour of the property.

Many newspapers that previously would not have been easily accessible were digitized and put online during the course of my research; newspapers.com, montananewspapers.org, and the Library of Congress website chroniclingamericaloc.gov were especially valuable.

Thanks also to my smart, steadfast, and patient husband, John Whalen, who read countless drafts of the manuscript and asked important questions. Friends and fellow writers Alicia Carlson, Becky Fitterling, Jan Guffin, Tom Harton, Andra Klemkosky, and Elizabeth Krajeck, along with my classmates and professors in the MFA program at Butler University, offered helpful suggestions. Voracious readers Cindy Munerol and Bonnie Simmons did the same. Authors and historians Eileen Janzen and Kathryn Lerch also offered their insight. Melinda MacAnally helped untangle the legalese in several documents, while her husband, David MacAnally, supplied me with historical railroad information. My brother, Peter Hendrickson, deserves all the credit for introducing me to Montana, his friend Sherry, and the story of

Julia Bennett. I also extend hearty thanks to his friends in the Treasure State who patiently answered my questions about locations, ranches, cattle, horses, vintage automobiles, and more.

I'm grateful for the new generation of historians and scholars who are beginning to tell the stories of the forgotten women who helped to settle and build the American West. Sherry Merica Pepper is carrying on their pioneering tradition and deserves a book of her own, but that's a story I'm saving for another day.

Notes

All unattributed quotes in this book are from Julia Bennett's unpublished memoir, written in the 1960s and part of Sherry Merica Pepper's private collection, or from Ruth Nave Duff's 1972 partial transcription of Lizzie Martin's 1867 diary, archived in the Nave Family Papers, 1865–1890, at the Montana Historical Society Research Center in Helena. Lizzie Martin's original diary has been lost.

Introduction

1. Annie Hanshew, "A 'Witty, Gritty Little Bobcat of a Woman': The Western Writings of Dorothy M. Johnson," *Montana Women's History* (blog), April 10, 2014, http://montanawomenshistory.org/a-witty-gritty-little-bobcat-of-a-woman -the-western-writings-of-dorothy-m-johnson.
2. "Novelist Visits Her Cody Home," *Billings* (MT) *Gazette*, February 15, 1928, https://www.newspapers.com/image/413316726/; see also Mary Shivers Culpin, "Caroline Lockhart Ranch, Bighorn Canyon National Recreation Area," unpublished draft, National Park Service, Rocky Mountain Regional Office, October 1981, https://web.archive.org/web/20120804124947/http://www .nps.gov/history/history/online_books/bica/caroline_lockhard_ranch.pdf.
3. Bruce Watson, "The Woman Who Said 'No' to War," *American Heritage* (blog), January 9, 2019, https://www.americanheritage.com/content/no-to-war.

Chapter 1

1. Adam Begley, "Side by Side," *New York Times*, September 27, 2009, https:// www.nytimes.com/2009/09/27/books/review/Begley-t.html.
2. Howard, *Montana*, 6.

Chapter 2

1. Eddy, *Christian Healing*, 10.
2. Advertisement in the *New Yorker*, May 18, 1929, https://archives.newyorker .com/newyorker/1929-05-18/flipbook/057/.
3. O'Neal, *Tex Ritter*, 19.

4. "For the Guild and Good Old Oklahoma," *New York Times*, March 1, 1931, https://timesmachine.nytimes.com/timesmachine/1931/03/01/118401151 .html?pageNumber=137.

5. "'Come Back, Cowboy, to Your Old Haunt,' Is Woman's Plaint," *Montana Standard* (Butte), March 22, 1932.

6. Marion Clyde McCarroll, "Dude Ranching Is Becoming a Profitable Profession, Says Julia A. Bennett, Who Runs One Out in Montana," *New York Evening Post*, April 18, 1931.

7. McCarroll, "Dude Ranching Is Becoming a Profitable Profession"; see also "Marion C. McCarroll, Ex-Columnist," *New York Times*, August 5, 1977, https://timesmachine.nytimes.com/timesmachine/1977/08/05/105375112 .html?pageNumber=24.

Chapter 3

1. Bell and Leeper bill of accounts, November 6, 1862, David R. Martin probate records, Livingston County Courthouse, Chillicothe MO.

2. Records are not consistent on the subject of Luly's age. Some show she was born on August 4, 1855, while others show she was born on August 4, 1856. The most reliable, the Nave family Bible, shows she was born in 1856, so I have chosen to use this date when calculating her age.

3. Margaret Butler transcription of deaths listed in Nave family Bible, n.d., 5. The family Bible indicates that David's death was at the age of "38 years, 11 months, and 18 days," which would be accurate relative to his date of birth.

4. "D. R. Martin Will," *Wills, Vol A-C, 1837–1890: Missouri, Wills and Probate Records, 1766–1988, Image 111*, https://www.ancestrylibrary.com/imageviewer /collections/9071/images/007631246_00111. Original data: Missouri, County, District, and Probate Courts.

5. *Missouri State Gazetteer and Business Directory*, 718.

6. George C. Rable, cited in Stiles, *Jesse James*, 23–24.

Chapter 4

1. Fellman, *Inside War*, 197.

2. Lieutenant A. J. Swan, "Statement of Melvin Gatheridge and Charges against James Nave of Livingston, Who Was in Poindexters Camp," August 28, 1862, Fold3, *Civil War Service Records* (CMSR)—*Confederate—Misc*, https://www .fold3.com/title/656/civil-war-service-records-cmsr-confederate-miscellaneous.

3. James Nave military records, database and images, Fold3, *Civil War Service Records* (CMSR)—*Confederate—Misc*, https://www.fold3.com/title/656/civil-war-service-records-cmsr-confederate-miscellaneous.

4. "Gratiot Street Prison," Civil War St. Louis, accessed August 21, 2020, http://www.civilwarstlouis.com/gratiot-street-prison/; see also Deb Houdek Rule, "Gratiot Street Prison: Then and Now," Civil War St. Louis, last updated June 7, 2013, http://www.civilwarstlouis.com/gratiot/gratiot-street-prison-then-and-now/.

5. "Union Provost Marshals' File of Papers Relating to Individual Citizens," October 31, 1864, F1305, Missouri State Archives.

6. The timing was fortuitous; in the winter of 1862 a smallpox epidemic broke out at the Alton Prison.

7. E. J. Crandall, "Hdqrs. Linn County Enrolled Missouri Militia, Brookfield," June 20, 1864, in "Linn County Civil War Reports," RootsWeb, accessed January 12, 2015, http://www.rootsweb.ancestry.com/~molinn/lccivil.html. The author of the *History of Caldwell and Livingston Counties* wrote, "The outrages perpetrated by certain of the militia stationed in this county may not be laid at the doors of the enrolled militia of Livingston, except in few cases. They were nearly always the work of men from other counties. Savage fighters there were among the Livingston men who did not make war a pastime, but there were the merest few who were murderers and robbers" (790).

8. *History of Caldwell and Livingston Counties*, 998.

9. Williams, *History of Northwest Missouri*, 545.

10. *History of Caldwell and Livingston Counties*, 991.

11. Fellman, *Inside War*, 6.

12. Although a family member wrote that Errendle Nave's daughter from a later marriage said that James Nave owned slaves, Nave's name does not appear on 1850 or 1860 U.S. Census schedules of slave owners in Livingston County, Missouri.

13. "Make Way for a Voice from Livingston County!" *Democratic Banner* (Pike County MO), July 30, 1849, https://chroniclingamerica.loc.gov/lccn/sn89066057/1849-07-30/ed-1/seq-1.

14. Fellman, *Inside War*, 5.

15. "Public Meeting," *Grand River Chronicle, Hannibal Journal and Union*, November 20, 1851.

16. *Missouri State Gazetteer and Business Directory*, 54.

17. *History of Caldwell and Livingston Counties*, 746.

18. *Organization and Status of Missouri Troops*, 239.

19. *History of Caldwell and Livingston Counties*, 991.

Chapter 5

1. *History of Caldwell and Livingston Counties*, 807. As the Civil War unfolded, the views of many Livingston County citizens evolved—or, at least, some claimed they did. "The only issue involved in the election of 1862 in Missouri was the question of emancipation," wrote the author. "Two years before, the advocate of emancipation did not reside in this county—at least he did not make himself known—but now the idea was seriously considered, and in many quarters was favorably considered.... The anti-emancipationists were slightly in the majority in this county. They opposed the agitation of the question of abolition in any form while the war lasted."

2. *History of Caldwell and Livingston Counties*, 37–42.

3. *History of Caldwell and Livingston Counties*, 792. By 1863 Jesse had become a Confederate recruiter and was imprisoned in a jail in Springfield, Missouri.

4. About 850 in the county served as Union soldiers. *History of Caldwell and Livingston Counties*, 804.

5. "Soldiers' Records: War of 1812—World War I, Nave, James" Missouri Digital Heritage, accessed January 17, 2015, https://s1.sos.mo.gov/records/archives/archivesdb/soldiers/.

6. "As told by Elsie Allinson"; Three Forks Area Historical Society, *Headwaters Heritage History*, 648.

7. "Escape of Prisoners," *Louisville Daily Democrat*, August 2, 1862.

8. Family lore says that Nave was once a member of Quantrill's Guerrillas of Missouri, but I could find no evidence to support that; handwritten report of memories by Elsie Nave Allinson, family collection.

9. Ronan and Baumler, *Girl from the Gulches*, 14. This incident took place in 1861, according to the book.

10. Fellman, *Inside War*, 73–74.

11. Fellman, *Inside War*, 74.

Chapter 6

1. Fellman, *Inside War*, 74.

2. "Pioneer Experiences Told at Meeting of Club Federation," *Townsend* (MT) *Star*, November 13, 1924.

3. Marcy, *Prairie Traveler*, 39.

4. Luchetti and Olwell, *Women of the West*, 141–42.

5. Marcy, *Prairie Traveler*, 24.

6. Marcy, *Prairie Traveler*, 24.

7. Ronan and Baumler, *Girl from the Gulches*, 9.

8. "Experiences at Meeting of Club Federation."

9. Ronan and Baumler, *Girl from the Gulches*, 15.

10. Lola Romine reminiscences, in Three Forks Area Historical Society, *Headwaters Heritage History*, 650.

11. "Experiences at Meeting of Club Federation."

12. Unruh, *Plains Across*, 386.

13. Ree Hester and Lola Romine, "The Nave Family," in *Pioneer Trails and Trials*, 837–38.

14. Unruh, *Plains Across*, 185.

15. [Ruth Nave Duff?], "Notes," n.d., Correspondence, NFP.

16. "Experiences at Meeting of Club Federation."

17. *History of Caldwell and Livingston Counties*, 964–67; see also "Shelton H. Brock (1837–1863)," RootsWeb, accessed May 15, 2015, http://freepages.genealogy .rootsweb.ancestry.com/~livcomo/roberts/shbrock.html.

Chapter 7

1. Marcy, *Prairie Traveler*, 23.

2. "Experiences at Meeting of Club Federation."

3. "Experiences at Meeting of Club Federation."

4. Charles D. Collins, *Atlas of the Sioux Wars*, 22.

5. Doyle, *Journeys to the Fields of Gold*, 4. John Bozeman successfully led a train to Virginia City in a second attempt during the summer of 1864.

6. "Experiences at Meeting of Club Federation."

7. "The Western Indians," *Rocky Mountain News Weekly* (Denver), April 9, 1863, 2.

8. "Experiences at Meeting of Club Federation."

Chapter 8

1. A few years earlier, L. C. Bishop and Paul Henderson, plotting the route of the Pony Express, had placed a marker at the site to aid the travelers in their journey.

2. Ronan and Baumler, *Girl from the Gulches*, xi.

3. "Union Provost Marshal's File of Papers Relating to Two or More Civilians," *Missouri's Union Provost Marshal Papers: 1861–1866*, reel number F1626, file number 13204, 740, accessed February 7, 2020, https://www.sos.mo.gov /cmsimages/Archives/Provost/f01626.pdf.

4. "Report of Lieut. Joseph M. Brown, Eighteenth Missouri Infantry," *United States Congressional Serial Set 2962* (Washington DC: U.S. Government Printing Office, 1891/92), 1031, https://babel.hathitrust.org/cgi/pt?id=hvd.hj1gww&view =1up&seq=1067.

5. *History of Linn County, Missouri*, 660.

6. Genealogical records, NFP. A transcription from another family Bible indicates that David's death was at the age of "38 years, 11 months, and 18 days," which would be accurate relative to his date of birth.

7. "Union Provost Marshal's File of Papers Relating to Two or More Civilians," 740.

Chapter 9

1. "Experiences at Meeting of Club Federation."

2. Originally named by its southern founders Varina, for the wife of Confederate president Jefferson Davis.

3. "Montana Emigration and Immigration," FamilySearch, accessed January 22, 2015, https://www.familysearch.org/wiki/en/Montana_Emigration_and_Immigration.

4. Federal Writers Project of the WPA, *WPA Guide to 1930s Montana*, 213.

5. Hosmer, *Montana*, 4.

6. Hosmer, *Montana*, 9.

7. Three Forks Area Historical Society, *Headwaters Heritage History*, 650.

8. *Pioneer Trails and Trials*, 837–38.

9. Langford, *Vigilante Days and Ways*, 185.

10. *Montana Post* (Virginia City), September 3, 1864, https://chroniclingamerica.loc.gov/lccn/sn83025293/1864-09-03/ed-1/seq-1/.

11. Rolle, *Road to Virginia City*, 77; see also Hosmer, *Montana*, 10.

Chapter 10

1. Hosmer, *Montana*, 17.

2. Hosmer, *Montana*, 17.

3. *Montana Post*, December 24, 1864, 3.

4. Hosmer, *Montana*, 9.

5. "Experiences at Meeting of Club Federation."

6. *Montana Post*, December 2, 1865, 2, https://chroniclingamerica.loc.gov/lccn/sn83025293/1865-12-02/ed-1/seq-2/.

7. Julia noted in her memoir that her mother was the "first white girl" to attend the school, although a class photo from the time does not seem to bear this out.

8. Eberstadt, *William Robertson Coe Collection of Western Americana*, 55.

9. A bill was introduced in the Montana Territory's legislature in 1867 to create a public school system. *Montana Post—Supplement*, November 16, 1867, https://chroniclingamerica.loc.gov/lccn/sn83025293/1867-11-16/ed-1/seq-9/; "Experiences at Meeting of Club Federation."

10. *Montana Post*, August 27, 1864, https://chroniclingamerica.loc.gov/lccn /sn83025293/1864-08-27/ed-1/seq-3/.

11. *Montana Post*, April 22, 1865, https://chroniclingamerica.loc.gov/lccn /sn83025293/1865-04-22/ed-1/seq-2/.

12. "Experiences at Meeting of Club Federation."

13. "Monetary," *Montana Post*, August 27, 1864, https://chroniclingamerica.loc .gov/lccn/sn83025293/1864-08-27/ed-1/seq-3/.

14. "Virginia City," *Montana Post*, August 27, 1864, https://chroniclingamerica.loc .gov/lccn/sn83025293/1864-08-27/ed-1/seq-3/.

15. "Experiences at Meeting of Club Federation."

16. Jacob Nave to Mollie Nave, October 16, 1865, NFP.

17. Jacob Nave to Mollie Nave, n.d., NFP.

Chapter 11

1. "Passenger Lists of Vessels Arriving at Philadelphia, Pennsylvania," *Records of the United States Customs Service, 1745–1997* (Washington DC: National Archives and Records Administration), record group number 36, series M425, roll 008, image 539, list number 178, https://www.ancestrylibrary.com /imageviewer/collections/8769/images/PAM425_8-0539 and https://search .ancestrylibrary.com/cgi-bin/sse.dll?indiv=1&dbid=7483&h=15751.

2. Maria gave birth to a final child, James, in 1831. "Frederick Benbrick," *Sixth Census of the United States, 1840*, Chariton, MO, Records of the Bureau of the Census, record group 29, National Archives (Washington DC: NARA), microfilm publication M704, roll 221, 309, https://www.ancestrylibrary.com/imageviewer /collections/8057/images/4409679_00631.

3. U.S. Department of the Interior, Bureau of Land Management, General Land Office Records, land titles, 1840 and 1848, https://glorecords.blm.gov /details/patent/default.aspx?accession=MO2760__.115&docClass=STA& sid=kcaivubw.ugh, and https://glorecords.blm.gov/details/patent/default.aspx ?accession=MO2970__.472&docClass=STA&sid=0bayreo5.tgs. This land is near the present-day town of Rothville.

4. Family lore has it that Ben left home at the age of twelve—a very good story, of course—but the U.S. Census and other records set his birth date as 1828.

5. *Glasgow* (MO) *Weekly Times*, October 5, 1848, https://chroniclingamerica.loc .gov/lccn/sn86063325/1848-10-05/ed-1/seq-3.

6. Stevens, *Journal of Rev. Benjamin Franklin Stevens*.

7. Milner and O'Connor, *As Big as the West*, 22.

8. Albert J. Galen, an associate justice of the Supreme Court of Montana, knew Doc Bembrick for more than forty years. He wrote that Doc "crossed the plains

from Kansas to the California gold fields in '49 and thereafter returned as far as St. Louis, Mo. on horseback, in 1853, consuming 67 days in making the trip." Albert J. Galen to David Hilger, May 18, 1925, NFP. See also "Golden Wedding Buffalo Hunter," *Powder River County Examiner* (Broadus MT), December 2, 1921, https://chroniclingamerica.loc.gov/lccn/sn84036256/1921-12-02/ed-1 /seq-7/.

9. Julia Bennett's report is consistent with Galen's, other than his age. She writes that he left for the gold fields at age twelve and returned out West again when he was sixteen.

10. Dodge, *Biographical Sketch of James Bridger*, 26.

11. Smiley, *History of Denver*, 171; see also Julia Bennett, memoir.

12. Smiley, *History of Denver*, 171.

13. Julia Bennett's memoir. The site is now within Yellowstone National Park. The Shoshone were also known as the Snake tribe.

14. Smiley, *History of Denver*, 162.

15. Smiley, *History of Denver*, 170.

16. Smiley, *History of Denver*, 209.

17. Smiley, *History of Denver*, 235.

18. City of Denver records show that on November 2, 1859, Ben Bembrick "bargained sold and put claimed" a fraction of lot 12, block 10, in Auraria City to John J. Riethmann, a baker and one of the first settlers in the area, and sold a "fraction of this lot to Luke Voorhees, same day." The 1866 *Business Directory of the City* showed that John J. Riethmann owned a bakery and confectionery located on Blake Street between E and F Streets in Denver; see Wilhelm, *Business Directory of the City*. Riethmann, one of the first settlers in the area, had built his first cabin "about October 27th or 28th, 1858," and his second in April 1859, but neither "was directly a part of the beginning of Denver," noted Smiley's *History of Denver*.

19. U.S. Department of the Interior, Bureau of Land Management, General Land Office Records, https://glorecords.blm.gov/details/patent/default.aspx?accession =0368-219&docClass=MW&sid=hufezyub.b1q#patentDetailsTabIndex=0.

20. Howard, *Montana*, 26.

21. *Powder River County Examiner*, December 2, 1921.

22. Golden City was founded in 1859 and named the state capital in 1862. Records show that Bembrick was the sixty-seventh person to cast a vote in Golden City's district 3, precinct 8, in the first Colorado territorial election, on August 19, 1861, https://history.denverlibrary.org/sites/history/files /Colorado1861TerritorialElection.pdf.

23. Galen to Hilger, May 18, 1925, NFP.

Chapter 12

1. *Montana Post*, August 27, 1864, https://chroniclingamerica.loc.gov/lccn/sn83025293/1864-08-27/ed-1/seq-3.
2. Three Forks Area Historical Society, *Headwaters Heritage History*, 650.
3. McClure, *Three Thousand Miles through the Rocky Mountains*.
4. *Montana Post*, December 24, 1864. By September of 1865 only twenty-two men, including James Nave and George Hale, were listed as voters in the Jefferson precinct, where Willow Creek was located.
5. McClure, *Three Thousand Miles through the Rocky Mountains*, 257.
6. "Willow Creek History," Headwaters Heritage Museum, http://www.tfhistory.org/history%20WC%2001.html.
7. Stanley, *Life of Rev. L. B. Stateler*, 190–91.
8. *Montana Post*, April 22, 1865, https://chroniclingamerica.loc.gov/lccn/sn83025293/1865-04-22/ed-1/seq-2/.
9. *Montana Post*, December 24, 1864.
10. *Montana Post*, August 27, 1864, https://chroniclingamerica.loc.gov/lccn/sn83025293/1864-08-27/ed-1/seq-4.
11. McClure, *Three Thousand Miles through the Rocky Mountains*, 282.

Chapter 13

1. "Experiences at Meeting of Club Federation."
2. Rover, "Prickly Pear Correspondence," *Montana Post*, April 22, 1865, https://chroniclingamerica.loc.gov/lccn/sn83025293/1865-04-22/ed-1/seq-1/; Gleaner, "From Last Chance," *Montana Post*, April 22, 1865, https://chroniclingamerica.loc.gov/lccn/sn83025293/1865-04-22/ed-1/seq-1/.
3. "Value of $1,000 from 1865 to 2020," CIP Inflation Calculator, https://www.officialdata.org/us/inflation/1865?amount=1000.
4. "Estate of Martin, David R., Deceased," no. 1790, David R. Martin probate records, Livingston County Courthouse, Chillicothe MO.
5. CHS, "A Trip through the New Mines," *Montana Post*, February 25, 1865, https://chroniclingamerica.loc.gov/lccn/sn83025293/1865-02-25/ed-1/seq-1/.
6. Nave family timeline, NFP.
7. Lucy Ann Nave and Lizzie Martin to parents, June 29, 1865, NFP.
8. Ronan and Baumler, *Girl from the Gulches*, 54.
9. "Experiences at Meeting of Club Federation."
10. Holmes, *Montana*, 104.
11. McClure, *Three Thousand Miles through the Rocky Mountains*, 285.
12. Ronan and Baumler, *Girl from the Gulches*, 54.

13. "Experiences at Meeting of Club Federation."

14. Lucy Ann Nave and Lizzie Martin to parents, June 29, 1865, NFP.

15. Hosmer, *Montana*, 18.

16. Lucy Nave and Lizzie Nave Martin to their parents, June 29, 1865, NFP.

17. According to the Society of Montana Pioneers, Enoch Wilson arrived in Virginia City on June 22, 1864, four days after the Naves.

18. Lucy Nave and Lizzie Nave Martin to their parents, June 29, 1865, NFP.

19. If Lucy accompanied them, Lizzie did not mention it; she already may have moved back to their parents' home.

20. Stoner, *Mammoth Springs and Plunket Lake*, 2. The journalist Alexander K. McClure may have stayed at the Naves' stage stop during his travels. He writes of a stagecoach trip through the valley where the Naves lived, describing a fifteen-mile journey through the foothills on a warm day, with no water available for either horses or passengers. "Finally we landed on Milton Creek," he wrote, "with clear, fresh water, and there we stopped to dine and rest. The inevitable Missourian was our host." McClure noted that his host's "photograph-album was not singular in that region for commencing with Jeff. Davis, following with General Price, and ending with Wilkes Booth." However, he continued, "We dined on our host's fresh vegetables and palatable bread and butter, rather than on his opinions, and got along very well."

21. "Experiences at Meeting of Club Federation."

Chapter 14

1. *Powder River County Examiner*, December 2, 1921.

2. "Stock-Raising in Montana," *Montana Post*, August 27, 1864, https://chroniclingamerica.loc.gov/lccn/sn83025293/1864-08-27/ed-1/seq-3/.

3. After six months, settlers had the option of buying the land for $1.25 per acre. Or after five years, they could "prove up" to show they had been good caretakers, pay a $10 filing fee, and be given a U.S. government land deed.

4. The U.S. government's 1868 plat map of the area shows Bembrick's cabin next to Crow Creek, identified as "Bunbrich's House."

5. McClure, *Three Thousand Miles through the Rocky Mountains*, 271.

6. Marshall Bennett, "Benjamin F. Bembrick's Knowledge of the Death of John Bozeman," John M. Bozeman Collection, 1866–1965, Merrill G. Burlingame Special Collections, Montana State University Library, Bozeman MT. Some historians now believe that Bozeman was murdered not by the Blackfeet but by Tom Cover.

7. Laura Gibson may have been the daughter of carpenter and farmer Nathan Gibson, who arrived in Virginia City from Indiana on February 9, 1863. By October 1865 the Virginia City post office was holding unclaimed letters in his

name. "Letter List," *Montana Post*, October 21, 1865, https://chroniclingamerica
.loc.gov/lccn/sn83025293/1865-10-21/ed-1/seq-2/.

8. "From Radersburg," *Montana Post*, April 25, 1868, https://chroniclingamerica
.loc.gov/lccn/sn83025293/1868-04-25/ed-1/seq-6/.

9. "The Crow Creek Mines," *Montana Post*, May 2, 1868, https://chronic
lingamerica.loc.gov/lccn/sn83025293/1868-05-02/ed-1/seq-5.

10. McClure, *Three Thousand Miles through the Rocky Mountains*, 283–84.

Chapter 15

1. Madison Lake is today called Ennis Lake.

2. "Woman Kills Bear," *Helena* (MT) *Daily Independent*, October 7, 1928, https://
www.newspapers.com/image/11733908/.

3. *Townsend Star*, May 21, 1925.

4. Although Julia Bennett identifies him only as "Mr. Murphy," he may have been
James H. "Rolls Royce" Murphy, who according to a November 3, 1922, article
in the *Chicago Tribune* was a "millionaire Board of Trade broker" and owner
of the J. H. Murphy Feed company of Chicago, https://www.newspapers.com
/image/355121338/.

5. "I went to Chicago later in February to book for the ranch" was the only reference to this trip in Julia's memoir.

6. "Dude Ranches Get Publicity," *Billings Gazette*, April 3, 1928, https://www
.newspapers.com/image/413249761.

7. The Northern Pacific Railroad served Bozeman, while the Milwaukee Railroad
served Gallatin Gateway.

8. William T. Dantz, "Theodore Roosevelt—Cowboy and Ranchman," *Harper's Weekly*, 1904, Theodore Roosevelt National Park, Theodore Roosevelt Digital Library, 474/644E, Dickinson State University, https://www
.theodorerooseveltcenter.org/Research/Digital-Library/Record?libID=o20444.

9. "Dude Ranch Is Removed," *Billings Weekly Gazette*, July 12, 1904, https://
www.newspapers.com/image/409274140/.

10. "History," Dude Ranchers Association, accessed February 6, 2020, https://
duderanch.org/history.

11. I. P. Larson, "The Evolution of the Dude Ranch Industry," *Montana Wildlife*,
February 1931.

12. "Coolidge Glad to Quit Office," *Montana Standard*, March 4, 1929, https://
www.newspapers.com/image/354607722/.

13. "Invitation Like Ticket to Heaven Says Schoolmam," *Montana Standard*, March
14, 1929, https://www.newspapers.com/image/354608437/.

14. Larson, "Evolution of the Dude Ranch Industry."

Chapter 16

1. Julia Bennett, memoir.
2. "Chick sale" is a slang term based on a vaudevillian and film star named Chic Sale, who told jokes about outhouses.
3. Jodi Hausen, "Fred Willson: A Modest Man Who Left a Big Mark," *Bozeman* (MT) *Daily Chronicle*, April 7, 2011, https://www.bozemandailychronicle .com/100/newsmakers/fred-willson-a-modest-man-who-left-a-big-mark/article _f30f2a9c-67b5-11e0-ba92-001cc4c002e0.html.
4. "Guest Cabins and Central Cabin, Diamond J Ranch," architectural drawings, January 30, 1930, and February 26, 1930, FWP.
5. See the U.S. Federal Census for the years 1900, 1910, 1920, 1930, in Madison and Gallatin Counties MT, https://www.ancestrylibrary.com/search/categories /usfedcen/.
6. Tom Lincoln to Julia Bennett, March 23, 1925, Sherry Merica Pepper private collection.

Chapter 17

1. In 1931 former millionaire James H. Murphy, who may have been the man Julia met, claimed to a judge that he had turned ownership of his company over to his son and his ex-wife and couldn't afford to repay the $925 he owed to a bank. See *Chicago Tribune*, November 7, 1931, https://www.newspapers.com/image /355152064/.
2. Minnie Paugh, "Dude Ranching on the Madison Started with Cunningham and Biering," draft manuscript, 8, MPRP.
3. Sherry Merica Pepper, in discussion with the author, June 21, 2012, Sonoita AZ.
4. Stursberg, *Your Dream Mentor*, 129.
5. Sherry Merica Pepper, in discussion with the author, June 24, 2012, Sonoita AZ.
6. "Bozeman Matron Dies When Car Goes through Ice," *Montana Standard*, January 2, 1931, https://www.newspapers.com/image/350768028/; see also the *Madisonian* (Virginia City MT), January 9, 1931.

Chapter 18

1. Northern Pacific advertisements for the North Coast Limited, 1930 and 1931.

Chapter 19

1. "Experiences at Meeting of Club Federation."
2. Carrie Adell Strahorn, *Fifteen-Thousand Miles by Stage*, xvi.

3. Langley, *San Francisco Directory*, 13.

4. Ross, *Resources of the Pacific Slope*, 273.

5. Ross, *Resources of the Pacific Slope*, 272.

6. Langley, *San Francisco Directory*, 14.

7. Langley, *San Francisco Directory*, 37.

8. Boardinghouses offered meals; lodging houses offered rooms only.

9. Ross, *Resources of the Pacific Slope*, 276.

10. Langley, *San Francisco Directory*, 1.

11. "News of the Morning," *Gold Hill Daily News*, October 11, 1866, https://cdnc
.ucr.edu/?a=d&d=SDU18661011.2.4.

12. "From Montana," *Sacramento Daily Union* (Nevada), August 11, 1866.

13. Advertisement, *Daily Alta California*, March 9, 1867, https://cdnc.ucr.edu/?a
=d&d=DAC18670309.2.24.7&srpos=21.

Chapter 20

1. William L. Lang, "James Cook (1728–1779)," *The Oregon Encyclopedia*, last
updated May 1, 2019, https://oregonencyclopedia.org/articles/cook_james/#
.XzwffS-ZNn4.

2. "Pacific Coast Correspondence," *Daily Alta California*, August 30, 1866, https://
cdnc.ucr.edu/?a=d&d=DAC18660830.

3. "Umatilla House," Historic The Dalles, accessed January 11, 2021, http://
historicthedalles.org/history/umatilla-house/.

4. Advertisement, *Walla Walla* (WA) *Statesman*, April 5, 1867, https://
chroniclingamerica.loc.gov/lccn/sn86072040/1867-04-05/ed-1/seq-1/.

5. Granville Stuart, "A Sketch," January 6, 1866, published in *Montana Post*, January 5, 1867, https://chroniclingamerica.loc.gov/lccn/sn83025293/1867-01
-05/ed-1/seq-4/.

6. *Idaho Tri-Weekly Statesman* (Boise), June 1, 1865; see also Larry R. Jones, "South
Boise Stage Lines," Idaho State Historical Society Reference Series, no. 465,
1983, 1, https://history.idaho.gov/wp-content/uploads/0465_South-Boise-Stage
-Lines.pdf.

7. Carrie Adell Strahorn, *Fifteen-Thousand Miles by Stage*, vii.

8. William A. Goulder, February 1877, quoted in Jones, "South Boise Stage Lines," 7.

9. Carrie Adell Strahorn, *Fifteen-Thousand Miles by Stage*, 291.

10. Howard, *Montana*, 47.

11. "Difference in Time," *Idaho World* (Idaho City), June 17, 1865, https://
chroniclingamerica.loc.gov/lccn/sn82015407/1865-06-17/ed-1/seq-2/.

12. "The Indian War," *Montana Post*, April 27, 1867, https://www.newspapers
.com/image/76888725/.

Chapter 21

1. "Indians," *Montana Democrat*, reprinted in *Walla Walla Statesman*, April 12, 1867, https://chroniclingamerica.loc.gov/lccn/sn86072040/1867-04-12/ed-1/seq-1/.
2. "The War Meeting," *Montana Post*, April 13, 1867, https://www.newspapers.com/image/76706068/.
3. "Indians."
4. "The Indian Movement," *Montana Post*, May 11, 1867, https://www.newspapers.com/image/76745350/.
5. "Indian Movement."
6. "Crow Creek Mines."
7. U.S. Federal Census, Radersburg, Jefferson, Montana Territory, 1870, roll M593_827; Family History Library film 552326, https://www.ancestrylibrary.com/search/collections/7163/.
8. *Daily Rocky Mountain Gazette* (Helena MT), November 1, 1871.
9. "Fort CF Smith Part 3 Abandonment," National Park Service, Bighorn Canyon, last updated February 24, 2015, http://www.nps.gov/bica/learn/historyculture/fort-cf-smith-part-3-abandonment.htm.

Chapter 22

1. Margaret Butler transcription of marriages listed in Nave family Bible, n.d., 4, NFP; see also "Enoch Wilson," Montana, County Marriages, 1865–1987, https://www.ancestrylibrary.com/imageviewer/collections/61578/images/48279_555431-00024.
2. "Estate of David R Martin rec'd in acct. with R. Matson Admn.," October 1867, David R. Martin probate records, Livingston County Courthouse, Chillicothe MO.
3. According to the 1870 U.S. Census records, the value of James Nave's personal estate was worth $11,725 (about $200,000 today)—substantially more than most other people in the area, with the exception of the Keating mine owners.
4. Jewell Peterson Wolk, quoted in "The Work Was Never Done: Farm and Ranch Wives and Mothers," *Montana Women's History Matters* (blog), July 17, 2014, http://montanawomenshistory.org/the-work-was-never-done-farm-and-ranch-wives-and-mothers/.
5. *Daily Rocky Mountain Gazette*, November 9, 1871.

Chapter 23

1. "How to Come," *New North-West* (Deer Lodge MT), April 8, 1870, https://www.newspapers.com/image/171620212/.

2. Harry, "A Visit to Radersburg," *New North-West*, September 30, 1871, https://www.newspapers.com/image/171927378/.

3. Lewis and Clark had noted its river when passing through the area in 1805.

4. *Pacific Coast Business Directory for 1867*, 353.

5. "The Lands on the Northern Pacific," *Times Herald* (Port Huron MI), May 13, 1874, https://www.newspapers.com/image/323841032/.

6. Federal Writers Project of the WPA, *WPA Guide to 1930s Montana*, 420.

7. Harlan Lucas, "Sentinel Rock," in *Yesteryears and Pioneers*, 325, https://mtmemory.org/digital/collection/p15018coll43/id/8089/rec/1. This rock, near the present-day town of Harlowton, was known as Bembrick Rock and then as Sentinel Rock.

8. Harry, "Visit to Radersburg."

9. Harry, "Visit to Radersburg."

10. John Dougherty mercantile store accounts book, 1876, Broadwater County Museum. For more on milk cows, see Howard, *Montana*, 143.

11. Dougherty mercantile store accounts book.

12. Leider, *Myrna Loy*, 9–11.

13. "Radersburg," *Bozeman* (MT) *Avant Courier*, August 8, 1872, https://www.newspapers.com/image/171825032/.

14. The estate was settled in 1874; see "Estate of David R. Martin dec'd.," June 4, 1874, David R. Martin probate records, Livingston County Courthouse, Chillicothe MO.

15. "Jefferson County Democratic Convention," *Bozeman Avant Courier*, August 1, 1873, https://www.newspapers.com/image/171959800.

16. "Notice to Miners," *Bozeman Avant Courier*, September 12, 1873, https://www.newspapers.com/image/171960825/.

17. *Daily Independent* (Helena MT), March 25, 1874.

18. *Helena* (MT) *Weekly Herald*, August 19, 1875, https://chroniclingamerica.loc.gov/lccn/sn84036143/1875-08-19/ed-1/seq-8/.

19. *Daily Independent*, March 22, 1874, https://www.newspapers.com/image/524687370/.

20. *Rocky Mountain Husbandman* (Diamond City MT), March 27, 1879, https://chroniclingamerica.loc.gov/lccn/sn83025309/1879-03-27/ed-1/seq-5.

21. "The Indians on Deep Creek," *Helena Weekly Herald*, August 5, 1875, https://chroniclingamerica.loc.gov/lccn/sn84036143/1875-08-05/ed-1/seq-8/.

22. "Indians on Deep Creek."

23. "Personal," *Helena Weekly Herald*, November 25, 1875, https://chroniclingamerica.loc.gov/lccn/sn84036143/1875-11-25/ed-1/seq-8/.

Chapter 24

1. "Editorial Correspondence," *Rocky Mountain Husbandman*, March 2, 1876, https://www.newspapers.com/image/167614833/.
2. "Jefferson County—Her Town and Mining Camps," *Helena Weekly Herald*, July 15, 1875, https://chroniclingamerica.loc.gov/lccn/sn84036143/1875-07-15/ed-1/seq-3/; "Radersburg Items," June 8, 1876, https://chroniclingamerica.loc.gov/lccn/sn84036143/1876-06-08/ed-1/seq-8/.
3. "Born," *Helena Weekly Herald*, June 15, 1876, https://chroniclingamerica.loc.gov/lccn/sn84036143/1876-06-08/ed-1/seq-7/; "In Radersburg, June 2d, 1876, to Mr. And Mrs. B. F. Bembrick, a daughter," *New North-West*, June 9, 1876.
4. "Indian War," *Helena Daily Independent*, July 6, 1876, reprinted from *Bozeman* (MT) *Times*, July 3, 1876, https://www.newspapers.com/image/11215614/.

Chapter 25

1. "Yellowstone Expedition," *Bozeman Avant Courier*, August 1, 1873, https://www.newspapers.com/image/171959800/.
2. Miller, *Adventures in Yellowstone*, 147.
3. Miller, *Adventures in Yellowstone*, 147.
4. Miller, *Adventures in Yellowstone*, 148.
5. The *Bozeman Avant Courier* and other newspapers, such as the *Butte Miner*, recounted a more lurid tale. "It was first decided upon to kill [Frank] Carpenter, who was tied to a tree to be shot," the *Miner* reported on September 4, 1877 (https://www.newspapers.com/image/354235311/). "Believing the last had come he made the sign of the cross as the final preparation for death, when the Indians, remembering the lessons of those who taught them that sign, released their prisoner and told him they would not hurt him if he would follow them without attempting to escape."
6. "More Murders," *Helena Daily Independent*, August 28, 1877, https://www.newspapers.com/image/18640407/.
7. "Tourists Killed," *Bozeman Avant Courier*, August 30, 1877, https://www.newspapers.com/image/343196206/.
8. "A Close Call," *Helena Daily Independent*, August 31, 1877, https://www.newspapers.com/image/18640760/, reprinted from *Bozeman Times*, August 30, 1877.
9. "Tourists Killed."
10. "Life with the Nez Perces," *New North-West*, September 14, 1877, https://www.newspapers.com/image/171820607/.
11. "The National Park Massacre," *Helena Daily Independent*, August 28, 1877, https://www.newspapers.com/image/18640407/.

12. Julia Bennett, memoir. Emma Cowan wrote in her reminiscences that she learned the news from "two acquaintances" who brought her a newspaper, but she did not mention their names.

Chapter 26

1. "The Dead Alive," *Bozeman Avant Courier*, September 6, 1877, https://www .newspapers.com/image/343196278/.
2. *Rocky Mountain Husbandman*, September 27, 1877, https://www.newspapers .com/image/167575089/.
3. Mrs. Geo. F. Cowan, "A Card of Thanks," *Bozeman Avant Courier*, September 20, 1877, https://www.newspapers.com/image/343196379/.

Chapter 27

1. *Helena Weekly Herald*, July 15, 1875.
2. *New North-West*, October 19, 1877, https://www.newspapers.com/image /171821859/. "The Butte *Miner* wishes to know why Musselshell is so frequently spelled Muscleshell. Because there is a good deal of muscle in Montana and mussels are very scarce. Let's all take a new start though and give the river its proper and correct name, Mussel Shell. It is shell-fish but bi-valves we can make it win."
3. *Rocky Mountain Husbandman*, June 6, 1878, https://www.newspapers.com /image/167421920/.
4. "The Grasshoppers," *Helena Daily Independent*, May 3, 1878, https://www .newspapers.com/image/22745691/.
5. "Grasshoppers."

Chapter 28

1. "Letter from Radersburg," *Helena Daily Independent*, May 29, 1880, https:// www.newspapers.com/image/525286859/.
2. "Death of James Nave," *Helena Daily Independent*, May 25, 1882, https://www .newspapers.com/image/11447990/.
3. "On the Road," *Helena Weekly Herald*, September 2, 1880, https://www .newspapers.com/image/343185896/.

Chapter 29

1. "Personals," *Helena Daily Independent*, August 5, 1881, https://www.newspapers .com/image/22749772/.

2. For more on the ferry acquisition, see "Poverty Flat Pencilings," *Helena Daily Independent*, March 30, 1882, https://www.newspapers.com/image/11443676/. For more on the Black Friday Mine acquisition, see U.S. Department of the Interior, Bureau of Land Management, General Land Office Records, https://glorecords.blm.gov/details/patent/default.aspx?accession=MTMTAA%20047395&docClass=SER&sid=zhge5ume.bxa.

3. "Where Cattle Is King," *Weekly Yellowstone Journal and Livestock Report*, July 22, 1882, https://www.newspapers.com/image/426141676/. Those named by the stock raiser were "the Northwestern company, Alfred Myers & Bro., Granville Stewart, Dr. Bembrick, Nelson Story and Hobson & Sweet." Earlier, cattle were sent east via the Dakota Territories or Wyoming and then through the Union Pacific Railroad. Later, the ranchers drove cattle 250 miles east to a railroad depot in Miles City.

4. Milner and O'Connor, *As Big as the West*, 263.

Chapter 30

1. "Doings in Helena," *Philipsburg* (MT) *Mail*, February 28, 1895, https://www.newspapers.com/image/50644561/.

2. "Christian Science," *Helena Daily Independent*, June 20, 1888, https://www.newspapers.com/image/523607579/.

3. As told to and recalled by Sherry Merica Pepper, in discussion with the author, June 22, 2012, Sonoita AZ. For a deeper explanation of Christian Science and its history, see Tony Lobl, "What's the History of Christian Science? How Christian Science Is Neither a Church nor a Denomination," New Statesman, February 13, 2007, https://www.newstatesman.com/blogs/the-faith-column/2007/02/christian-science-church.

4. "The History of Toston," *Townsend Star*, January 26, 1967.

Chapter 31

1. Hanshew, *Border to Border*, 92–93.

2. "The Great Northwest," *Anaconda* (MT) *Standard*, April 25, 1891, https://www.newspapers.com/image/354700535/.

3. "Local and Personal," *Townsend* (MT) *Messenger*, May 10, 1900, http://montananewspapers.org/lccn/sn84036075/1900-05-10/ed-1/seq-5/.

4. Free, *Progressive Cook Book*, 17.

5. "If the present rate of [bison] destruction is continued the race will be extinct within a few years," "The Buffalo," *Helena Weekly Herald*, September 1, 1881, https://www.newspapers.com/image/343161476/.

6. Sherry Merica Pepper, in discussion with the author, February 10, 2014, Sonoita AZ.

Chapter 32

1. A cutting horse is one trained to separate a cow from the herd.
2. "Radersburg Cemetery and Macomber Field Cemetery," Townsend Montana, http://www.townsendmt.com/wp-content/uploads/2019/01/BR -RADERSBURG.pdf; "Territorial News," *Rocky Mountain Husbandman*, July 1, 1880, https://www.newspapers.com/image/167614833/.
3. *Montana Advertising Directory*.
4. Sherry Merica Pepper, in discussion with the author, June 15, 2012, Sonoita AZ.

Chapter 33

1. "She leaves to-day on a tour of the territory and will endeavor to visit every farmer, stockgrower and fine stock breeder in Montana"; *Rocky Mountain Husbandman*, April 11, 1889.
2. "Notes by the Way," *Rocky Mountain Husbandman*, May 9, 1889.
3. Holley, *My Opinions and Betsey Bobbet's*, 237.
4. T. A. Larson, "Montana Women and the Battle for the Ballot," *Montana* 23, no. 1 (1973): 24–41, http://montanawomenshistory.org/wp-content/uploads/2013 /11/Larson-T.A.-Montana-Women-and-the-Battle-for-the-Ballot.pdf.
5. "The Suffrage Question," *Helena Daily Independent*, July 19, 1889, https:// www.newspapers.com/image/148149815/.
6. *Helena Daily Independent*, July 23, 1881, https://www.newspapers.com/image /22749030/.
7. "Radersburg Rays," *Townsend Tranchant*, November 28, 1888, http:// montananewspapers.org/lccn/sn85053289/1888-11-28/ed-1/seq-3/.
8. "Death of Mrs. Nave," *Townsend Tranchant*, July 11, 1888, http:// montananewspapers.org/lccn/sn85053289/1888-07-11/ed-1/seq-4/.
9. "Radersburg Rays," *Townsend Messenger*, September 21, 1894, http:// montananewspapers.org/lccn/sn84036075/1894-09-21/ed-1/seq-3/.
10. *Townsend Messenger*, December 7, 1894, http://montananewspapers.org/lccn /sn84036075/1894-12-07/ed-1/seq-5/.
11. *Townsend Messenger*, November 9, 1894, http://montananewspapers.org/lccn /sn84036075/1894-11-09/ed-1/seq-5/.
12. "Local and Personal," *Townsend Messenger*, October 12, 1894, http:// montananewspapers.org/lccn/sn84036075/1894-10-12/ed-1/seq-3/.
13. *Townsend Tranchant*, October 3, 1884, http://montananewspapers.org/lccn /sn85053289/1884-10-03/ed-1/seq-4/.
14. *Townsend Messenger*, November 9, 1886.
15. *Helena Weekly Herald*, November 14, 1889, https://chroniclingamerica.loc.gov /lccn/sn84036143/1889-11-14/ed-1/seq-4.

Chapter 34

1. "Ministerial Meekness," *Winston* (MT) *Prospector*, January 5, 1899, http://montananewspapers.org/lccn/sn85053012/1899-01-05/ed-1/seq-4/.

2. "Will Be Heard in This County," *Winston Prospector*, January 5, 1899, http://montananewspapers.org/lccn/sn85053012/1899-01-05/ed-1/seq-5/.

3. *Winston Prospector*, June 22, 1899, http://montananewspapers.org/lccn/sn85053012/1899-06-15/ed-1/seq-1/.

4. "No Bridge," *Townsend Messenger*, September 13, 1900, http://montananewspapers.org/lccn/sn84036075/1900-09-13/ed-1/seq-4/.

5. "The Local News," *Townsend Forum*, October 10, 1900, http://montananewspapers.org/lccn/sn84036076/1900-10-10/ed-1/seq-7/.

6. "Mortuary Record," *Daily Inter Mountain* (Butte MT), February 26, 1901, https://chroniclingamerica.loc.gov/lccn/sn85053057/1901-02-26/ed-1/seq-3/.

7. *Townsend Forum and Townsend Messenger*, March 6, 1901, http://montananewspapers.org/lccn/sn84036077/1901-03-06/ed-1/seq-3/.

8. "Death of Enoch Wilson," *Chillicothe Constitution*, February 10, 1902, https://www.newspapers.com/image/10170456/.

Chapter 35

1. Willard Bennett, *1900 United States Federal Census*, Radersburg, Broadwater MT, 16, https://www.ancestrylibrary.com/imageviewer/collections/7602/images/4120359_00194.

2. "Additional Locals," *Townsend Star*, November 29, 1902, http://montananewspapers.org/lccn/sn86075288/1902-11-29/ed-1/seq-2/; "Crow Creek," *Townsend Star*, December 6, 1902, http://montananewspapers.org/lccn/sn86075288/1902-12-06/ed-1/seq-2/.

3. "Toston Topics," *Townsend Star*, January 24, 1903, http://montananewspapers.org/lccn/sn86075288/1903-01-24/ed-1/seq-3/.

4. National Park Service, National History of Historic Places Registration Form, Toston Bridge, July 20, 2005, http://focus.nps.gov/nrhp/GetAsset?assetID=44ac9871-3e72-44af-be23-9d87e35bff6e.

5. "Toston," *Broadwater County Citizen* (Townsend MT), May 6, 1904, http://montananewspapers.org/lccn/sn85053283/1904-05-06/ed-1/seq-3/.

6. "Toston," *Townsend Star*, July 29, 1905, http://montananewspapers.org/lccn/sn86075288/1905-07-29/ed-1/seq-1/.

7. *Broadwater County Citizen*, May 6, 1904, 3.

8. "Toston," *Townsend Star*, October 28, 1905, http://montananewspapers.org/lccn/sn86075288/1905-10-28/ed-1/seq-4; "Toston," *Townsend Star*, December

23, 1905, http://montananewspapers.org/lccn/sn86075288/1905-12-23/ed
-1/seq-1/.

9. "Toston," *Townsend Star*, December 30, 1905, http://montananewspapers.org
/lccn/sn86075288/1905-12-30/ed-1/seq-4/.

Chapter 36

1. "Toston," *Townsend Star*, October 22, 1904, http://montananewspapers.org
/lccn/sn86075288/1904-10-22/ed-1/seq-4/.

2. Stoner, *Mammoth Springs and Plunket Lake*, 4; see also U.S. Department of the
Interior, Bureau of Land Management, General Land Office Records, Desert
Lands Certificate No. 632, May 12, 1905, https://glorecords.blm.gov/details/cdi
/default.aspx?doc_id=1182941&sid=cflef0dh.n5y#cdiDetailsTabIndex=1.

3. *Townsend Star*, May 11, 1907, http://montananewspapers.org/lccn/sn86075288
/1907-05-11/ed-1/seq-1/.

4. Bruce Bembrick Huntley, Montana, Birth Records, 1897–1988, https://
www.ancestrylibrary.com/imageviewer/collections/61591/images/48414
_302022005556_1199-00221.

5. "Toston," *Townsend Star*, February 25, 1905, http://montananewspapers.org
/lccn/sn86075288/1905-02-25/ed-1/seq-1/.

6. "Toston," *Townsend Star*, February 18, 1905, http://montananewspapers.org
/lccn/sn86075288/1905-02-18/ed-1/seq-1/.

7. "Toston," *Townsend Star*, March 4, 1905, http://montananewspapers.org/lccn
/sn86075288/1905-03-04/ed-1/seq-4/.

8. The Wilsons' neighbors were a Welshman named David Williams, his wife,
Ann, and their three young children. Their granddaughter Myrna, who later
would change her last name and become the movie star Myrna Loy, had not
yet been born.

9. "Our Advertisers," *Crow Creek Journal*, June 19, 1907, http://montananewspapers
.org/lccn/sn85053284/1907-06-19/ed-1/seq-1/.

10. "Largest Department Store in Broadwater County," *Townsend Star*, May 11, 1907,
http://montananewspapers.org/lccn/sn86075288/1907-05-11/ed-1/seq-12/.

11. "Of Local Interest," *Crow Creek Journal*, August 22, 1907, http://
montananewspapers.org/lccn/sn85053284/1907-08-22/ed-1/seq-3/.

12. "A Merry Crowd," *Crow Creek Journal*, September 5, 1907, http://
montananewspapers.org/lccn/sn85053284/1907-09-05/ed-1/seq-3/.

13. "Display of Good Marksmanship," *Crow Creek Journal*, September 12, 1907,
http://montananewspapers.org/lccn/sn85053284/1907-09-12/ed-1/seq-3/.

14. "Montana Mining," *Boston* (MA) *Evening Transcript*, September 2, 1911, https://news.google.com/newspapers?nid=sArNgO4T4MoC&dat=19110902&printsec=frontpage&hl=en.

15. *1910 United States Federal Census*, Toston, Broadwater MT, roll T624_829, Enumeration District 0005, FHL microfilm 1374842, https://www.ancestrylibrary.com/imageviewer/collections/7884/images/31111_4330776-00646.

16. "A Broadwater Tragedy," *River Press* (Fort Benton MT), October 27, 1909, https://chroniclingamerica.loc.gov/lccn/sn85053157/1909-10-27/ed-1/seq-3/.

17. *1910 United States Federal Census*.

18. "Toston Incorporation," *Broadwater Opinion* (Townsend MT), February 21, 1913, http://montananewspapers.org/lccn/sn85053286/1913-02-21/ed-1/seq-2/.

19. Sherry Merica Pepper, in discussion with the author, February 10, 2014, Sonoita AZ. The details are scarce, because Julia never discussed or recorded them.

20. "Toston Notes," *Townsend Star*, February 19, 1910, http://montananewspapers.org/lccn/sn86075288/1910-02-19/ed-1/seq-3/. A week earlier Julia's sister Diddy had been confined at the same hospital, recovering from "the effects of la grippe."

21. "Newsy Toston Letter," *Townsend Star*, March 16, 1912, http://montananewspapers.org/lccn/sn86075288/1912-03-16/ed-1/seq-4/.

22. *Townsend Star*, January 26, 1967.

23. "Suffragist Speaker Coming to Toston," *Missouri Valley Index* (Toston MT), October 15, 1914, http://montananewspapers.org/lccn/sn85053288/1914-10-15/ed-1/seq-1/.

24. "Millinery," *Suffrage Daily News* (Helena MT), November 2, 1914, https://chroniclingamerica.loc.gov/lccn/sn85053121/1914-11-02/ed-1/seq-4/.

25. "Female Suffrage Has Carried the Treasure State," *Daily Missoulian*, November 6, 1914, https://www.newspapers.com/image/168537951/.

26. Statewide, suffrage carried the day by a slightly higher margin of 52.35 percent: "Montana Amendment 1, Women's Suffrage Measure," Ballotpedia, accessed January 11, 2021, https://ballotpedia.org/Montana_Amendment_1,_Women%27s_Suffrage_Measure_(1914). ArcGIS, "1914 Suffrage Vote," accessed July 18, 2016, http://ceic.maps.arcgis.com/home/webmap/viewer.html?webmap=ae30931850f24c85b8e06c13135e7bbd&extent=-119.3983,39.448,-99.0517,51.6548.

27. "Broadwater Election," *Townsend Star*, November 10, 1914, http://montananewspapers.org/lccn/sn86075288/1914-11-10/ed-1/seq-2/.

28. In 1913, women in Illinois had won the right to vote in only municipal and presidential elections.

29. Native American women in Montana did not earn the right to vote until 1924. Mary Pickett, "Jeannette Rankin and the Path to Women's Suffrage in Montana: Nov. 3 Marks 100 Years since Women in Montana Secured the Right to Vote," *Billings Gazette*, November 2, 2014, http://billingsgazette.com/news /government-and-politics/jeannette-rankin-and-the-path-to-women-s-suffrage -in/article_83307d2b-2888-558d-9e1d-907d6518101f.html.

Chapter 37

1. Howard, *Montana*, 5.

2. Howard, *Montana*, 183.

3. "Toston Notes," *Townsend Star*, July 25, 1918, http://montananewspapers.org /lccn/sn86075288/1918-07-25/ed-1/seq-7/.

4. "Toston Notes," *Townsend Star*, July 11, 1918, http://montananewspapers.org /lccn/sn86075288/1918-07-11/ed-1/seq-7/.

5. United States Weather Bureau, *Climatological Data for the United States by Sections*, vol. 5, no. 13 (Washington DC: United States Weather Bureau, 1918), 101–8, https://books.google.com/books?id=qytEAAAAYAAJ.

Chapter 38

1. Julia's house was at 502 S. Fifth Ave., Bozeman.

2. Howard, *Montana*, 197.

3. Linderman, *Plenty Coups*, 311, 313.

4. "Help Wanted—Male," *Great Falls* (MT) *Daily Tribune*, July 7, 1920, https:// www.newspapers.com/image/239623371/.

5. "Could You Be a Fuller Man?" *Billings Gazette*, December 21, 1924, https:// www.newspapers.com/image/409594957/.

6. "Golden Wedding Buffalo Hunter," *Powder River County Examiner*, December 2, 1921, https://www.newspapers.com/image/343184604/.

7. "Mr. Bennett Is Improving," *Toston Times*, January 28, 1923, http:// montananewspapers.org/lccn/sn85053285/1923-01-18/ed-1/seq-4/; see also "Toston News," *Helena Daily Independent*, November 30, 1922, https://www .newspapers.com/image/527994849/.

8. Raymond B. Lewis (director, James Farm and Mining Corporation), sues A. B. Bennett, Julia A. Bennett, and Lulu A. Bembrick for Note (Bozeman). April 16, 1924, "Judgment on above—472.18," November 16, 1923, Gallatin County MT court records.

9. "Dr. B. F. Bembrick of Toston Is Dead," *Helena Daily Independent*, May 15, 1925, https://www.newspapers.com/image/11503993/.

10. Albert J. Gallatin to David Hilger, May 18, 1925, NFP.

11. 722 S. Seventh Ave., Bozeman.

12. *1920 United States Federal Census*, Violet Ray Marshall, Bozeman Ward 3, Gallatin MT, roll T625_970, p. 7B, Enumeration District 73, https://www .ancestrylibrary.com/imageviewer/collections/6061/images/4313238-00993.

Chapter 39

1. "Return of Sheriff or Constable," May 22, 1931, in district court filing, Writ of Attachment 9449, Gallatin County MT, June 12, 1931, Gallatin County MT court records.

2. "Woman Married for 29 Years Seeking Divorce," *Montana Standard*, June 12, 1931, https://www.newspapers.com/image/349194189/.

3. "Guests from East," *Madisonian*, June 12, 1931, http://montananewspapers.org /lccn/sn86075314/1931-06-12/ed-1/seq-8/.

4. "Buffaloes Included in Ranch Attachment," *Montana Standard*, June 13, 1931, https://www.newspapers.com/image/350768028/.

5. "Dude Ranches Finding It Tough These Times," *Helena Daily Independent*, June 13, 1931, https://www.newspapers.com/image/527633884/.

Chapter 40

1. Sherry Merica Pepper, in discussion with the author, June 22, 2012, Sonoita AZ.

Chapter 41

1. In keeping with the time period of this story, I chose to use American Indian, the term in use during the 1930s, rather than the contemporary term Native American.

2. I. H. Larson, "The Evolution of the Dude Ranch Industry," *Montana Wildlife*, February 1931.

3. "Max Big Man Pays Call on President," *Billings Gazette*, March 13, 1932, https:// www.newspapers.com/image/414950376/.

4. *New York World Telegram*, April 4, 1932.

Chapter 42

1. Burlington Northern advertisement, *Town and Country*, April 15, 1932, https:// www.google.com/books/edition/Town_Country/2gdVAAAAYAAJ.

Chapter 43

1. Sherry Merica Pepper, in discussion with the author, June 22, 2012, Sonoita AZ.

2. Sherry Merica Pepper, in discussion with the author, June 22, 2012, Sonoita AZ. Quoting Pepper's recollection of her conversation with Charlie Anceney Jr.

3. "Newly-Weds Are Home for Visit," *Montana Standard*, August 1, 1937, https://www.newspapers.com/image/349435078/.

4. Also along for the trip were the Stursbergs' friends Marjorie Cuthbert and Betty and Dot McDermid.

5. Choate School 1932 yearbook, *Brief*, 98, 176, Choate Rosemary Hall archives.

6. Excerpt of letter from George St. John, n.d., in Pete Stursberg's 1932 scrapbook. All Stursberg scrapbooks are from Sherry Merica Pepper's private collection.

7. Sherry Merica Pepper, in discussion with the author, June 22, 2012, Sonoita AZ.

8. Excerpt of letter from Herbert Stursberg to Pete Stursberg, n.d., in Pete Stursberg's 1932 scrapbook.

9. Albert Stursberg obituary (unidentified newspaper, n.d.), in Pete Stursberg's 1933 scrapbook.

10. *1920 United States Federal Census*, Albert Stursberg, Manhattan Assembly District 15, New York NY, roll T625_1213, p. 25B, Enumeration District 1087, https://www.ancestrylibrary.com/imageviewer/collections/6061/images/4313936-00753.

11. *Bernardsville News*, n.d., in Pete Stursberg's 1932 scrapbook.

12. "Livingston Rodeo Revives the Spirit of the Old West," *Philipsburg Mail*, June 24, 1932, http://phm.stparchive.com/Archive/PHM/PHM06241932p02.php.

13. From Pete Stursberg's 1932 scrapbook.

14. Victoria and Genevieve Brady's father had married three times. His first wife, Elizabeth, had died in a train accident in 1912.

15. "Four DePew Cousins Drop Fight on Will," *New York Times*, June 2, 1931, https://timesmachine.nytimes.com/timesmachine/1931/06/02/96201162.html?pageNumber=5.

16. "Roy Sieger Killed in Auto Crash," *Helena Daily Independent*, August 27, 1932, https://www.newspapers.com/image/527454571/.

Chapter 44

1. Madison County MT Clerk and Recorder's Office, records, 51109—Bennett-Stursberg contract, August 30, 1932, book 121, 400–403.

2. Madison County MT Clerk and Recorder's Office, records, 48493—bargain and sale deed, October 18, 1932, book 124, 87–88.

3. "United States Personal Income Per Capita, 1928–2008," Demographia, accessed March 21, 2020, http://demographia.com/db-pc1929.pdf.

4. "Federal Income Tax Brackets (Tax Year 1932) Archives," Tax-Brackets, accessed March 21, 2020, https://www.tax-brackets.org/federaltaxtable/1933.

5. Rates at the Diamond J in 1933 were $160 per week for two adults in a cabin, not including fees for horseback riding and other extras. Rates for a guest's servant were $75 per week.

6. Dr. Millet may have been Dr. John A. P. Millet, a physician at 770 Park Avenue—the only Dr. Millet listed in the 1933 *Polk's New York City Directory*.

7. Stursberg, *Your Dream Mentor*, 133.

8. Betty Cass, Day by Day, *Wisconsin State Journal* (Madison), April 10, 1940, https://www.newspapers.com/image/397118952/.

9. Handwritten note by Pete Stursberg, n.d., and Babette Stursberg to Pete Stursberg, n.d., both in Pete Stursberg's 1933 scrapbook.

10. Diamond J Ranch advertisement, *Yale Daily News*, May 11, 1933, in Pete Stursberg's 1933 scrapbook; see also http://digital.library.yale.edu/digital/collection/yale-ydn/id/151055/rec/2.

11. Bordman and Norton, *American Musical Theater*, 533.

12. Babs Stursberg to Pete Stursberg, n.d., in Pete Stursberg's 1933 scrapbook.

13. "The White Sister," Internet Movie Database, accessed June 2, 2014, http://www.imdb.com/title/tt0024770/?ref_=fn_al_tt_4.

14. "Circus Fans Admit Explorer to Fold," *New York Times*, March 30, 1933, https://timesmachine.nytimes.com/timesmachine/1933/03/30/105121846.html.

15. "3,000 Attend Ball in Circus Setting," *New York Times*, April 26, 1933, https://timesmachine.nytimes.com/timesmachine/1933/04/26/99229034.html.

16. "3,000 Attend Ball."

Chapter 45

1. Jackson, *Time Exposure*, 102.

2. Jackson diary, February 24, 1932, WHJP.

3. The Ciné-Kodak was the world's first 16 mm movie camera.

4. Jackson diary, May 25, 1933.

5. Jackson diary, May 26, 1933.

6. Jackson diary, May 27, 1933.

7. Unidentified newspaper article, n.d., in Pete Stursberg's 1933 scrapbook; see also "Two in State Benefit by Will of New Yorker," *Boston Globe*, April 30, 1936, https://www.newspapers.com/image/431949572/.

Chapter 46

1. Jackson diary, June 12, 1933.

2. Jackson diary, July 7, 1933.

3. Marilynn Johnson, "Ethel Augustus Maynard," Find a Grave, March 28, 2009, http://findagrave.com/cgi-bin/fg.cgi/pages.suddenlink.net/www.findagrave .com/cgi-bin/fg.cgi?page=gr&GRid=35281722.

4. Robert Beck, "History of the Jumping Horse Ranch," with Nancy Lein Griffin and Helene Beck, *Wagon Tongue*, 12, no. 2 (April 2014): 5, http:// madisonvalleyhistoryassociation.org/Vol12%20Iss2.pdf.

5. Jackson diary, July 10 and 11, 1933.

6. Jackson diary, July 25, 1934.

Chapter 47

1. Rees, "Dude Ranch Tourism," 176.

2. "Star Land, Sun Land, Rope, Spur and Gun Land—That Is the Glowing Southwest," *Brooklyn* (NY) *Daily Eagle*, December 2, 1934, https://www.newspapers .com/image/58335064/.

3. U.S. Department of Commerce, *Population*, vols. 2–3.

4. *Tucson, Arizona, City Directory*, 1936, https://www.ancestrylibrary.com /imageviewer/collections/2469/images/15444919.

5. Violet Westinghouse also owned property in her native Cumbria, England. George Westinghouse IV, email message to author, February 16, 2015.

6. Their fears weren't unwarranted; just a few months earlier, a man matching the description of the kidnapper of the nine-year-old son of lumber magnate J. P. Weyerhaeuser in Washington State had turned up begging for food on a woman's doorstep in nearby Livingston, Montana. "Woman's Story Spurs Montana Hunt for Kidnaping Suspect," *Chicago Tribune*, June 14, 1935, https:// www.newspapers.com/image/372725001/.

7. Photograph, circa 1935, Sherry Merica Pepper private collection.

8. *Madisonian*, October 18, 1935, http://montananewspapers.org/lccn/sn86075314 /1935-10-18/ed-1/seq-8/; George Westinghouse IV, email message to author, February 7, 2015.

9. George Westinghouse IV, email message to author, February 11, 2015.

10. George Westinghouse IV, email message to author, February 9, 2015.

11. "Anson Bennett," *Montana Standard*, October 26, 1935, https://www .newspapers.com/image/349163335/.

12. Westinghouse email, February 11, 2015.

Chapter 48

1. "The 'King and Queen' of the Movies," *Kansas City Times*, December 10, 1937, https://www.newspapers.com/image/656947126/.

2. Leider, *Myrna Loy*, 60.

3. *Santa Rita Hotel*, vintage color postcard (Kansas City MO: C. T. Art Colortone, n.d.), https://images.app.goo.gl/rRtLstGE7RP8i2Az9, accessed August 31, 2020.

4. Westinghouse email, February 16, 2015.

5. "Appliance Magnate Wintered in the Old Pueblo," *Tucson (AZ) Citizen*, December 9, 2006, https://www.newspapers.com/image/580208087/.

6. *Arizona Daily Star*, April 8, 1934, in Julia Bennett's scrapbook.

7. "Wetmore Hodges, Industrialist, Dies at 69; Developer of Food-Freezing Process," *New York Times*, April 4, 1957, https://timesmachine.nytimes.com/timesmachine/1957/04/04/90789491.pdf.

8. "Hodges Mentioned for Commerce Post," *Billings Gazette*, July 10, 1935, https://www.newspapers.com/image/411276788/.

9. "New Guest Ranch Opens near Here," *Arizona Daily Star* (Tucson), January 21, 1936, https://www.newspapers.com/image/163659816/.

Chapter 49

1. "Escape Winter on the California Desert," *Spokane (WA) Daily Chronicle*, October 19, 1934, https://www.newspapers.com/image/562114158/.

2. Julia does not specifically say how she came up with the name of the ranch, but it fits the pattern.

3. Saguaro National Monument is now Saguaro National Park.

Chapter 50

1. Francis H. Sisson, "To the Members of the Town Hall Club," *Town Crier*, July 1, 1929, back cover, https://ia600309.us.archive.org/28/items/towncrier1929town/towncrier1929town.pdf.

2. Grace Sartwell Mason, "You're Not the Only One!," letter to the editor, *Town Crier*, July 1929, https://ia600309.us.archive.org/28/items/towncrier1929town/towncrier1929town.pdf.

3. "Becomes Bride," *Montana Standard*, July 18, 1937, https://www.newspapers.com/image/349425332/.

4. Unidentified newspaper clipping, n.d., in Pete Stursberg's 1936 scrapbook.

Chapter 51

1. Betty Cass, Day by Day, *Wisconsin State Journal*, August 17, 1939, https://www.newspapers.com/image/396790457/.

2. Sherry Merica Pepper, telephone discussion with the author, February 16, 2015.

3. Betty Cass, Day by Day, *Wisconsin State Journal*, August 16, 1939, https://www.newspapers.com/image/396790513/.

4. Carey Orr cartoon, February 9, 1949, Sherry Merica Pepper private collection.

5. Cass, Day by Day, *Wisconsin State Journal*, August 16, 1939.

6. "'Yellowstone' Song by Gene Quaw from 1937," YouTube video, 4:30, posted by "bearmauled," November 23, 2018, https://www.youtube.com/watch?v=1MgnNev1Z84.

7. Sherry Merica Pepper, in discussion with the author, June 22, 2012, Sonoita AZ.

8. "Myrna Loy's Mother Dances," *Montana Standard*, August 9, 1936, https://www.newspapers.com/image/349448224/.

9. "Ennis Residents Guests at Annual Barn Dance Event," *Montana Standard*, September 3, 1939, https://www.newspapers.com/image/350810107/.

10. "Friends Gather at Diamond W Sunday," unidentified newspaper clipping, 1937, in Julia Bennett's scrapbook.

11. Sherry Merica Pepper, in discussion with the author, June 22, 2012, Sonoita AZ.

12. Sherry Merica Pepper, in discussion with the author, June 22, 2012, Sonoita AZ.

13. Alexander Bing, telephone discussion with the author, June 7, 2012.

14. Sherry Merica Pepper, telephone discussion with the author, February 16, 2015.

15. Frank Seitz, telephone discussion with the author, February 2, 2016.

16. Sherry Merica Pepper, telephone discussion with the author, February 16, 2015.

17. Sherry Merica Pepper, telephone discussion with the author, February 16, 2015.

18. "Anceney Too Weak Yet to Be Given X-Ray Examination," *Helena Daily Independent*, January 26, 1936, https://www.newspapers.com/image/528020016/; "C. L. Anceney, Noted Montana Stockman, Dies," *Billings Gazette*, February 25, 1936, https://www.newspapers.com/image/411303819/.

19. "Anceney Is Given Chance to Recover," *Great Falls Tribune*, January 25, 1936, https://www.newspapers.com/image/239094339/.

20. Sherry Merica Pepper, in discussion with the author, June 24, 2012, Sonoita AZ.

21. Sherry Merica Pepper, in discussion with the author, June 24, 2012, Sonoita AZ.

Chapter 52

1. Unidentified newspaper advertisement, n.d., in Julia Bennett's scrapbook.

2. "Eagle Speaker Tells Wonders of Great Area," *Brooklyn Daily Eagle*, December 2, 1934, https://bklyn.newspapers.com/image/58335064/.

3. "Pleasant Stay Awaits Guests at Diamond-W," *Arizona Daily Star*, February 20, 1937, https://www.newspapers.com/image/169469143/.

4. Sherry Merica Pepper, in discussion with the author, June 22, 2012, Sonoita AZ.

5. "Diamond W's Parties Held," *Arizona Daily Star*, January 4, 1942, https://www.newspapers.com/image/163561036/; "Mrs. Bennett Is Hostess at Fete for 'Diamond W,'" *Arizona Daily Star*, March 27, 1940, https://www.newspapers.com/image/163537428/.

Chapter 53

1. Lisbeth, "Dressed for Vacation on Dude Ranch," *Times Herald* (Middletown NY), June 21, 1937, https://www.newspapers.com/image/40196527/.
2. Mary Nichols, "A Unique Shop Full of New Ideas," *Arizona Daily Star*, February 18, 1940, https://www.newspapers.com/image/164048836/. The Stable was located at 108 S. Sixth in Tucson.
3. Nichols, "A Unique Shop Full of New Ideas."
4. Sherry Merica Pepper, in discussion with the author, June 22, 2012, Sonoita AZ.
5. "Bad Weather Does Not Ruin Auction," *Arizona Daily Star*, January 22, 1939, in Pete Stursberg's 1939 scrapbook.
6. Sherry Merica Pepper, in discussion with the author, June 22, 2019, Bozeman MT.
7. Unidentified advertisement, n.d., in Pete Stursberg's 1939 scrapbook.
8. Sherry Merica Pepper, in discussion with the author, June 22, 2012, Sonoita AZ.

Chapter 54

1. Olary's name is variously spelled in newspaper articles as Olary, O'Lary and O'Leary. I have used the most widely used version.
2. "Two Men Held after Shooting of a Man at Toston," *Billings Gazette*, October 2, 1939, https://www.newspapers.com/image/410428524/.
3. "Self-Defense Plea Made by Bembrick Being Tried on Charge of Killing," *Townsend Star*, January 18, 1940.
4. "Toston Man Killed, Jim Bembrick Held," *Townsend Star*, October 5, 1939.
5. "Jury Selection Moves Slowly," *Billings Gazette*, January 16, 1940, https://www.newspapers.com/image/410114390/. See also "Not Guilty," *Missoulian*, November 4, 1911, https://www.newspapers.com/image/167693328/.
6. "Trial of Toston Resident Begins," *Montana Standard*, January 16, 1940, https://www.newspapers.com/image/354232429/.
7. Jeannette Rankin was elected to Congress in 1916 and 1940. She was the only U.S. representative who voted against the United States entering the war after the Japanese bombed Pearl Harbor.
8. "James Bembrick Is Free: Cleared of Murder Charge," *Townsend Star*, January 25, 1940.
9. Sherry Merica Pepper, in discussion with the author, June 22, 2012, Sonoita AZ; canceled check from Pete Stursberg to Jim Bembrick, in Stursberg's 1940 scrapbook, along with newspaper articles about the murder trial.
10. "Self-Defense Plea Made by Bembrick."
11. Steele, *Wellington Rankin*, 131.

12. "Self-Defense Plea Made by Bembrick." The *Townsend Star* reported that the trial was delayed "when juror Homer Henry of Confederate was drifted in when he attempted to drive in from his ranch in the storm. He was 45 minutes late."

13. "Self-Defense Plea Made by Bembrick." Although the newspaper article reported it had been twenty years since the last murder, other articles noted that it had been twenty-seven years.

14. "Self-Defense Plea Made by Bembrick."

15. "Self-Defense Plea Made by Bembrick."

16. "James Bembrick Is Free."

17. "Last of State Evidence Is Presented in Murder Trial," *Helena Daily Independent*, January 18, 1940, https://www.newspapers.com/image/11492068/.

18. "Self-Defense Plea Made by Bembrick."

19. "Bembrick Killing Case Is Given to Jurors Saturday," *Helena Daily Independent*, January 21, 1940, https://www.newspapers.com/image/528528832/.

20. "Self-Defense Plea Made by Bembrick."

21. "'Realistic' Response in Murder Trial Costs Witness Fine of $10," *Billings Gazette*, January 19, 1940, https://www.newspapers.com/image/410116911/.

22. "Last of State Evidence Is Presented."

23. "James Bembrick Is Free."

24. "James Bembrick Is Free."

25. "James Bembrick Is Free."

26. "J. J. Bembrick of Bozeman Dead," *Montana Standard-Post*, October 22, 1965, https://www.newspapers.com/image/353044103/.

Chapter 55

1. Minutes of Diamond Ranches Corporation special board meeting, March 20, 1941, Diamond Ranches Corporation record book, Marshall Bennett private collection.

2. In 1940, $45,000 would have equaled more than $825,000 today. "Certificate of Incorporation of Diamond Ranches Corporation," *Arizona Daily Star*, July 16, 1940, https://www.newspapers.com/image/163785876/.

3. Diamond Ranches Corporation record book.

4. Diamond Ranches Corporation record book, July 21, 1940.

5. Diamond Ranches to Herbert Stursberg, August 30, 1940, Diamond Ranches Corporation record book.

6. Diamond Ranches to Herbert Stursberg, December 1, 1940, Diamond Ranches Corporation record book.

7. "Charlie's Jaw Wags—Nothing Comes Out," *Ogden Standard Examiner*, July 4, 1940, https://www.newspapers.com/image/596722212/.

8. Cass, Day by Day, *Wisconsin State Journal*, August 17, 1939.

9. "Kirsten Flagstad's Daughter Married by Bozeman Pastor," *Missoulian*, August 12, 1940, https://www.newspapers.com/image/352185406/.

10. "U.S. Sugar Rationing Is Begun," *Arizona Republic* (Phoenix), May 5, 1942, https://www.newspapers.com/image/117201386/.

11. "War Simplifies Women's Lives," *Arizona Republic*, January 11, 1942, https://www.newspapers.com/image/117050332/.

12. "Officers May Use Ranches," *Tucson* (AZ) *Daily Citizen*, May 30, 1942, https://www.newspapers.com/image/10506971/.

13. "Facilities of Dude Ranches Available Yet," *Tucson Daily Citizen*, December 8, 1942, https://www.newspapers.com/image/10573473/.

14. "For Sale," *Tucson Daily Citizen*, September 5, 1944, https://www.newspapers.com/image/9846295/.

15. Unidentified newspaper clipping, n.d., in Pete Stursberg's 1941 scrapbook.

16. "In Butte Rodeo Parade," *Madisonian*, August 5, 1938, http://montananewspapers.org/lccn/sn86075314/1938-08-05/ed-1/seq-8/.

17. In this musical, Dorothy Lamour, clad "in a feathered headdress and scanties," performed the culturally insensitive production number "Injun Gal Heap Hep." "Dude Ranches' Guests Taking Part in Film," *Tucson Daily Citizen*, January 6, 1943, https://www.newspapers.com/image/16100153/; "'Riding High,' a Knockabout Musical Film, with Dorothy Lamour, Dick Powell, Victor Moore, Opens at Paramount," *New York Times*, December 23, 1943, https://timesmachine.nytimes.com/timesmachine/1943/12/23/88589070.html?pageNumber=26.

18. "Movie Shooting Begins Tuesday," *Arizona Daily Star*, October 31, 1943, https://www.newspapers.com/image/162511773/.

19. "Audience Hails Local Premier," *Arizona Daily Star*, February 17, 1939, https://www.newspapers.com/image/163759002/.

Chapter 56

1. "Air Force's Firemen Save Most of Ranch," *Tucson Daily Citizen*, February 24, 1943, https://www.newspapers.com/image/18731770/.

2. "Air Base Firemen Save Structure by Effective Work," *Arizona Daily Star*, February 25, 1943, https://www.newspapers.com/image/164066473/.

3. "Air Force's Firemen Save Most of Ranch."

4. "Fire Destroys Schley Tower," *Bernardsville* (NJ) *News*, May 4, 1933, https://www.newspapers.com/image/95677107/; "Eleven Fires Keep Firemen on Jump," *Bernardsville News*, March 28, 1935, in Pete Stursberg's 1935 scrapbook.

5. Sherry Merica Pepper, in discussion with the author, June 22, 2012, Sonoita AZ.

6. "Fire Thrills Fifth Avenue," *Sun* (New York), April 1, 1917, https://www.newspapers.com/image/88271909/.

7. "The Old West Kept Alive by Grazing Feuds," *Chicago Tribune*, March 21, 1943, https://www.newspapers.com/image/370957834/.

8. Clipping from *Yale Daily News*, n.d., in Pete Stursberg's 1943 scrapbook.

9. "Laird Stursberg of Livingston Mills Ends Life," unidentified newspaper, n.d., in Pete Stursberg's 1943 scrapbook.

10. Charles A. Rheinstrom to director of naval officer procurement, New York City, May 3, 1943, in Pete Stursberg's 1943 scrapbook.

11. Telegram excerpts, in Pete Stursberg's 1943 scrapbook.

12. "Five Die as Planes Collide in Mid-Air above Miami; Officer and Wife Victims," *Cincinnati Enquirer*, April 6, 1942, https://www.newspapers.com/image/103168769/.

13. Photographs in Pete Stursberg's 1943 scrapbook.

14. Sherry Merica Pepper, in discussion with the author, June 22, 2012, Sonoita AZ.

15. Montana State Divorce Records, 1943–1986, certificate no. Br. 4, https://www.ancestrylibrary.com/imageviewer/collections/61477/images/47793_554232-01008. Original data: Montana Department of Public Health and Human Services.

16. "Captain Dashiel Speaks to Navy Graduating Class," *Arizona Daily Star*, November 12, 1943, https://www.newspapers.com/image/162909158/.

17. Florence B. Stursberg v. Edward A. Stursberg, C27502 (Pima County AZ, Super. Ct., September 12, 1946).

18. Sherry Merica Pepper, telephone discussion with the author, April 24, 2019.

19. Sherry Merica Pepper, in discussion with the author, June 22, 2012, Sonoita AZ.

20. Sherry Merica Pepper, in discussion with the author, February 10, 2014, Sonoita AZ.

Chapter 57

1. Sherry Merica Pepper, in discussion with the author, June 22, 2012, Sonoita AZ.

2. "Dude Rancher Asks Tests for Hunters," *Independent Record*, November 24, 1949, https://www.newspapers.com/image/393673837/.

3. Cass, Day by Day, *Wisconsin State Journal*, April 10, 1940.

4. Paul Salopek, "Ghosts of a Vanished Frontier," *Chicago Tribune*, July 27, 1997, https://www.newspapers.com/image/167458993/.

5. Cornelius C. Smith, *Tanque Verde*, 103.

6. Cornelius C. Smith, *Tanque Verde*, 105.

7. Cornelius C. Smith, *Tanque Verde*, 104.

8. "Rancher Faces Arraignment in Man's Death," *Tucson Daily Citizen*, October 1, 1945, https://www.newspapers.com/image/10627920/; "Converse Jury Hears Three Pistol Experts," *Tucson Daily Citizen*, February 13, 1946, https://www.newspapers.com/image/10489590/. Just ten days before the shooting, Pete Stursberg had written Romero, the ranch hand, a check for $30, probably for doing some work at the Diamond W; see Pete Stursberg's 1945 scrapbook.

9. "J. P. Converse Renamed to School Board," *Tucson Daily Citizen*, October 30, 1945, https://www.newspapers.com/image/10646655/; "Dude Ranchers Choose Allen as President," December 8, 1945, https://www.newspapers.com/image/10668110/.

10. "Third Motion Made in Court for Converse," *Tucson Daily Citizen*, December 11, 1945, https://www.newspapers.com/image/10669989/.

11. "Mrs. Converse Is Found Dead," *Tucson Daily Citizen*, June 9, 1947, 15; "Self-Inflicted Gunshot Fatal," *Arizona Republic*, June 9, 1947, https://www.newspapers.com/image/117367408/.

Chapter 58

1. John Frey of Washington DC was head of the Department of the Allied Metal Trades of the American Federation of Labor. Diamond W guest book, April 20, 1947; see also "John Frey, Labor Statesman, Holds No Fears for America," *Arizona Daily Star*, April 7, 1948, https://www.newspapers.com/image/162434747/.

2. Dick and Peggy Pollard, "Mr. and Mrs. America Take You to Montana Dude Ranch," *Philadelphia Inquirer*, August 18, 1946, https://www.newspapers.com/image/171530400/.

3. Sherry Merica Pepper, in discussion with the author, June 22, 2012, Sonoita AZ.

4. "Utahn Gains Big Loan," *Salt Lake Tribune* (Salt Lake City UT), August 4, 1946, https://www.newspapers.com/image/598776926/. Just two months later Gardner was advertising in the *Los Angeles Times* to trade the Diamond W for property in Los Angeles. In February 1950 he used the Diamond W as partial payment for his purchase of the Robinson Hotel in Long Beach. It then was purchased by Hula Braden Oldfield.

5. "Ranch Owners Remodeling," *Tucson Daily Citizen*, September 28, 1950, https://www.newspapers.com/image/17567436/.

6. Julia and Don invested the proceeds from the sale of the Diamond W in two large Phoenix motels—the Greenway and the Palomine—that he and three other Montana businessmen were buying from Gardner for $1.2 million. The group formed a corporation called Palomine Realty, and each of the five investors held one share in the new organization. "Articles of Incorporation of Palomine

Realty Co.," *Arizona Republic*, January 14, 1949, https://www.newspapers.com/image/117307065/.

7. Sherry Merica Pepper, text message to the author, May 15, 2019.

8. Sherry Merica Pepper, telephone discussion with the author, April 24, 2019.

Chapter 59

1. John Uihlein, whose family was one of the founders of the Schlitz Beer Company, owned a ranch near the Diamond J. Sherry Merica Pepper, in discussion with the author, June 22, 2012, Sonoita AZ.

2. Marshall Bennett, in discussion with the author, June 20, 2012, Bozeman MT.

3. Engen, *Skiing a Way of Life*, 100.

4. Marshall Bennett, in discussion with the author, June 30, 2012, Bozeman MT.

5. Sherry Merica Pepper, telephone discussion with the author, April 24, 2019.

6. "Diamond J House Burns to Ground," *Madisonian*, October 9, 1953, http://montananewspapers.org/lccn/sn86075314/1953-10-09/ed-1/seq-1/.

7. Sherry Merica Pepper, telephone discussion with the author, April 24, 2019.

Chapter 60

1. Sherry Merica Pepper, in discussion with the author, June 22, 2012, Sonoita AZ.

2. "Sleep Pills Kill Woman," *Arizona Republic*, April 4, 1957, https://www.newspapers.com/image/117631252/.

3. Sherry Merica Pepper, in discussion with the author, June 22, 2012, Sonoita AZ.

4. Eddy, *Science and Health with Key to the Scriptures*, 466.

5. Eddy, *Science and Health with Key to the Scriptures*, 468.

6. "Bridge and Pinochle Tournament Sponsored by Sheridan Hospital Guild Has First Session," *Montana Standard*, November 4, 1956, http://www.newspapers.com/image/354794382/; "Novel Auction Planned by Lions at Ennis," *Montana Standard*, February 10, 1957, https://www.newspapers.com/image/350636140/.

7. Sherry Merica Pepper, telephone discussion with the author, October 27, 2016.

8. Stursberg, *Your Dream Mentor*, 114.

9. Sherry Merica Pepper, telephone discussion with the author, February 12, 2019.

10. Eddy, *First Church of Christ, Scientist, and Miscellany*, 149–50.

11. Sherry Merica Pepper, telephone discussion with the author, December 6, 2013.

Bibliography

Archives

BFP. Bates Family Papers, 1754–1973, box 7, Letter from Barton Bates to Edward Bates, October 10, 1861. Missouri Historical Society Archives, St. Louis MO. https://mohistory.org/collections/item/D02032.

FWP. Fred F. Willson Papers, 1889–1956, Diamond J Ranch, series 6. Merrill G. Burlingame Special Collections, Montana State University Library, Bozeman MT.

NFP. Nave Family Papers, 1865–1890. Montana Historical Society Research Center, Archives, Helena MT.

MPRP. Minnie Paugh Madison Valley Research Papers, 1964–1965. Merrill G. Burlingame Special Collections, Montana State University Library, Bozeman MT.

WHJP. William Henry Jackson Papers. Manuscripts and Archives Division, New York Public Library, Astor, Lenox, and Tilden Foundations, New York City NY.

Publications

Barnsess, Larry. *Gold Camp: Alder Gulch and Virginia City, Montana*. New York: Hastings House, 1962.

Bates, Grace. *Gallatin County: Places and Things Present and Past*. 2nd ed. Bozeman MT: Grace Bates, 1994.

Beal, Merrill D. *The Story of Man in Yellowstone*. Caldwell ID: Caxton Printers, 1949.

Bordman, Gerald, and Richard Norton. *American Musical Theater: A Chronicle*. United Kingdom: Oxford University Press, 2010. https://www.google.com/books/edition/_/OVdShkzkX74C.

Broadwater County Historical Society. *Broadwater Bygones: A History of Broadwater County*. Townsend MT: Broadwater County Historical Society, 1977.

Browne, J. Ross. *Resources of the Pacific Slope*. New York: D. Appleton and Company, 1869. https://www.google.com/books/edition/Resources_of_the_Pacific_Slope/YXRAru3nICsC.

Burlingame, Merrill G. *Gallatin County's Heritage: A Report of Progress 1805–1976*. Bozeman MT: Gallatin County Bicentennial Committee, 1976.

———. *The Montana Frontier*. Bozeman MT: Big Sky Books, 1980.

Burlingame, Merrill G., and J. Ross Toole, *A History of Montana*. New York: Lewis Historical Publishing, 1957.

Carter, Sarah, ed. *Montana Women Homesteaders*. Helena MT: Farcountry Press, 2009.

Collins, Arian E. *The Nave Family: From Switzerland to Montana, 1590s to 1990s*. San Diego CA: Bordertown Publications, 2003. Available through the Montana Historical Society Research Center archives and online at http://www.usgwarchives.net/tn/cocke/nave/nave01.htm.

Collins, Charles D., Jr. *Atlas of the Sioux Wars*. Fort Leavenworth KS: Combat Studies Institute Press. https://www.armyupress.army.mil/Portals/7/educational-services/staff-rides/atlas-of-the-sioux-wars-second-edition.pdf.

Colton, J. H. *The Western Tourist, or Emigrant's Guide through the States of Michigan, Indiana, Illinois, and Missouri, and the Territories of Wisconsin and Iowa*. New York: Self-published, 1845. https://books.google.com/books?id=Tp01AQAAMAAJ.

Cronin, Janet, and Dorothy Vick. *Montana's Gallatin Canyon: A Gem in the Treasure State*. Missoula MT: Mountain Press Publishing, 1992.

Dippie, Brian W., ed. *Charles M. Russell, Word Painter*. Fort Worth TX: Amon Carter Museum, 1993.

Dodge, Grenville M. *Biographical Sketch of James Bridger: Mountaineer, Trapper, and Guide*. New York: Unz, 1905. https://archive.org/stream/biographicalsket00dodg#page/26/mode/2up/.

Doyle, Susan Badger. *Journeys to the Fields of Gold: Emigrant Diaries from the Bozeman Trail, 1863–1866*. Helena: Montana Historical Society Press, 2000.

Eberstadt, Edward. *The William Robertson Coe Collection of Western Americana*. New Haven CT: Yale University Library Gazette, 1948.

Eddy, Mary Baker. *Christian Healing: A Lecture Delivered at Boston*. 23rd ed. Cambridge MA: John Wilson and Son, University Press, 1905. https://books.google.com/books?id=JUg0vwEACAAJ.

———. *The First Church of Christ, Scientist, and Miscellany*. Boston: Christian Science Publishing Society, 1913. https://books.google.com/books?id=qwSGxQEACAAJ.

———. *Science and Health with Key to the Scriptures*. Boston: Allison V. Stewart, 1912. https://www.google.com/books/edition/Science_and_Health_with_Key_to_the_Scrip/MRkqAAAAYAAJ.

Egan, Ken, Jr. *Montana 1864*. Helena MT: Riverbend Publishing, 2014.

Engen, Sverre. *Skiing a Way of Life*. Sandy UT: Sciotto Enterprise, 1976.

Federal Writers Project of the WPA. *The WPA Guide to 1930s Montana*. Tucson: University of Arizona Press, 1994. Originally published as *Montana: A State Guide Book*. New York: Viking Press, 1939.

Fellman, Michael. *Inside War: The Guerilla Conflict in Missouri during the American Civil War*. New York: Oxford University Press, 1989.

Free, Alice Lloyd, ed. *Progressive Cook Book*. Billings MT: First Methodist Episcopal Church, 1893. Archives and Special Collections—Maureen and Mike Mansfield Library, http://exhibits.lib.umt.edu/omeka/items/show/508.

Groth, Paul. *Living Downtown: The History of Residential Hotels in the United States*. Berkeley: University of California Press, 1999.

Hanshew, Annie. *Border to Border: Historic Quilts and Quiltmakers of Montana*. Helena: Montana Historical Society Press, 2009.

Hassrick, Peter H. *Charles M. Russell*. New York: Harry N. Abrams, 1989.

History of Caldwell and Livingston Counties, Missouri. St Louis MO: National Historical Company, 1886. https://books.google.com/books?id=cs8yAQAAMAAJ.

The History of Linn County, Missouri: An Encyclopedia of Useful Information. Kansas City MO: Birdsall and Dean, 1882. https://www.google.com/books/edition/The_History_of_Linn_County_Missouri/B30UAAAAYAAJ?gbpv=0.

A History of Montana. Vol. 3. New York: Lewis Historical Publishing, 1957.

History of Montana 1739–1885. Chicago: Warner, Beers, 1885.

Holley, Marietta. *My Opinions and Betsey Bobbet's*. Hartford CT: American Publishing, 1884. http://www.gutenberg.org/files/55594/55594-h/55594-h.htm.

Holley, Marietta. *Samantha Rastles the Woman Question*. Edited by Jane Curry. Urbana: University of Illinois Press, 1983.

Holmes, Krys. *Montana: Stories of the Land*. Helena: Montana Historical Society Press, 2008. https://books.google.com/books?id=-FahazPXm3YC.

Hosmer, Hezekiah L. *Montana: An Address*. New York: New York Printing Company, 1866. Archives and Special Collections, Mansfield Library, University of Montana-Missoula. https://cdm16013.contentdm.oclc.org/digital/collection/p16013coll56/id/67.

Howard, Joseph Kinsey. *Montana: High, Wide, and Handsome*. New Haven CT: Yale University Press, 1943.

Jackson, William Henry. *Time Exposure: The Autobiography of William Henry Jackson*. New York: Van Rees Press, 1940. Reprinted, Albuquerque: University of New Mexico Press, 1989.

Knowlton, Christopher. *Cattle Kingdom: The Hidden History of the Cowboy West*. Boston: Mariner Books, 2017.

Kotsilibas-Davis, James, and Myrna Loy. *Myrna Loy: Being and Becoming*. New York: Donald L. Fine, 1987.

Langford, Nathaniel Pitt. *Vigilante Days and Ways: The Pioneers of the Rockies, the Makers and Making of Montana, Idaho, Oregon, Washington, and Wyoming*.

Vol. 2. New York: D. D. Merrill, 1893. https://books.google.com/books?id=8Ns
_AQAAMAAJ.

Langley, Henry G., comp. *The San Francisco Directory for the Year Commencing September, 1867: Embracing a General Directory of Residents and Business Directory; Also a Directory of Streets, Public Offices, Etc., and a Map of
the City*. San Francisco: Henry G. Langley, 1867. https://archive.org/details
/sanfranciscodire1867lang/page/n103/mode/2up.

Leider, Emily. *Myrna Loy: The Only Good Girl in Hollywood*. Berkeley: University
of California Press, 2011.

Linderman, Frank B. *Plenty Coups: Chief of the Crows*. Lincoln: University of
Nebraska Press, 1962.

Luchetti, Cathy, and Carol Olwell. *Women of the West*. Berkeley CA: Antelope
Island Press, 1982.

Marcy, Randolph B. *The Prairie Traveler: A Hand-book for Overland Expeditions*.
New York: Harper and Brothers, 1859. https://www.gutenberg.org/ebooks
/23066.

McClure, A. K. *Three Thousand Miles through the Rocky Mountains*. Philadelphia PA: J. B. Lippincott, 1869. https://books.google.com/books?id=
HpIzAQAAMAAJ.

Meyers, Jeffrey. *Gary Cooper, American Hero*. New York: Morrow, 1998.

Miller, M. Mark. *Adventures in Yellowstone: Early Travelers Tell Their Tales*. Guil-
ford CT: Morris Book Publishing, 2009.

Milner, Clyde A., II, and Carol A. O'Connor. *As Big as the West: The Pioneer Life
of Granville Stuart*. New York: Oxford University Press, 2009.

The Missouri State Gazetteer and Business Directory. St. Louis MO: Sutherland
and McEvoy, 1860. https://books.google.com/books?id=s80yAQAAMAAJ.

Montana Advertising Directory. Helena MT: Steele, 1884. https://books.google
.com/books?id=guwCAAAAYAAJ.

Nell, Donald F., and John E. Taylor. *Lewis and Clark in the Three Rivers Valleys,
Montana, 1805–1806*. Tucson AZ: Headwaters Chapter Lewis and Clark Trail
Heritage Foundation, Patrice Press, 1996.

O'Neal, Bill. *Tex Ritter: America's Most Beloved Cowboy*. Austin TX: Eakin Press,
1998.

*Organization and Status of Missouri Troops, Union and Confederate, in Service
during the Civil War*. Washington DC: Government Printing Office, 1902.
https://archive.org/details/organizationstat00unit/page/n8.

The Pacific Coast Business Directory for 1867. San Francisco CA: H. G. Langley,
1867. https://archive.org/stream/cihm_17457.

Parker, Nathan H. *The Missouri Hand-Book.* St. Louis MO: P. M. Pinckard, 1865. https://books.google.com/books?id=JAYyAQAAMAAJ.

Pioneer Trails and Trials. Virginia City MT: Madison County History Association, 1978.

Pioneer Trails and Trials 3_7_77. Virginia City MT: Madison County History Association, 1976. https://mtmemory.org/digital/collection/p15018coll43/id/25205.

Polk's New York City Directory (Boroughs of Queens and Richmond). Vol. 1933–34. New York: R. L. Polk and Co., 1933. New York Public Library Digital Collections, https://digitalcollections.nypl.org/items/c2862c40-c050-0137-6c84 -3dce233ea3bd.

Progressive Years Madison County Montana. Vol. 2. Virginia City MT: Madison County History Association, 1983.

Rees, Amanda. "Dude Ranch Tourism, Hollywood, and the Production of Regional Identity in the American West, 1922–1950." *Aether* 11 (February 2013): 170–203.

Rolle, Andrew, ed. *The Road to Virginia City: The Diary of James Knox Polk Miller.* Norman: University of Oklahoma Press, 1960.

Ronan, Margaret, and Ellen Baumler. *Girl from the Gulches: The Story of Mary Ronan.* Helena: Montana Historical Society Press, 2003.

Russell, Charles M. *Trails Plowed Under: Stories of the Old West.* Introductions by Will Rogers and Brian W. Dippie. Lincoln: University of Nebraska Press, 1996.

Sanders, Helen Fitzgerald. *A History of Montana.* Vol. 2. Chicago: Lewis Publishing, 1913. https://books.google.com/books?id=OT84AQAAMAAJ.

Sanders, James U., ed. *Society of Montana Pioneers: Constitution, Members, and Officers; Register.* Vol. 1. Helena: Society of Montana Pioneers, 1899. https:// www.familysearch.org/library/books/records/item/210973-society-of-montana -pioneers-constitution-members-and-officers-with-portraits-and-maps-vol-1.

Schlissel, Lillian. *Women's Diaries of the Westward Journey.* New York: Schocken Books, 2004.

Schwantes, Carlos A. "The Steamboat and Stagecoach Era in Montana and the Northern West," *Montana the Magazine of Western History* 49, no. 4 (1999): 2–15.

Sievert, Ken, and Ellen Sievert. *Virginia City and Alder Gulch.* Helena MT: Farcountry Press, 1993.

Smiley, Jerome C., ed., *History of Denver.* Denver CO: Times-Sun Publishing, 1901.

Smith, Cornelius C. *Tanque Verde: The Story of a Frontier Ranch, Tucson, Arizona.* Tucson AZ: Self-published, 1978.

Smith, Phyllis. *The Flying D Ranch Lands of Montana: A History.* Bozeman MT: Gallatin County Historical Society and Pioneer Museum, 2001.

———. *Montana's Madison County—A History*. Bozeman MT: Gooch Hill Publishing, 1999.

Smits, David D. "The Frontier Army and the Destruction of the Buffalo: 1865–1883." *Western Historical Quarterly* 25, no. 3 (1994): 312–38.

Speelman, Mike. *Historic Photos of Tucson*. Nashville TN: Turner Publishing, 2007.

Stanley, Edwin James. *Life of Rev. L. B. Stateler: A Story of Life on the Old Frontier*. Rev. ed. Nashville TN: Publishing House of the M. E. Church, South, 1916. https://books.google.com/books?id=gEY3AAAAMAAJ.

Stearns, Harold Joseph. "History of the Upper Musselshell Valley to 1920." Master's thesis, University of Montana, 1966. http://scholarworks.umt.edu/cgi/viewcontent.cgi?article=3594&context=etd.

Steele, Volney. *Wellington Rankin—His Family, Life and Times*. Bozeman MT: Bridger Creek Historical Press, 2002.

Stevens, Benjamin Franklin. *The Journal of Rev. Benjamin Franklin Stevens*, 1849, Hannibal MO, Free Public Library, http://hannibal.lib.mo.us/digital/Rev%20Stevens/journal_of.htm.

Stiles, T. J. *Jesse James: Last Rebel of the Civil War*. New York: Alfred A. Knopf, 2002.

Stoner, John. *Mammoth Springs and Plunket Lake: A Bozeman to Helena Watering Hole*. Self-published, Broadwater County Historical Society, 2004.

Strahorn, Carrie Adell. *Fifteen-Thousand Miles by Stage*. New York: G. P. Putnam's Sons, 1911. https://books.google.com/books?id=7OQTAAAAYAAJ.

Strahorn, Robert E. *The Resources of Montana Territory and Attractions of Yellowstone Park*. Helena: Montana State Legislature, 1879. http://mtmemory.org/cdm/pageflip/collection/p16013coll56/id/73/type/singleitem/pftype/pdf.

Stuart, Granville. *Forty Years on the Frontier As Seen in the Journals and Reminiscences of Granville Stuart, Gold-Miner, Trader, Merchant, Rancher, and Politician*. Cleveland OH: Arthur H. Clark, 1925. Lincoln: University of Nebraska Press, 1977.

Stursberg, Peter. *Your Dream Mentor: How Role Models Can Help*. Salt Lake City UT: Northwest Publishing, 1994.

Swartout, Robert R., Jr., and Harry W. Fritz, eds. *The Montana Heritage: An Anthology of Historical Essays*. Helena: Montana Historical Society Press, 1992.

Taliaferro, John. *Charles M. Russell: The Life and Legend of America's Cowboy Artist*. Boston: Little, Brown, 1996.

Three Forks Area Historical Society. *Headwaters Heritage History*. 2nd ed. Butte MT: Three Forks Area Historical Society, 1983.

United Daughters of the Confederacy, Missouri Division, comp. *Reminiscences of the Women of Missouri during the Sixties*. Jefferson City MO: United Daugh-

ters of the Confederacy, Missouri Division, 1913. https://archive.org/details
/womenofmissouri00missrich/.

United States Congressional Serial Set. Vol. 1003. Washington DC: U.S. Government
Printing Office, 1859.

Unruh, John D., Jr. *The Plains Across: The Overland Emigrants and the Trans-
Mississippi West, 1840–60.* Urbana: University of Illinois Press, 1979. https://
archive.org/details/plainsacross00unru/.

U.S. Department of Commerce. *Population.* Vol. 2, *General Report Statistics by
Subject.* 15th Census of the United States: 1930. Washington DC: U.S. Government Printing Office, 1933. https://www.census.gov/library/publications/1933
/dec/1930a-vol-02-population.html.

U.S. Department of Commerce. *Population.* Vol. 3, *Reports by States, Showing
the Composition and Characteristics of the Population for Counties, Cities, and
Townships or Other Minor Civil Divisions.* 15th Census of the United States:
1930. Washington DC: U.S. Government Printing Office, 1932. https://www
.census.gov/library/publications/1932/dec/1930a-vol-03-population.html.

Van West, Carroll. *A Travelers Companion to Montana History.* Helena: Montana
Historical Society Press, 1986.

Vostral, Sharra L. *Under Wraps: A History of Menstrual Hygiene Technology.* Lan-
ham MD: Lexington Books, 2008.

Watry, Elizabeth A. *Women in Wonderland.* Helena MT: Riverbend Publishing,
2012.

Wetmore, Alphonso, comp. *Gazetteer of the State of Missouri.* St. Louis MO: C.
Keemle, 1837. https://books.google.com/books?id=6H8UAAAAYAAJ.

Wilhelm, D. O. *Business Directory of the City.* Denver: Byers and Dailey, 1866.
https://www.ancestrylibrary.com/imageviewer/collections/2469/images
/15341358.

Williams, Walter. *A History of Northwest Missouri.* Vol. 1. Chicago: Lewis Publishing, 1915. https://books.google.com/books?id=ZmIUAAAAYAAJ.

Yesteryears and Pioneers. Harlowton MT: Harlowton Woman's Club, 1972.

Index

Page numbers in italics indicate illustrations.

Bennett, Donald, *xv, 85, 164, 165, 175*; birth of, 160; in Bozeman, 273; child of, 251; death of, 279; investments of, 326n6; Julia's plans worrying, 228; marriage of, 181; in New York, 238; sister living with, 198; as student, 178, 180, 181; work of, 178; in youth, 168–69, 171, 175, 177

Bennett, Elizabeth, *xv*, 159, 167–68, 177

Bennett, Julia Bembrick, in personal life, xiii–xiv, *xv, 85, 149, 155, 164, 239, 245*; animals and, 147–48, 150; background of, 4, 77; beliefs of, 7, 278–79, 280; birth of, 137; at brother's trial, 255; character of, 275–76, 278–81, 283; childhood memories of, 38, 44, 133, 141–46, 150–52; as community member, 172; death and burial of, 283; divorce of, 183–84; education of, 151–52; on father, 50, 53, 300n9; as fisher, 169, 219; friendships of, 84, 90, 166, 270; in frightening situations, 169–70; as grandparent, 251, 274, 280, 285; hard times for, 181, 278–81; home of, 315n1 (chap. 38); as household manager, 170; as hunter, 75–76, 152, 167–68, 219; Indians and, 146; legacy of, 286–87; in legal proceedings, 180; loneliness of, 158; love interests of, 245–46; marriage of, 159–60, 168–73, 177–78; miscarriages of, 170–71; on mother, 298n7 (chap. 10); moves of, 168–69; as parent, 160, 171, 177, 178, 180, 185, 229–30; Pete Stursberg and, 267; practical jokes played on, 171–72; as ranch wife, 174–76

Bennett, Julia Bembrick, in work life, xiii–xiv, *xv*, 227, 237, 243, 260, 281; animals and, 268; as association director, 262; boardinghouse of, 177; character of, 80, 196, 204–5, 219, 240–42, 243–46, 252, 275–77; as corporation president, 258–59; dude ranch ideas of, 77, 224; dude ranch preparation by, 81–83, 87–89, 231–32, 247; financial situation of, 77, 184, 236, 261, 273; fires and, 264–65, 276–77; funding strategies of, 81, 87, 207–9, 224, 226–28, 232–33, 258–59; as hostess at Diamond J Ranch, 186–87, 201–2, 205–6, 219–23, 225–26, 241–42, 244–45; as hostess at Diamond W Ranch, 235–36, 241, 244, 248–51, 261–62, 268–70, 272–73; as hotel manager, 178; ignored, 266; investments of, 326n6; in legal proceedings, 182–84, 187–88; marriage proposal to, 194; as Nine Quarter Circle and Rising Sun Ranch employee, 77–78, 79–80, 81–82, 83–84, 180, 280, 303n5; promotion of Diamond J Ranch by, 3–9, 10–11, 91–92, 191–94, 195–97, 208–9, 211, 212–13, 216–17, 238, 262; promotion of Diamond W Ranch by, 234–35, 238, 247–48, 262; as salesperson, 179; as shop owner, 252–53; as stenographer, 180; stories of, 133, 202

Bennett, Marjorie "Marge," *xv, 175*, 227, 239; at Barber camp, 216–17; birth of, 171; burial of, 279; character of, 198, 278; in childhood, 175, 177; children of, 251, 253; custody of, 184;

Bennet, Marjorie (*cont.*)

death of, 278; Diamond J Ranch and, 273; Diamond W Ranch and, 231, 232, 233, 235, 251; divorces of, 267, 278; in dude ranch publicity, 9, 10; with grandparents, 178, 180; marriages of, 238–39, 274; in movies, 262; on Nine Quarter Circle Ranch, 81; Pete and, 199, 201, 202–3, 210, 211–13, 217; retail shop, 252–53; as student, 76, 81, 92, 178, 198; traveling with mother, 229–30; "Unk" on, 200–201; Westinghouse family and, 226, 227–28; William Henry Jackson and, 220, 221, 222–23

Bennett, Marshall, *xv*, 251, 273, 275, 276, 283, 285, 286

Bennett, Violet Marshall, *xv*, 181, 198, 251, 273

Bennett, Willard, 159

Bennett Construction Company, 170

Bennett family, *xv*

Bergen, Edgar, 259, 260

Bernardsville Fire Department, 265

Bernardsville NJ, 200, 239

Biering and Cunningham ranch, 177

Big Belt Mountains, 67, 74, 116

Big Horn County MT, 174, 178

Big Man, Chief Max, 192

Billings Gazette, 78, 92

Billings Weekly Gazette, 79

bison. *See* buffalo

Bitter Creek, 35–36

Blackfeet Indians, 67, 73, 108, 115, 302n7

Black Friday Mine, 139, 168

Bloody Dick stream, 169

Bloom, Jerome, 30

Blue Mountains, 94, 102

boardinghouses, 40, 95, 177, 305n8 (chap. 19)

Boise ID, 103

Bottler ranch, 132

Bozeman, John, 32, 67, 106, 297n5, 302n6

Bozeman Avant Courier, 123, 128, 131, 133, 308n5

Bozeman Daily Chronicle, 177

Bozeman MT, 74, 76, 82, 133, 177, 179, 201, 220, 303n7

Bozeman Times, 128

Bozeman Trail, 32, 97, 109, 111

Brady, Genevieve, 203–4

Brady, James Cox, 204, 317n14

Brady, Victoria, 203–4

Brady, Victoria May Pery, 204

Bridger, Jim, 50, 214

Broadwater County MT, 157, 173, 254, 255, 256

Brock, Shelton, 30

buffalo, 27–28, 49, 50–51, 52, 115, 179, 185, 192

Burial Hill (Virginia City MT), 39

Butler, Julius, 8, 78, 79–80, 81, 83

Butler family, 76, 180, 185

Butte Miner, 159, 308n5

cabins: guest, 82, 87–89, 186, 187, 201, 221, 277; as homes, 39, 56, 62, 168, 300n18; homestead, 67, 302n4; as schools, 61, 151

California, 48, 49–50, 93, 94–95

California, Oregon and Mexico Steamship Company, 98

cameras, 216, 223, 318n3 (chap. 45)

Camp Fortunate, 169

Camp GY-BA-JK, 209–10

Penrod, Adaline "Addie." *See* Bembrick, Adaline "Addie"
Penrod, Frank, 158
Penrod, Lulu, 158
Penrod, Samuel, 151, 158
Pepper, Sherry Merica. *See* Stursberg, Sherry
Peterson, Ernest, 183, 187
Peyton, Mr., 107
Pfiester, F. J., 128
Philadelphia Inquirer, 272–73
photograph albums, 41, 96, 302n20
photographers, 166, 192, 219, 242. *See also* Jackson, William Henry
pigs, 147, 148, 174–75
Pima Indians, 48, 234
Pine Lodge Camp, 146, 173
pistols. *See* guns
Pittsburgh Press, 193
Place, Lew, 231
Place, Roy, 231
Planter's House, 106
Plenty Coups (Crow chief), 178–79
Plummer, Henry, 38–39
pneumonia, 204, 217
Poindexter's Army, 15–16
Poker Joe (Nez Perce man), 125, 127
Pony Express, 35, 297n1 (chap. 8)
Pool, Reverend, 157
Portland OR, 98, 99
The Prairie Traveler (Marcy), 24, 25
Price, Sterling, 57, 302n21
Prickly Pear valley, 60
Princeton NJ, 217
Prohibition, 186, 211

Quantrill's Guerrillas, 296n8
quartz, 66, 112–13, 121

Quaw, Gene, 241–42
quilt-making, 28, 40, 61, 110, 144

Radersburg MT, 67, 68, 74, 111–13, 116–17, 134–35, 137
railroad, 78, 100, 106, 111, 168, 169–70, 178, 195, 199. *See also* Milwaukee Railroad; Northern Pacific Railroad; Santa Fe Railroad; Southern Pacific Railroad; Union Pacific Railroad
Rankin, Jeannette, xiv, 173, 255, 322n7 (chap. 54)
Rankin, Wellington D., 255–56, 257
rationing, 261, 263–64, 266
rattlesnakes, 138, 148, 169, 171
Redmond, Elliott, 279
Red White and Blue Lode, 56
reporters, xiv, 10–11, 115, 154, 168, 254, 263–64, 265
Republican Party, 79–80, 181, 255
Resources of the Pacific Slope, 95
revolvers. *See* guns
Riethmann, John J., 300n18
rifles. *See* guns
Rincon Mountains, 234
Ringling Brothers, 212
Rising Sun Ranch, 76, 185, 245, 280
Ritter, Tex, 9–10
Robber's Roost, 201–2
Rocky Mountain Husbandman, 121, 123, 132, 153
Rocky Mountain News, 53–54
Rocky Mountain News Weekly, 33
rodeos, 10, 202–3, 219–20
Romero, Francisco, 270–71
Ronan, Mary Sheehan, 22, 26–27, 28, 36, 61–62, 62–63

steamships, 96, 98, 99

Steele, William L., 31

Stevens, Benjamin Franklin, 48, 49

Stewart, Robert Marcellus, 20

Stinson airplane, 259

St. Louis Hotel (Helena MT), 118

St. Louis MO, 16, 17, 50, 142, 300n8

stock market crash, 3, 87

Stonehyrst, 200

Stony Creek station (New York NY), 213

Story, Nelson, 310n3 (chap. 29)

Strahorn, Carrie Adell, 94, 103, 105

Stuart, Granville, 50, 101, 104, 140, 310n3 (chap. 29)

Stursberg, Albert, 199, 201, 217–18

Stursberg, Babs, 210, 211–12, 239

Stursberg, Edward "Pete," xv, 200; background of, 199–201; Bennett family and, 238, 255; brother of, 266; character of, 199, 253, 266–67; comparisons to, 274; death of, 279–80; Diamond W Ranch and, 251, 258; in early adulthood, 217–18; Edgar Bergen and, 259; fires and, 263–66; Marge and, 202–3, 238–39; marriages of, 238–39, 267

Stursberg, Herbert "Unk," 196–97, 199–201, 205–8, 218, 224, 238, 253, 258–59, 279

Stursberg, Laird, 199, 265, 266

Stursberg, Louise, 199

Stursberg, Marie Louise, 199

Stursberg, Peter (Marge's son), xv, 251, 267, 273, 274, 278, 280, 285; Your Dream Mentor, 286

Stursberg, Sherry (Sherry Merica Pepper), xv; birth of, 253; on camping preparations, 242; at Diamond W Ranch, 273; on father, 267; fire

affecting, 276–77; on grandmother, 240, 245, 276, 280, 281, 283; marriage of, 285–86; mother and, 274, 278, 279; in youth, 267, 285

Sublette-Greenwood Cutoff, 35

suffrage, women's, 153, 154, 173

Suffrage Daily News, 173

Sun, 265

Sun Ranch. See Rising Sun Ranch

Sutherlin, R. N., 121

Switzer, Miss, 136

syphilis, 226–27

Tanque Verde Creek and area, 234

Tanque Verde Ranch, 232, 234, 270

Taylor, Bellevernon, 6–7

Taylor Lode, 56

teachers, 12, 43, 61–62, 80, 97, 136, 142, 151–52, 164

telegraph and telegrams, 128, 132, 156, 217, 232

Tennessean, 193

Teton Sioux Indians, 32, 67

Thomas and Ruckel Road, 102

time zones, 106

Tinsley, William, 96, 108

Toston MT, 74, 150, 160–61, 162, 173, 177, 179, 180, 254

Toston Times, 180

Town Hall Club (New York NY), 238

Townsend Messenger, 154, 157

Townsend Star, 161, 166, 171, 173, 254, 255, 257, 323nn12–13

Townsley, Benjamin, 139

trapping, 51

treaties, 52, 111, 124

trials, 255–57, 270–71, 323n12

Tucson AZ, 224–25, 230–31, 234–35, 238, 261, 262, 263